T0215423

How Open Source Ate Software

Understand the Open Source Movement and So Much More

Second Edition

Gordon Haff

Apress®

How Open Source Ate Software

Gordon Haff
Lancaster, MA, USA

ISBN-13 (pbk): 978-1-4842-6799-8
https://doi.org/10.1007/978-1-4842-6800-1

ISBN-13 (electronic): 978-1-4842-6800-1

Managing Director, Apress LLC: Welmoed Spahr
Acquisitions Editor: Louise Corrigan
Development Editor: James Markham
Coordinating Editor: Nancy Chen

Cover designed by eStudioCalamar

Cover image by SevenStorm JUHASZIMRUS from Pexels

Distributed to the book trade worldwide by Springer Science+Business Media New York, 233 Spring Street, 6th Floor, New York, NY 10013. Phone 1-800-SPRINGER, fax (201) 348-4505, e-mail orders-ny@springer-sbm.com, or visit www.springeronline.com. Apress Media, LLC is a California LLC and the sole member (owner) is Springer Science + Business Media Finance Inc (SSBM Finance Inc). SSBM Finance Inc is a **Delaware** corporation.

For information on translations, please e-mail booktranslations@springernature.com; for reprint, paperback, or audio rights, please e-mail bookpermissions@springernature.com.

Apress titles may be purchased in bulk for academic, corporate, or promotional use. eBook versions and licenses are also available for most titles. For more information, reference our Print and eBook Bulk Sales web page at http://www.apress.com/bulk-sales.

Any source code or other supplementary material referenced by the author in this book is available to readers on GitHub via the book's product page, located at www.apress.com/9781484267998. For more detailed information, please visit http://www.apress.com/source-code.

Printed on acid-free paper

To my dad.

Table of Contents

About the Author

Gordon Haff is a technology evangelist for Red Hat, the leading provider of commercial open source software, where he works on emerging technology product strategy; writes about tech, trends, and their business impact; and is a frequent speaker at customer and industry events. Among the topics he works on are edge, blockchain, AI, cloud-native platforms, and next-generation application architectures. He writes for a variety of publications including The Enterprisers Project, opensource.com, Connections, and TechTarget. Prior books include *From Pots and Vats to Programs and Apps*. His Innovate @Open podcast includes interviews with a wide range of industry experts on the topic of open source innovation.

Prior to Red Hat, as an IT industry analyst, Gordon wrote hundreds of research notes, was frequently quoted in publications such as *The New York Times* on a wide range of IT topics, and has advised clients on product and marketing strategies. Earlier in his career, he was a product manager who brought a wide range of computer systems, from minicomputers to large Unix servers, to market while at Data General.

He lives west of Boston, Massachusetts, in apple orchard country and is an avid hiker, skier, sea kayaker, and photographer. He can be found on Twitter as @ghaff and reached via email at gordon@alum.mit.edu. His website and blog are at `www.bitmasons.com`.

Gordon has engineering degrees from MIT and Dartmouth and an MBA from Cornell's Johnson School.

Acknowledgments

I'd like to thank my employer, Red Hat, for its support in writing this book. Red Hat also contributes to many of the open source projects that I discuss throughout these pages.

Over the years, many Red Hatters have contributed to and helped to develop many of the ideas and concepts explored here, as well as to build the business practices that have demonstrated how open source can anchor effective business models. A number of my past and current colleagues have also provided specific feedback and contributed content, including William Henry, David Neary, Joe Brockmeier, Ross Turk, Robyn Bergeron, Deb Bryant, Thomas Cameron, Diane Mueller, Yan Fisher, Ben Fischer, and Gina Likins, among others. I would especially like to thank Richard Fontana on Red Hat's legal team who provided a detailed review and feedback on Chapter 3.

The Linux Foundation executive, event, and public relations teams contributed through public resources, interviews, and the many fertile discussions that their events have been a catalyst for.

I'd also like to thank my editors at Apress—Nancy Chen, Louise Corrigan, and James Markham—for their efforts in bringing this manuscript to the page, as well as managing director Welmoed Spahr for agreeing to take on this project.

Finally, I express my appreciation to all the interview subjects, researchers, editors, and other authors, without whom this book would not be possible.

Introduction

Information wants to be free. Users in control. I have rights to the code I depend on. That's one way to view free and open source software.

Those are important things. Software freedoms matter. But it's a lens that highlights open source as largely a personal movement that was probably never to have a truly widespread impact so long as it remained so constrained.

But open source also has practical applications relating to how software gets developed and used. It's part of an evolution in how individuals and organizations cooperatively innovate. That's why open source, and open more broadly, is a topic worth serious attention.

Open source software as we know it today arose in a time and place when and where norms that had once prioritized sharing were giving way to a more proprietary and closed computer industry. Open source software helped to change that, and, in so doing, it illuminated processes for creating software that were *better* and not just preferable for mostly abstract reasons relating to software freedom.

Open source became an integral part of a world transitioning from traditional industrial structures and embedding software into more and more of its fabric.

This second edition provides you with the context to understand the historical forces that shaped open source including the legal framework within which open source operates then and now. While something vaguely like open source software may well have been inevitable, the form it took and the concerns that it tackled grew out of specific events and market dynamics. But many of those events lie far in the past, and the market landscape looks much different. Will open source software start to wither in such a changed world? Or, conversely, can its lessons be applied to broader questions of collaboration and culture that go far beyond computer source code?

In the course of asking questions such as these, I explain how open source works from community, development, and business perspectives through the eyes and words of both practitioners and researchers. I delve into the differences between community projects and commercial products. I share current thinking about project governance and community health. I highlight research that informs our understanding of why developers and others contribute to open source and how contributors can be best encouraged and nurtured. One of the big changes that open source software has seen is a shift from a primary focus on individual user freedoms to one that takes a broader view. What are the best ways of developing software? How can users best access software innovation and flexibly make use of software in the context of their specific business needs? How can they use open source and open source–inspired processes to adapt to a faster-paced and more digital world?

This book examines the challenges facing open source given that some of the conditions that gave rise to it no longer apply. Business models built on open source software have never been easy, but today's market landscape including, not least of all, the major public cloud providers creates new obstacles to monetization and sustainability. I take a look at some paths to navigate around those obstacles including some of the new licensing approaches that attempt to—but mostly don't—address business model challenges using that particular tool.

It's perhaps a reflection of the rapid evolution of open source software and open source principles that this second edition has added so much new content. There's the revisiting of licenses as a business license tool, however mostly ill-directed. On the other hand, we've also seen a newfound recognition that trademarks may be useful as part of a legal toolkit for supporting business models based on open source development. I also delve into open governance and community management practices that have started to be more systematically laid out just within the past few years. The contrast between projects and products has also assumed outsized importance of late, especially in light of the ascendance of DevSecOps, an increasingly hostile threat landscape, and new open source–based security tools related to machine learning and trusted execution environments.

Beyond software is more of a mixed bag. Some areas, like open education, haven't advanced much with online education, for example, having largely failed to live up to its initial hype. (Remote pandemic learning has only served to illustrate the challenges of distance teaching.) At the same time, in the open hardware area, RISC-V is showing considerable potential as a serious hardware architecture that is truly open.

But beyond software, open source approaches are taking root in data, hardware, education, and organizations more broadly. Not everything is transparent and open, nor can it realistically be. Business models depend on unique capabilities and knowledge. However, open source software both reflects and informs trends and practices that are becoming increasingly important and pervasive in business and elsewhere. Understand how open source came to be and how it works, and you'll be closer to understanding how to innovate through working together with others in the modern world.

The Beginnings of Free and Open Source Software

Origin stories are often messy. What you are about to read is no exception.

The story of open source software is a maze of twisty streams feeding into each other and into the main channel. They're part and parcel with the history of the Unix operating system, which itself is famously convoluted. In this chapter, we'll take a look at open source's humble beginnings.

In the Beginning

The sharing of human-readable source code was widespread in the early days of computing. A lot of computer development took place at universities and in corporate research departments like AT&T's Bell Labs. They had long-established traditions of openness and collaboration, with the result that even when code wasn't formally placed into the public domain, it was widely shared.

Computer companies shipping software with their systems also often included the source code. Users frequently had to modify the software themselves so that it would support new hardware or because they needed to add a new feature. The attitude of many vendors at the time was that software was something you needed to use the hardware, but it wasn't really a distinct thing to be sold.

Indeed, users of computer systems often had to write their own software in the early days. The first operating system for the IBM 704 computer (Figure 1-1), the GM-NAA I/O input/output system, was written in 1956 by Robert L. Patrick of General Motors

© Gordon Haff 2021
G. Haff, *How Open Source Ate Software*, https://doi.org/10.1007/978-1-4842-6800-1_1

Research and Owen Mock of North American Aviation. (An operating system is the software that supports a computer's basic functions, such as scheduling tasks, executing applications, and controlling peripherals such as storage devices.)

Figure 1-1. *IBM 704 at NASA Langley in 1957. Source: Public domain*

The culture of sharing code—at least in some circles—was still strong going into the late 1970s when John Lions of the University of New South Wales in Australia annotated the Sixth Edition source code of the Unix operating system. Copies of this "Lions' Commentary" were circulated widely among university computer science departments and elsewhere. This sort of casual and informal sharing was the norm of the time even when it wasn't technically allowed by the code's owner, AT&T in the case of Unix.

Ah, Unix

The idea of modifying software to run on new or different hardware gained momentum around Unix. Unix was rewritten in 1973–1974 (for its V4 release) in C, a programming language newly developed by Dennis Ritchie at Bell Labs. Using what was, by the standards of the time, a high-level programming language for this purpose, while not absolutely unique, was nonetheless an unusual, new, and even controversial approach.

More typical would have been to use the assembly language specific to a given machine's architecture. Because of the close correspondence between the assembler code and an architecture's machine code instructions (which execute directly on the hardware), the assembler was extremely efficient, if challenging and time consuming to write well. And efficiency was important at a time when there wasn't a lot of spare computer performance to be wasted.

However, as rewritten in C, Unix could be modified to work on other machines relatively easily; that is, it was "portable." This was truly unusual. The norm of the day was to write a new operating system and a set of supporting systems and application software for each new hardware platform.

Of course, to make those modifications, you needed the source code.

AT&T was willing to supply this for several reasons. One was especially important. After the Sixth Edition was released in 1975, AT&T began licensing Unix to universities and commercial firms, as well as the US government. But the licenses did not include any support or bug fixes, because to do so would have been "pursuing software as a business," which AT&T did not believe that it had the right to do under the terms of the agreement by which it operated as a regulated telephone service monopoly. The source code let licensees make their own fixes and "port" Unix to new and incompatible systems. (We'll return to the topic of copyright and licenses in Chapter 3.)

However, in the early 1980s, laid-back attitudes toward sharing software source code started to come to an end throughout the industry.

No More Free Lunches?

In AT&T's specific case, 1982 was the year it entered into a consent decree with the US Federal Trade Commission providing for the spin-off of the regional Bell operating companies (Figure 1-2). Among other things, the decree freed AT&T to enter the computer industry. Shortly thereafter, AT&T commenced development of a commercial version of Unix.

UNITED STATES DISTRICT COURT
FOR THE DISTRICT OF COLUMBIA

UNITED STATES OF AMERICA,   )
)
                Plaintiff,   )
)
          v.   )   Civil Action No.
)   82-0192
)
WESTERN ELECTRIC COMPANY,   )
INCORPORATED, AND AMERICAN   )
TELEPHONE AND TELEGRAPH   )
COMPANY,   )   FILED.
)
                Defendants.   )   AUG 24 1982
)
                                      JAMES E. DAVEY, Clerk.

MODIFICATION OF FINAL JUDGMENT

Plaintiff, United States of America, having filed its
complaint herein on January 14, 1949; the defendants having
appeared and filed their answer to such complaint denying the
substantive allegations thereof; the parties, by their
attorneys, having severally consented to a Final Judgment which
was entered by the Court on January 24, 1956, and the parties
having subsequently agreed that modification of such Final

Figure 1-2. *AT&T entered into a consent decree in 1982 that allowed it to pursue software as a business. This led to the increasing commercialization of Unix. Source: Public domain*

This would lead, over the course of about the next decade, to the messy "Unix wars" as AT&T Unix licensees developed and shipped proprietary Unix versions that were all incompatible with each other to greater or lesser degrees. It's an *extremely* complicated and multi-threaded history. It's also not all that relevant to how open source has evolved other than to note that it created vertical silos that weren't all that different from the minicomputers and mainframes that Unix systems replaced. The new boss looked a lot like the old boss.

During the same period, AT&T—in the guise of its new Unix System Laboratories subsidiary—got into a legal fight with the University of California, Berkeley, over their derivative (a.k.a. "fork") of Unix, the Berkeley Software Distribution (BSD). Specifically, it was a squabble with the Computer Systems Research Group (CSRG) at Berkeley, but I'll just refer to the university as a whole here.

Berkeley had been one of AT&T's educational licensees. Over time, it modified and added features to its licensed version of Unix and, in 1978, began shipping those add-ons as BSD. Over time, it added significant features, involving the outright re-architecting and rewriting of many key subsystems and the addition of many wholly new components. As a result of its extensive changes and improvements, BSD was increasingly seen as an entirely new, even better, strain of Unix; many AT&T licensees would end up incorporating significant amounts of BSD code into their own Unix versions. (This contributed further to the Unix wars as different companies favored predominantly the AT&T strain or the Berkeley strain in their products.)

Berkeley continued developing BSD to incrementally replace most of the standard Unix utilities that were still under AT&T licenses. This eventually culminated in the June 1991 release of Net/2, a nearly complete operating system that was ostensibly freely redistributable. This in turn led to AT&T suing Berkeley for copyright infringement.

Suffice it to say that the commercialization of Unix, which had been the hub around which much source code sharing had taken place, helped lead to a more balkanized and closed Unix environment.

PCs Were a Different Culture

But the sharing ethos was also eroding more broadly.

During the 1980s, the personal computer space was increasingly dominated by the IBM PC and its clones running a Microsoft operating system. Nothing that looked much like open source developed there to a significant degree. In part, this probably reflected the fact that the relatively standardized system architecture of the PC made the portability benefits of having source code less important.

Furthermore, most of the tools needed to develop software weren't included when someone bought a PC, and the bill for those could add up quickly. The BASIC programming language interpreter was included with Microsoft's DOS operating system, but that was seen as hopelessly outdated for serious use even by the not-so-demanding standards of the time. When Borland's more modern Turbo Pascal debuted in 1984 for only $50, it was a radical innovation given that typical programming language packages went for *hundreds* of dollars. Programming libraries and other resources—including information that was mostly locked up in books, magazines, and other offline dead tree sources—added to the bill. Making a few changes to a piece of software was not for the relatively casual hobbyist.

People did program for the IBM PC, of course, and over time a very healthy community of freeware and shareware software authors came into being.

I was one of them.

Shareware, at least as the term was generally used at the time, meant try-before-you-buy software. Remember, this is a time when boxed software sold at retail could go for hundreds of dollars with no guarantee that it would even work properly on your computer. And good luck returning it if it didn't.

The main software I wrote was a little DOS file manager, 35KB of assembler, called Directory Freedom, derived from some assembly code listings in *PC Magazine* and another developer's work. It never made a huge amount of money, but it had its fan base, and I still get emails about it from time to time. I also uploaded to the local subscription bulletin board system (BBS) various utility programs that I originally wrote for my own use.

But distributing source code was never a particularly big thing.

Breaking Community

Similar commercializing dynamics were playing out in other places. The MIT Artificial Intelligence (AI) Lab, celebrated by Steven Levy in *Hackers* as a "pure hacker paradise, the Tech Square monastery where one lived to hack, and hacked to live," was changing. Here, it was Lisp that was commercializing.

The Lisp programming language was the workhorse of artificial intelligence research, but it required so much computing horsepower that it didn't run well on the ordinary computers of the day. As a result, for close to a decade, members of the AI Lab had been experimenting with systems that were optimized to run Lisp. By 1979, that work had progressed to the point where commercialization looked like a valid option.

Eventually two companies, Symbolics and Lisp Machines Inc., would be formed. But it ended up as a messy and acrimonious process that led to much reduced open collaboration and widespread departures from the Lab.

Richard Stallman was one member of the AI Lab who did not head off to greener corporate Lisp pastures but nonetheless felt greatly affected by the splintering of the Lab community. Stallman had previously written the widely used Emacs editing program.

With Emacs, as Glyn Moody writes in *Rebel Code* (Perseus Publishing, 2001), "Stallman established an 'informal rule that anyone making improvements had to send them back' to him."

His experiences with the effects of proprietary code in the Symbolics vs. Lisp Machines Inc. war led him to decide to develop a free and portable operating system, given that he had seen a lack of sharing stifling the formation of software communities. In another widely told story about Stallman's genesis as a free software advocate, he was refused access to the source code for the software of a newly installed laser printer, the Xerox 9700, which kept him from modifying the software to send notifications as he had done with the Lab's previous laser printer.

Free Software Enters the Fray

In 1983, Richard Stallman announced on Usenet, the Internet's (still called the ARPANET at the time) newsgroup service, that "Starting this Thanksgiving I am going to write a complete Unix-compatible software system called GNU (for Gnu's Not Unix), and give it away free to everyone who can use it." See Figure 1-3.

Figure 1-3. *Stallman's Free Software Foundation (FSF) and GNU Project are generally taken as the beginning of free and open source software as a coherent movement. Source: Victor Siame (vcopovi@wanadoo.fr) under the Free Art License*

As justification, he went on to write that

I consider that the golden rule requires that if I like a program I must share it with other people who like it. I cannot in good conscience sign a nondisclosure agreement or a software license agreement. So that I can continue to use computers without violating my principles, I have decided to put together a sufficient body of free software so that I will be able to get along without any software that is not free.

It was to be based on the Unix model, which is to say that it was to consist of modular components like utilities and the C language compiler needed to build a working system. The project began in 1984. To this day, there is in fact no "GNU operating system" in that the GNU Hurd operating system kernel has never been completed. Without a kernel, there's no way to run utilities, applications, or other software as they have no way to communicate with the hardware.

However, Stallman did complete many other components of his operating system. These included, critically, the parts needed to build a functioning operating system from source code and to perform fundamental system tasks from the command line. It's a hallmark of Unix that its design is very modular. As a result, it's entirely feasible to modify and adapt parts of Unix without wholesale replacing the whole thing at one time (a fact that would be central to the later development of Linux).

Establishing the Foundations of Free

However, equally important from the perspective of open source's origins were the GNU Manifesto that followed in 1985, the Free Software Definition in 1986, and the GNU General Public License (GPL) in 1989, which formalized principles for preventing restrictions on the freedoms that define free software.

The GPL requires that if you distribute a program covered by the GPL in binary, that is, machine-readable form, whether in original or modified form, you must also make the human-readable source code available. In this way, you can build on both the original program and the improvements of others, but, if you yourself make changes and distribute them, you also have to make those changes available for others to use. It's what's known as a "copyleft" or reciprocal license because of this mutual obligation.

Free and open source software was still in its infancy in the late 1980s. (Indeed, the "open source" term hadn't even been coined yet.) Linux was not yet born. BSD Unix would soon be embroiled in a lawsuit with AT&T. The Internet was not yet fully commercialized. But, especially with the benefit of hindsight, we can start to discern patterns that will become important: collaboration, giving back, and frameworks that help people to know the rules and work together appropriately.

But it was the Internet boom of the 1990s that would really put Linux and open source on the map even if this phase of open source would turn out to be just the first act of an ultimately more important story. This is the backdrop against which open source would rise in prominence while the computer hardware and software landscape would shift radically.

Fragmented Hardware and Software

Turn the clock back to 1991. A Finnish university student by the name of Linus Torvalds posted in a Usenet newsgroup that he was starting to work on a free operating system in the Unix mold as a hobby. Many parts of Stallman's initial GNU Project were complete. In sunny California, Berkeley had shipped the first version of its Unix to be freely distributable.

Free software had clearly arrived. It just wasn't a very important part of the computing landscape yet.

Vertical Silos Everywhere

It was a very fragmented computing landscape. The Unix market was embroiled in internecine proprietary system warfare. Many other types of proprietary computer companies were also still around—if often past their prime.

The most prominent were the "Route 128" Massachusetts minicomputer companies, so called because many were located on or near the highway by that name, which partially encircled the adjacent cities of Boston and Cambridge on the northeast coast of the United States. However, there were also many other vendors who built and sold systems for both commercial and scientific computing. Most used their own hardware designs from the chips up through disk drives, tape drives, terminals, and more. If you bought a Data General computer, you also bought memory, reel-to-reel tape drives, disk drives, and even cabinets from either the same company or a small number of knock-off add-on suppliers.

Their software was mostly one-off as well. A typical company would usually write its own operating system (or several different ones) in addition to databases, programming languages, utilities, and office applications. When I worked at Data General during this period, we had about five different non-Unix minicomputer operating systems plus a couple of different versions of Unix.

Many of these companies were themselves increasingly considering a wholesale shift to their own versions of Unix. But it was mostly to yet another customized hardware and Unix operating system variant.

Most computer systems were still large and expensive in those days. "Big Iron" was the common slang term. The analysis and comparison of their complicated and varied architectures filled many an analyst's report.

Even "small business" or "departmental" servers, as systems that didn't require the special conditions of the "glass room" datacenter were often called, could run into the tens of thousands of dollars.

Silos Turn On Their Side

However, personal computers were increasingly starting to be stuck under desks and used for less strenuous tasks. Software from Novell called NetWare, which specialized in handling common tasks like printing or storing files, was one common option for such systems. There were also mass-market versions of Unix. The most common came from a company called Santa Cruz Operation that had gotten into the Unix business by buying an AT&T-licensed variant called Xenix from Microsoft. Many years later, a descendent company using the name SCO or SCO Group would instigate a series of multiyear lawsuits related to Linux that would pull in IBM and others.

More broadly, there was a pervasive sea change going on in the computer systems landscape. As recounted by semiconductor maker Intel CEO Andy Grove in *Only the Paranoid Survive* (Penguin Random House, 1999), a fundamental transformation happened in the computer industry during the 1990s.

As we've seen, the historical computer industry was organized in vertical stacks. Those vertical stacks were increasingly being rotated into a more horizontal structure (Figure 1-4).

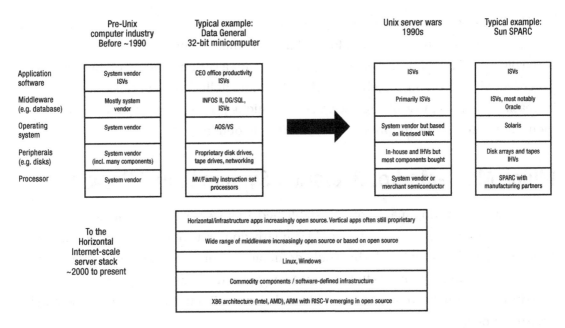

Figure 1-4. *The Unix wars era saw some shift from tightly integrated proprietary server stacks tied to a single vendor. But it took the rise of the Internet and many of the market forces associated with it to truly turn vertical stacks on their side*

It wasn't a pure transformation; there were (and are) still proprietary processors, servers, and operating systems.

But more and more of the market was shifting toward a model in which a system vendor would buy the computer's central processing unit from Intel, a variety of other largely standardized chips and components from other suppliers, and an operating system and other software from still other companies. They'd then sell these "industry standard" servers through a combination of direct sales, mail order, and retail.

During this period, Advanced Micro Devices (AMD) was also producing compatible x86 architecture processors under license from Intel although the two companies would become embroiled in a variety of contractual disputes over time. AMD would later enjoy periods of success but has largely remained in Intel's shadow.

The PC model was taking over the server space.

Grove described this as the 10X force of the personal computer. The tight integration of the old model might be lacking. But in exchange for a certain amount of do-it-yourself to get everything working together, for a few thousand dollars you got capabilities that increasingly rivaled those of engineering workstations you might have paid *tens* of thousands to one of the proprietary Unix vendors to obtain.

Which Mass-Market Operating System Would Prevail?

With the increasing dominance of x86 established, there was now just a need to determine which operating system would similarly dominate this horizontal stack. There was also the question of who would dominate important aspects of the horizontal platform more broadly such as the runtimes for applications, databases, and areas that were just starting to become important like web servers. But those were less immediately pressing concerns.

The answer wasn't immediately obvious. Microsoft's popular MS-DOS and initial versions of Windows were designed for single-user PCs. They couldn't support multiple users like Unix could and therefore weren't suitable for business users who needed systems that would let them easily share data and other resources. Novell NetWare was one multiuser alternative that was very good at what it did—sharing files and printers— but it wasn't a general-purpose operating system. (Novell's various attempts to expand NetWare's capabilities mostly fizzled.) And, while there were Unix options for small systems, they weren't really mass market and suffered from the Unix fragmentation described earlier.

Microsoft Swings for the Fences

Microsoft decided to build on its desktop PC domination to similarly dominate servers.

Microsoft's initial foray into a next-generation operating system ended poorly. IBM and Microsoft signed a "Joint Development Agreement" in August 1985 to develop what would later become OS/2. However, especially after Windows 3.0 became a success on desktop PCs in 1990, the two companies increasingly couldn't square their technical and cultural differences. For example, IBM was primarily focused on selling OS/2 to run on its own systems—naming its high-profile PC lineup PS/2 may have been a clue— whereas Microsoft wanted OS/2 to run on a wide range of hardware from many vendors.

As a result, Microsoft had started to work in parallel on a re-architected version of Windows. CEO Bill Gates hired Dave Cutler in 1988. Cutler had led the team that created the VMS operating system for Digital's VAX computer line among other Digital operating systems. Cutler's push to develop this new operating system is well chronicled in G. Pascal Zachary's *Showstopper! The Breakneck Race to Create Windows NT and the Next Generation at Microsoft* (Free Press, 1994) in which the author describes him as a brilliant and, at times, brutally aggressive chief architect.

Cutler had a low opinion of OS/2. He was said by some to also have a low opinion of Unix. In *Showstopper!* a team member is quoted as saying

> *He thinks Unix is a junk operating system designed by a committee of Ph.D.s. There's never been one mind behind the whole thing, and it shows, so he's always been out to get Unix. But this is the first time he's had the chance.*

Cutler undertook the design of a new operating system that would be named Windows NT upon its release in 1993.

IBM continued to work on OS/2 by itself, but it failed to attract application developers, was never a success, and was eventually discontinued. This Microsoft success at the expense of IBM was an early-on example of the growing importance of developers and developer mindshare, a trend that Bill Gates and Microsoft had long recognized and played to considerable advantage. And it would later become a critical factor in the success of open source communities.

Windows NT Poised to Take It All

Windows NT on Intel was a breakout product. Indeed, Microsoft and Intel became so successful and dominant that the "Wintel" term was increasingly used to refer to the most dominant type of system in the entire industry. By the mid-1990s, Unix was in decline, as were other operating systems such as NetWare.

Windows NT was mostly capturing share from Unix on smaller servers, but many thought they saw a future in which Wintel was everywhere. Unix system vendors, with the notable exception of Sun Microsystems under combative CEO Scott McNealy, started to place side bets on Windows NT. There was a sense of inevitability in many circles.

The irony was that, absent Windows NT, Unix would likely have conquered all. Jeff Atwood wrote that

> *The world has devolved into Unix and NT camps exclusively. Without NT, I think we'd all be running Unix at this point, for better or worse. It certainly happened to Apple; their next-generation Copland OS never even got off the ground. And now they're using OS X which is based on Unix.*

Unix might still have remained the operating system of choice for large systems with many processors; Windows NT was initially optimized for smaller systems. But it was easy to see that Windows NT was fully capable of scaling up and had been architected by Cutler to be able to serve as a Unix replacement. Once it got there, it was going to be very difficult not to rally around something that had become an industry standard just as Intel's x86 processor line had. Products selling in large volumes have lower unit costs and find it far easier to establish partnerships and integrations up and down the new stack with its horizontal layers.

The Internet Enters the Mainstream

But wait. It wasn't quite "Game over, man." A couple other things were happening by now. The Internet was taking off, and the first versions of Linux had been released.

By 1990, the Internet had been in existence, in some form, for a couple of decades. It originated with work commissioned by the US Defense Advanced Research Projects Agency (DARPA) in the 1960s to build fault-tolerant communication with computer networks. However, you probably hadn't heard of it unless you were a researcher at one of the handful of institutions connected to the early network. The Internet emerged from this obscurity in the 1990s for a variety of reasons, not least of which was the invention of the World Wide Web—which for many people today is synonymous with the Internet—by English scientist Tim Berners-Lee while working at CERN, the European research organization that operates the largest particle physics laboratory in the world.

From Scale-Up to Scale-Out

The great Internet build-out of the late 1990s lifted many boats, including the vendors of high-end expensive hardware and software. The quartet of Sun, networking specialist Cisco, storage disk array vendor EMC, and database giant Oracle was nicknamed the "four horsemen of the Internet." It seemed as if every venture capital–backed startup needed to write a big check to those four.

However, a lot of Internet infrastructure (think web servers)—as well as high-performance scientific computing clusters—ran on large numbers of smaller systems instead. Unix vendors, most notably Sun, were happy to sell their own smaller boxes for these purposes, but those typically carried a much higher price tag than was the norm for "industry standard" hardware and software.

The use of more and smaller servers was part of a broader industry shift in focus from "scale-up" computing to "scale-out." Distributed computing was driven by the maturation of the client/server and network/distributed computing styles that first emerged and gained popularity in the 1980s. This seemed like something that played to the Microsoft wheelhouse.

Internet Servers Needed an Operating System

Yet, Windows NT wasn't really ideal for these applications either. Yes, it was rapidly taking share from Unix in markets like small businesses and replicated sites in larger businesses—to the point where a vendor like Santa Cruz selling primarily into those markets was facing big losses. However, network infrastructure and scientific computing roles had mostly favored Unix historically for both reasons of custom and technology. For example, the modular mix-and-match nature of Unix had long made it popular with tinkerers and do-it-yourselfers. Transitioning to Windows NT was therefore neither natural nor easy.

BSD Unix was one obvious alternative. It did make inroads but only limited ones. The reasons are complicated and not totally clear even with the benefit of hindsight. Lingering effects of the litigation with AT&T. Licensing that didn't compel contributing back like the GPL does. A more centralized community that was less welcoming to outside contributions. I'll return to some of these later, but, in any case, BSD didn't end up having a big effect on the software landscape.

Enter Linux

Into this gap stepped Linux paired with other open source software such as GNU, the Apache web server, and many other types of software over time.

Recall our Finnish university student Linus Torvalds. Working on and inspired by MINIX, a version of Unix initially created by Andrew Tanenbaum for educational purposes, Torvalds began writing an operating system kernel.

The kernel is the core of a computer's operating system. Indeed, some purists argue that a kernel *is* the operating system with everything else part of a broader operating environment. In any case, it is usually one of the first programs loaded when a computer starts up. A kernel connects application software to the hardware of a computer and generally abstracts the business of managing the system hardware from the "userspace" things that someone trying to use the computer to do something cares about.

A New *nix

Linux is a member of the Unix-like (or sometimes "*nix") family of operating systems. The distinction between Unix and Unix-like is complicated, unclear, and, frankly, not very interesting. Originally, the term "Unix" meant a particular product developed by AT&T. Later it extended to AT&T licensees. Today, the Open Group owns the Unix trademark, but the term has arguably become generic with no meaningful distinction between operating systems that are indisputably a true Unix and those that are better described as Unix-like for reasons of trademark or technical features.

Torvalds announced his then-hobby project in 1991 to the broader world in the comp. os.minix Usenet newsgroup, Usenet being the popular distributed discussion board on the early Internet. He soon released version 0.01, which was mostly just the kernel.

By the next year, Torvalds had relicensed Linux under the GPL. Others had created the first Linux distributions to simplify installing it and to start packaging together the many components needed to use an operating system. By 1993, over 100 developers were working on the Linux kernel; among other things, they adapted it to the GNU environment. The year 1994 saw version 1.0 of Linux, the addition of a graphical user interface from the XFree86 project, and commercial Linux distributions from Red Hat and SUSE.

Linux Grows in Popularity

Initially, Linux was popular especially in university and computing research organizations, much as Unix more generally had been in the mid-1970s and Solaris, Sun's Unix flavor, had in the mid-1980s. Linux also started finding its way into many network infrastructure roles for file and print sharing, Web and file serving, and similar tasks.

You could download it for free or buy it on a disk for cheap. It's worth being explicit about what "cheap" meant in this context. The early to mid-1990s were still the era of the retail software stores like Egghead Software and hefty publications like *Computer Shopper*, a large format magazine filled with ads for computer gear and software that hit over 800 pages at its peak. Consumers were accustomed to buying boxed software, including the aforementioned Windows NT, at prices that easily ran into the hundreds of dollars. For a company accustomed to buying business applications from the likes of Oracle, this might have seemed like a bargain. But not many university students or even young professionals saw it that way. One of my former colleagues recalls being blown away by the fact that he could buy Red Hat Linux on a CD from a discount retailer for about $6. That's cheap.

Eclipsing Unix

Linux was also compatible with Unix programs and skills. A wide range of software development tools were available for it (again, for free or cheap). It had all the applications needed to run it as either part of a big cluster or in a server closet somewhere. The low costs involved also meant that Linux could be and frequently was brought in the back door of companies without IT management even having to know, much less approve.

By the close of the 1990s, Linux and open source more generally were not yet the dominant force and influence that they are today. But the market share of Linux was already eclipsing Unix on x86 servers. It was running some of the largest supercomputers in the world on the TOP500 list. It was the basis for many of the infrastructure products like "server appliances" sold during the dot-com boom.

And even just by the year 2000, it had attracted thousands of developers from all over the world. The open source development model was working.

Was Linux Inevitable?

At this point, it's worth taking a brief pause as we look back to the year 2000 to ask a rather simple question: "Are we looking at a landscape that was fated, at least in terms of broad strokes, or was the computer industry circa 2000 the result of an improbable chain of events?" After all, as we've seen, the industry as a whole was ready to cede the operating system market, and by extension a large chunk of the computer software market, to Microsoft. Surely almost everyone couldn't have been wrong. Was the arrival of Linus Torvalds and Linux a random improbable event that sent the computer industry off in a radically different direction?

Part of the answer depends upon whether you subscribe to the hero or the great man idea. The theory is primarily attributed to the Scottish philosopher and essayist Thomas Carlyle who gave a series of lectures on heroism in 1840, later published as *On Heroes, Hero-Worship, and The Heroic in History*. Carlyle stated that "The history of the world is but the biography of great men," reflecting his belief that heroes shape history through both their personal attributes and divine inspiration.

But it also depends upon how you view the computer industry at the height of the Internet dot-com era. One view might focus on a hard-charging Microsoft that was sweeping all before it. But another might correctly observe that the Internet was upending everything. And Microsoft was slow to react to a technology that came out of Unix and networking roots that were largely divorced from the PC world from which Microsoft sprang.

And as for all that industry common wisdom? Longtime Sun engineer and co-founder of Oxide Computer Bryan Cantrill is one person not impressed by industry wisdom. He argues that

> ...the industry was wrong. And the industry's been wrong many times before, so this should not be earth shattering or a newsflash. But the companies that embraced Windows had very serious deep structural problems. It was an act of capitulation. And it was not forward thinking at all. They were from all of them. From DEC, from HP, from IBM, and then I mean, probably the most pathetic one is SGI just because SGI absolutely should have been an independent thinker but felt that it needed to forego its future to Windows.

He goes on to add that

> I think if it's not Linux, it would have been one of the BSD variants that would have been the de facto Unix on x86. It is the rise of the Internet and it is the the rise of SMP [symmetrical multiprocessing] to a lesser degree, and then the the rise of a commodity microprocessors as the highest performing microprocessors to which Linux grabbed a ride, drafted on those economic mega-trends, but did not really contribute to them.

Open Source Accelerates

Open source software was born in the 20th century, but its great impact has been as a 21st-century phenomenon.

In part, this is because computing changed in a way that was beneficial to open source software such as Linux. Open source has also surely acted as something of a feedback loop to amplify many of those trends.

As we've seen, many of the major early open source projects had an affinity for networked, scale-out computing. Initially, this seemed at odds with the way many enterprise IT departments approached their infrastructure and applications, which tended toward the scale-up and monolithic. Need more capacity? Upgrade your server. Big check, please.

A New Enterprise IT Model

However, by the early 2000s, many organizations were revising how they thought about enterprise IT. As my then-analyst colleague Jonathan Eunice would write in a 2001 research note:

> *...we must understand that what constitutes enterprise computing today is in fact evolving quite rapidly. Every day it moves a little more toward, and morphs a little further into, the realm of network computing. Enterprise IT is increasingly implemented with standardized infrastructure, as well as increasingly is delivered over an Internet Protocol network connection. IT departments increasingly structure themselves, their missions, and their datacenters [this way] as do services providers.*

In the world of the Big Iron Unix vendors, an enormous amount of work went into vertical scalability, failover clustering, resource management, and other features to maximize the performance and reliability of single servers. Linux (and Windows) plugged away at features related to these requirements over time. But the world increasingly placed a lower priority on those needs and shifted its attention to the more distributed and network-centric workloads that were closer to the initial open source sweet spot. In fact, there's an argument to be made that at least some of the Linux development work funded by companies like IBM in the early 2000s focused far too obsessively on making Linux a better scale-up Unix.

Born on the Web

The demand for open source software in the new millennium has also been accelerated by a new class of businesses, which it is no exaggeration to say would not have been possible in the absence of open source. Just one cloud service provider, Amazon Web Services (AWS), likely has millions of servers. At that scale, presumably Amazon could have licensed the source code for an operating system or other software and then adapted them to their needs. However, like Google, Facebook, and essentially all Internet companies of any size, they primarily run open source software.

In part, this is simply a matter of cost. Especially for those companies offering services that they monetize only indirectly through advertising or other means (think free consumer Gmail from Google), it's unclear that the economics would work if they needed to pay for software in the traditional historical manner.

That's not to say that everything these companies use is free. It often makes sense for even technologically sophisticated organizations to establish commercial relationships with some of their suppliers. These companies also require many of the same kinds of specialized financial and other categories of software and software services all large businesses need. It rarely makes sense to do everything in-house.

Nonetheless, these companies are in a sense almost a new category of system vendor, producing and building much of the software (and even optimized hardware) for their internal use.

Build or Buy?

Still, every company needs to make decisions about where it focuses internal research and development. This was the central thesis of Nick Carr's 2003 article in *Harvard Business Review* entitled "IT Doesn't Matter" The incredible permeation of software into almost every aspect of business makes some of Carr's specific arguments seem increasingly overstated. (Many felt this was the case at the time as well.) As software plays into competitive differentiation at many levels, it's increasingly rare for companies to treat it as a pure commodity that can all be easily outsourced. However, his broader point that firms should focus on those areas where they can truly differentiate and capture value nonetheless applies.

Open source software makes it easier to trade off build and buy decisions because it's no longer a binary choice. Historically, software tended to be a take-it-or-leave-it proposition. If it didn't work *quite* like you wanted it to, you could put in a feature request to a vendor who might do something about it in a release or two. At least if you were an important enough customer. There was often the option of paying for something custom from your supplier, but that still put a lot of process in the way of getting the changes made.

With open source, companies can choose where to use available open source code unchanged—perhaps with the full support of a vendor. Or they can tweak and augment for their particular needs without the need to build the whole thing from scratch.

Disrupting the Status Quo

But, really, these arguments about economics, especially in the context of individual companies, skirt around the most important reasons why open source has accelerated so quickly. These reasons involve moving beyond a narrow view of open source as being just about code. It requires thinking about open source as both a very good development model and the means for individuals and companies to work together in ways that just weren't possible previously.

And that's been the real story of open source in this millennium. It increasingly isn't about being cheaper than proprietary software. Oh, open source software often is. And in some respects, it's classic Disruptive Innovation, which isn't all about price, but usually involves it to some degree (Figure 1-5).

The Disruptive Innovation Model

This diagram contrasts *product performance trajectories* (the red lines showing how products or services improve over time) with *customer demand trajectories* (the blue lines showing customers' willingness to pay for performance). As incumbent companies introduce higher-quality products or services (upper red line) to satisfy the high end of the market (where profitability is highest), they overshoot the needs of low-end customers and many mainstream customers. This leaves an opening for entrants to find footholds in the less-profitable segments that incumbents are neglecting. Entrants on a disruptive trajectory (lower red line) improve the performance of their offerings and move upmarket (where profitability is highest for them, too) and challenge the dominance of the incumbents.

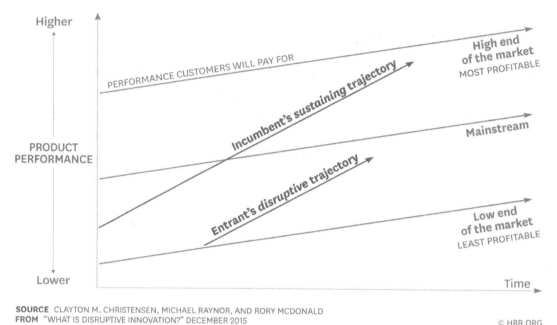

SOURCE CLAYTON M. CHRISTENSEN, MICHAEL RAYNOR, AND RORY MCDONALD
FROM "WHAT IS DISRUPTIVE INNOVATION?" DECEMBER 2015

© HBR.ORG

Figure 1-5. *The Disruptive Innovation model. Source: Clayton M. Christensen, Michael Raynor, and Rory McDonald, Copyright hbr.org*

Disruptive Innovation is the term coined by Harvard Business School Professor Clayton Christensen to "describe a process by which a product or service takes root initially in simple applications at the bottom of a market and then relentlessly moves up market, eventually displacing established competitors."

We've already seen an example in this book. The personal computer and the servers that evolved from it disrupted the traditional Unix vendors. The Unix vendors themselves often disrupted earlier forms of proprietary systems such as minicomputers.

Christensen also writes that "An innovation that is disruptive allows a whole new population of consumers at the bottom of a market access to a product or service that was historically only accessible to consumers with a lot of money or a lot of skill."

Relative to Unix, Linux fits this definition (as does Windows). And, indeed, a great deal of existing Unix business has shifted to Linux over time. This benefited large and technically sophisticated users who simply wanted to spend less money.

But it also allowed new categories of users and businesses that might well not have been able to afford proprietary Unix. Linux has arguably also been a disrupter to Windows by largely keeping it out of network infrastructure and scientific commuting markets that it might have eventually captured by default in the absence of an alternative like Linux or another free Unix.

We could apply similar arguments to many other categories of open source software—databases, application servers and other enterprise middleware, programming tools, virtualization, and so on. For many examples, the major virtue in their early years was that you could download them off the Internet and try them out for free. They weren't actually better in other respects than the proprietary alternatives.

From Disruption to Where Innovation Happens

However, during the past decade or so, things started to shift. Early cloud computing projects aimed at those who wanted to build their own clouds were probably the first big inflection point. Big data was another. Today, it's cloud-native, containers, artificial intelligence, the many projects related to them, and more. The common thread is that the manner in which open source allows innovations from multiple sources to be recombined and remixed in powerful ways has created a situation in which a huge number of the interesting innovations are now happening *first* in open source.

This is, in part, perhaps because otherwise independent open source communities can integrate and combine in powerful ways.

The Rise of Ecosystems

The cloud-native application development and infrastructure space is probably the most striking example of both complementary and competitive projects coming together in an area of technology. It started out being mostly about containers themselves, which are an efficient, lightweight way to isolate applications and application components within an operating system. But it's expanded with projects like Kubernetes, Prometheus, and hundreds more that encompass container orchestration, monitoring, logging, tracing, testing and building, service discovery, and just about anything else you can imagine might be useful to develop, secure, deploy, and manage distributed applications at scale. We also see the continuing intersection between cloud-native and other areas. For example, both software-defined storage and software-defined networking functionality are being containerized in various ways.

Artificial intelligence and machine learning (AI/ML) is another important area in which many of the tools and building blocks are dominated by open source. This includes the programming languages like Python, event systems like Kafka, tools for collaboration and sharing like Jupyter notebooks, and distributed storage like Ceph. You also see an intersection between this space and cloud-native as projects like Open Data Hub use container platforms to simplify complex software deployments.

Breaking Up Monoliths

Open source broadly has also evolved in step with a computing landscape that has grown far more distributed and flexible.

Software both molds the computing environment it runs in and reflects it. A great deal of proprietary software development historically focused on big programs with big license fees that would be (expensively) installed and customized and then left to run for years. Connections between programs and between programs and data required more expensive, complex software going by acronyms like EDI (Electronic Data Interchange). This fit with proprietary business models.

Complexity was actually a good thing (at least from the vendor's perspective). It tied customers to a single vendor, generated consulting fees, and created lots of upsell opportunities with all the options needed to make everything work together. Complexity also meant that there was no real way to determine up front if software was going to work as advertised. In practice, I've seen more than one high-end computer systems management program end up as a very expensive bookend sitting on a shelf because it never really quite did the job it was purchased to do.

Even once the Web came onto the scene, initial efforts to have less rigid integrations still reflected traditional ways of doing things, for example, service-oriented architecture (SOA), at least in its initial form. Many of the core ideas behind SOA, such as separating functions into distinct units that communicate with each other by passing data in a well-defined, shared format, are part of modern architectural patterns such as microservices. However, as implemented at first, SOA was often mired down by heavyweight web service standards and protocols.

By contrast, today's distributed systems world is more commonly characterized by lightweight protocols like REST; open source software components that can be mixed, matched, and adapted; and a philosophy that tends to favor coding reference implementations rather than going through heavyweight standards-setting processes. Open source has brought Unix-flavored approaches like highly modular design to both platform software and applications more broadly.

Linux and Open Source Had Arrived

In 2003, IBM aired a TV commercial titled "Prodigy." It featured a young boy sitting and absorbing pearls of wisdom. Hollywood director Penny Marshall: "Everything's about timing, kid." Harvard professor Henry Louis Gates: "Sharing data is the first step toward community." Muhammad Ali: "Speak your mind. Don't back down." The commercial ends with someone asking who the kid is. "His name is Linux."

The ad, created by Ogilvy & Mather, was a don't-change-the-channel ad with arresting imagery. Then-head of IBM's worldwide advertising, Lisa Baird, said it was targeted at "CEOs, CFOs, and prime ministers." The investment in this ad reflected how forward-looking individuals and organizations were starting to view open source at the turn of the century.

Irving Wladawsky-Berger, who recognized the potential of Linux early on and ran Linux strategy for IBM at the critical turn-of-the-century juncture, noted in a 2011 LinuxCon keynote that "We did not look at Linux as just another operating system any more than we looked at the Internet as just another network." He went on to say that we viewed it as "a platform for innovation into the future, just like we viewed the Internet."

Many view IBM's Linux investment as, at a minimum, an important endorsement for large enterprises to consider Linux a safe choice. Matt Asay of Amazon Web Services told me that "One of the biggest things that happened for open source was IBM's billion dollar commitment to Linux… Almost overnight, the conversations changed." Technology journalist Steven Vaughan-Nichols agrees saying, "What the IBM acceptance does is it gives an official Fortune 50 blessing to an operating system, which previously was still seen as this thing that only really nerdy academic sorts were going to do anything with."

As Wladawsky-Berger recounted to me in 2020:

And I still remember very well in December of '99, I called Sam Palmisano, the head of IBM Systems Group. And I said, Sam, the task force recommends that we should embrace Linux. And Sam said, okay, Irving, we will do that... And I said to Sam, when do you want to announce it? And Sam said, how about now? And I said, Sam, it's the Christmas holidays. Maybe we should wait until the new year. And in the second week of January of 2000, we made a major announcement saying that IBM would embrace Linux across all of these offerings.

Equally notable were the smaller companies like Red Hat, SUSE, and others who were starting to build businesses that not only used but were explicitly based on open source.

It may not have been clear to many in 2000 that Linux was anything more than a Unix-like operating system with an unusual license or that open source more broadly was a significant part of the software or business equation. However, here in 2020, it's clear that Linux and open source broadly are playing a major role in pushing software innovation forward. And that really means pushing business capabilities forward given how inextricably linked they are to software.

CHAPTER 2

From "Free" to "Open Source" to Products

We've seen how free and open source software not only came onto the scene but became an essential part of the computing landscape. Not just cheaper than proprietary software but a model that encourages the creation of software ecosystems and new innovations.

And this shift from being largely about less expensive software to being about *strategically* important things gets reflected in how organizations think about open source software today. For example, research conducted by Illuminas and published in Red Hat's "The State of Enterprise Open Source" in 2020 found 95% of IT leaders saying that enterprise open source is important to their enterprise infrastructure software strategy. And 75% said it was "very important" or "extremely important," up from 69% in the previous year's survey.

However, in the process of telling this story, I've moved quickly past some details. Are the oft-conflated "free" and "open source" one and the same, or do they capture an important distinction? Is open source software safe to use? How are community open source projects and commercial products related to each other?

Words Matter

Richard Stallman and his Free Software Foundation have long emphasized the word "free." But Stallman didn't intend that to mean someone had to give you a copy of software without charging for it. Rather, as he would later add in a footnote to the GNU Manifesto:

> *I have learned to distinguish carefully between "free" in the sense of freedom and "free" in the sense of price. Free software is software that users have the freedom to distribute and change. Some users may obtain copies*

G. Haff, *How Open Source Ate Software*, https://doi.org/10.1007/978-1-4842-6800-1_2

at no charge, while others pay to obtain copies—and if the funds help support improving the software, so much the better. The important thing is that everyone who has a copy has the freedom to cooperate with others in using it.

The oft-repeated shorthand is that free software is about free as in freedom rather than free as in beer.

Free as in Freedom

The GNU Manifesto was a reaction to what was happening in the computer industry more broadly at the time. Convivial academic collaborations were giving way to fragmented and proprietary commercial products.

As Steven Weber writes in *The Success of Open Source* (Harvard University Press, 2005):

The Free Software Foundation was fighting a battle with this narrative on philosophical grounds. To reverse the decline, Stallman sought to recapture what he thought was essential about software—the ideology of cooperative social relations embedded within the knowledge product. The philosophy implanted in the software was as important as the code.

There were a variety of terms floating around for this new type of software. Brian Behlendorf of the Apache web server project, an early open source software success that became an important element in the Internet build-out, favored "source code available software." But free software became the common term. And, for newcomers, distinguishing free as in freedom from free as in beer was often confusing.

For example, in the personal computer world, "freeware" typically *did* mean that there was no charge for a program and programs typically weren't bundled with their corresponding source code.

The Coining of "Open Source"

In 2018, writing on the 20th anniversary of the coining of the term "open source," Christine Peterson—who had been the executive director of the Foresight Institute—recounts how she was focused

...on the need for a better name and came up with the term "open source software." While not ideal, it struck me as good enough. I ran it by at least four others: Eric Drexler, Mark Miller, and Todd Anderson liked it, while a friend in marketing and public relations felt the term "open" had been over-used and abused and believed we could do better. He was right in theory; however, I didn't have a better idea, so I thought I would try to go ahead and introduce it.[1]

At a meeting later that week, the terminology again came up when discussing promotion strategy related to Netscape's plan to release its web browser code under a free software type of license. A loose, informal consensus developed around the open source term.

Influential publisher and event organizer Tim O'Reilly would soon popularize it. In addition to using the term himself, "on April 7, 1998, O'Reilly held a meeting of key leaders in the field. Announced in advance as the first Freeware Summit, by April 14 it was referred to as the first 'Open Source Summit,'" writes Peterson.

Pragmatism and Commercialism

The initial motivation for this shift in terminology was primarily practical. People were tired of explaining that it was perfectly well and good to charge for "free software."

However, it also served another purpose that one suspects many proponents such as O'Reilly realized from the beginning. It helped to distance open source as a broader movement for organization, collaboration, innovation, and development from the narrower and more philosophical bent of free software which was primarily focused on user freedoms.

O'Reilly would note the following year that "the Free Software Foundation represents only one of the traditions that make up the open source movement" with university software development traditions—most notably Berkeley's BSD—also being significant. Furthermore, for various reasons, free software had a particular focus on licenses as a tool to guarantee user freedom. This may have been important (especially at first), but it was only one component of the many things playing into openness, user freedoms, and collaborative development.

---

[1]https://opensource.com/article/18/2/coining-term-open-source-software

The shift in terminology also reflected how open source software, including but hardly limited to Linux, was becoming commercially interesting to established vendors, new vendors, and end users. Some traditional IT suppliers like IBM were making huge investments in open source. New companies that were inextricably linked to open source were aborning.

The first Internet wave in the latter half of the 1990s was built on open source. Large-scale hosting providers, those building specialized software appliances for serving email and web pages, and the early iterations of search engines and other now familiar services were usually at least partly built on open source software foundations. Many wanted to customize the software they depended on. Furthermore, the scale at which they operated increasingly made alternatives to proprietary software an economic necessity.

Commercialism led to something of a schism between hobbyists and those focused more on the ideological roots of free software on the one hand and the more pragmatic and profit minded on the other. A focus on free as in freedom software vs. software developed collaboratively and in the open because it was more effective to do so. The two aspects were by no means mutually exclusive, but there was clearly tension for both philosophical and pragmatic reasons.

Today, one interpretation is that the two perspectives have mostly reached a rapprochement; the practical benefits of open source software include user flexibility and freedoms that at least overlap their ideological counterparts. A more cynical view is that pragmatism and profit have come to dominate open source—at least with respect to where much of the attention, effort, and certainly money flows. In reality, it's a bit of both, and whether it's closer to one or the other is going to depend on your priorities and point of view.

In the next chapter, you'll see how this played out and continues to do so with respect to software licensing (although the free vs. open source dichotomy, such as it is, isn't just a matter of license choice).

Projects vs. Products

I've been mostly talking about open source software in terms of just the software code itself. For a hobbyist project, that may be a reasonable simplification. For Linus Torvalds, it was bits on a desktop computer at the University of Helsinki. These days, it's more commonly files stored in an online repository like GitHub. No one is selling the software. No one is promising support in any sort of formal way.

However, for most products that companies sell, it's important to distinguish between projects and products.

Upstream and Downstream

In its simplest form, there is an "upstream" community project and a "downstream" product based on the upstream. (The upstream may just be a "community" of one person or a small group for newer or smaller projects.)

For this discussion, assume that the product is also fully open source software although some companies practice partial open source development by combining core open source components with proprietary ones in various ways. Downstream products may also bring together and integrate independent and quasi-independent upstreams, but the same general principle applies.

Upstream is the catch-all term for the ultimate source of the project. It's the core group of contributors, their mailing lists, website, and so on. Ideally, it's where most of the development happens. By contrast, the product is something that a customer buys to solve a business problem.

Innovation, rate of improvement, wide acceptance, and other aspects of the product may derive in large part from the fact that a vibrant upstream community exists. But don't confuse the two. As Paul Cormier, Red Hat's CEO, puts it, "Too often, we see open source companies who don't understand the difference between projects and products. In fact, many go out of their way to conflate the two."[2]

Usually, the open source project comes first. Sometimes the process gets reversed when a company acquires a proprietary product and releases it as open source. But most of the same principles apply to the relationship of the project to the product.

---

[2]www.redhat.com/en/blog/what-makes-us-red-hat

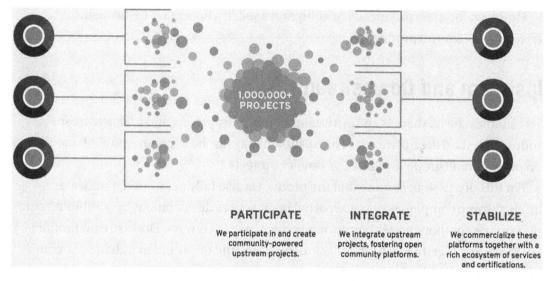

Figure 2-1. *The open source product development process. Source: Red Hat*

Projects and Products Depend on Each Other

To be clear, there are strong linkages between successful projects and successful products. As Figure 2-1 shows, integrated and stabilized products based on open source flow from broad participation in upstream community projects.

For example, as I'll cover in more detail in a later chapter, metrics for community success often include measures of community breadth; how many contributors work for someone other than the project's creator? This is important because a community with no outside contributors is, in some respects, an open source project in name only. Others can look at the code, but there's none of the broader participation that makes the open source development model work so well.

It's also good to have a strong relationship between project and product from a development perspective. "Upstream first" is a best practice, meaning that code changes go into the project from whence they subsequently flow downstream into the product.

It's a best practice, in part, because it means less work. There's less code to maintain that's not part of the upstream. This isn't always possible. The most vibrant and independent projects won't always accept code that, for example, is specific to a particular customer's product requirement and isn't of broader interest. But companies that work effectively with and participate in upstream projects stand to have the most influence when it comes to decisions that are important to them.

What Support Means

However, many attributes that are part of a product aren't necessarily in a project.

Many assume that the main difference is that people pay for support in the case of a product. That's not wrong; customers still call and email for support in the case of software products based on open source just as they do for software products that aren't based on open source.

Support has also broadened since the days when it meant mostly picking up the phone to get a question answered.

When things go wrong in a production software environment, the ability to access the right information quickly can be the difference between a fast return to normal operations and a costly outage. And sometimes, the best support call is one you don't need to make. For example, customers today like to search to locate articles, technical briefs, and product documentation that are most relevant to the problem at hand. System architects like to browse detailed technical case studies that engineers have designed, tested, and benchmarked.

Reducing Risk

But, more broadly, what customers are looking for from enterprise software companies is reduced risk. In addition to the support itself, this falls into several different areas including the creation of a long and stable life cycle, certifications, and process rigor that often goes beyond what is found in even a well-run project.

Supporting the Complete Life Cycle

First is life cycle support. In a project, it's common to have an unstable branch and a stable branch. At some point of development, the unstable branch is deemed to be stable, it replaces the current stable branch, and the cycle begins again. At that point, the prior stable branch is typically retired. It's still available, but work on it is usually frozen. (This isn't a hard and fast rule; sometimes developers will retrofit a fix for a particularly serious bug, but, generally speaking, community projects tend to focus on the latest and greatest.)

However, enterprise customers often want long life cycles. This can mean five years, seven years, or even longer. Longer life cycles mean more choice and flexibility, reduced cost and risk, and greater ease of planning. To meet this requirement, enterprise software companies "backport" fixes and feature enhancements into older versions of their software.

Everything Working Together

Certifications are also an important part of an enterprise software product. This includes certifying hardware, certifying software, and certifying providers like public clouds. These types of certifications are based on joint testing with partners, established business relationships, and other agreements both to reduce the number of potential issues and to have processes in place to resolve problems when they happen.

While well-run projects incorporate automated tests and other processes intended to reduce the number of bugs introduced into the code base, downstream products tend to have more robust quality assurance testing with many engineers dedicated to that role. For example, Red Hat's program includes acceptance, functionality, regression, integration, and performance testing.

Other product features can include legal protections such as defending customers against intellectual property (IP) lawsuits or dealing with certain other legal issues.

The Intersection of Security and Risk

A final area of product assurance that is often top of mind today is security. This is a particular area of concern for just about any software user today, and open source software users are no exception. Many aspects of open source product security are similar to those associated with enterprise software products generally. For example, it's important to have a dedicated team of engineers who proactively monitor, identify, and address potential risks. This lets them give accurate advice to quickly assess risk and minimize business impact.

There are also some real or perceived differences between considering security in the context of open source software and proprietary software.

Securing Open Source

This discussion requires teasing apart several different concepts.

The first is the concept of IT security overall which is generally relevant to commercial software products, whether open source, proprietary, or a blend of the two (and which also applies to projects to a greater or lesser degree). The second is the question of whether there are security challenges or advantages that are specific to open source software. And finally, what recent hot security topics relate to open source software?

What Is IT Security?

Security is a big topic, and it gets even bigger if one pulls in adjacent subjects such as data governance, data protection, incident management, regulatory compliance, and so forth. An in-depth treatment is beyond the scope of this book, but let's take a look at some highlights.

For our purposes here, IT security refers to protecting data and systems from unauthorized access and implementing processes that prevent misuse, modification, or theft of sensitive information. Cybersecurity covers the protection of data on the Internet from hackers and other cybercriminals. IT and cybersecurity are methods of establishing a set of security strategies that work together to help protect your digital data from unauthorized access, use, misuse, disclosure, destruction, modification, or disruption.

Traditionally, security was focused on perimeter-based security, but that perimeter is increasingly dissolving as organizations disperse their workloads outside of their on-prem datacenter into a public cloud. Security is also transforming from something often done as a one-off checkpoint at the end of a development cycle to something continuous starting at the very beginning of the cycle.

Business as Usual: Patch and Automate

An open source software vendor needs to provide security patches and advice in much the same manner as any other software vendor—though the open source company has the added advantage of being better able to collaborate closely with customers, partners, and other vendors.

Many projects also do an effective job of developing and making available security fixes and best practices—especially when fixes are pushed upstream quickly—but the process may take longer and be less formalized.

Misconfigurations and inadequate change control are a top threat to security. Misconfigurations can leave systems vulnerable to attack. Change control is critical for understanding who modified configurations, when, and what was changed throughout system life cycles.

Automation can help you streamline daily operations as well as integrate security into processes, applications, and infrastructure from the start. In fact, fully deploying security automation can reduce the average cost of a breach by 95%, but only 16% of organizations have done so according to a report from IBM Security, "2019 Cost of a Data Breach Report."

Does Open Source Hurt Security or Help It?

Does access to source code by both the "good guys" and the "bad guys" help or hurt security? When people ask whether open source is more or less secure than proprietary software, this question is often the one they're asking whether explicitly or otherwise.

One can get a sense of the debate from two different statements attributed to the US Department of Homeland Security's Luke McCormack in 2016. A week after his statement that opening up federal source code would be like giving the Mafia a "copy of all FBI system code" set off a minor firestorm, he walked it back to say, "Security through obscurity is not true security: we cannot depend on vulnerabilities not being exploited just because they have not been discovered yet."

Does Code Help the Bad Guys?

The hurts-security side of the argument is rooted in physical analogies.

When many people think about security, they probably think of something like a home security system. Physical security systems do typically depend to at least some degree on "security through obscurity." They may actively protect against a wide range of threats, but they often also depend on, to at least to some degree, the would-be burglar not knowing precisely what types of sensors there are, where they are placed, and how the property is being monitored.

The degree to which obscurity makes software more secure is controversial, and the answer probably boils down to "it depends" to some degree. As Daniel Miessler has noted, "It's utterly sacrilegious to base the security of a cryptographic system on the secrecy of the algorithm."[3] At the same time, he argues that "The key determination for whether obscurity is good or bad reduces to whether it's being used a layer on top of good security, or as a replacement for it. The former is good. The latter is bad."

Even the National Institute of Standards and Technology (NIST) in the United States equivocates. On the one hand, it has stated that "System security should not depend on the secrecy of the implementation or its components." However, it also recommends (in the same document) that

---

[3]https://danielmiessler.com/study/security-by-obscurity/

For external-facing servers, reconfigure service banners not to report the server and OS type and version, if possible. (This deters novice attackers and some forms of malware, but it will not deter more skilled attackers from identifying the server and OS type.)[4]

The general consensus seems to be that obscurity doesn't help much (if any) and you shouldn't depend on it in any case. Attacks mostly come through probing for weaknesses en masse. They exploit configuration errors, the use of default or weak passwords, and *known* vulnerabilities that haven't been patched yet. Any vulnerability that a white hat security researcher finds by combing through source code could be found by a black hat one first. But that's not a common pattern.

Or Is "Many Eyes" the Secret Sauce?

At the same time, it's not clear to what degree the common argument favoring open source for security reasons—"with many eyes, all bugs are shallow"—applies either. One problem is that many eyes can still miss things. The other is that not all projects have many eyes on them.

In early 2017, I sat down with then-CTO of the Linux Foundation, Nicko van Someren, to talk about the Core Infrastructure Initiative (CII), a group set up in the wake of the Heartbleed bug, a security vulnerability that potentially affected about 70% of the world's web servers.

In the case of Heartbleed specifically, the bug (discovered by a Google engineer) was quickly fixed, but it exposed the fact that a number of key infrastructure projects were underfunded. As van Someren put it:

Probably trillions of dollars of business were being done in 2014 on OpenSSL [the software with the Heartbleed bug], and yet in 2013, they received 3 thousand bucks worth of donations from industry to support the development of the project. This is quite common for the projects that are under the hood, not the glossy projects that everybody sees.

---

[4]http://nvlpubs.nist.gov/nistpubs/Legacy/SP/nistspecialpublication800-123.pdf

He went on to say that

We try to support those projects with things like doing security audits where appropriate, by occasionally putting engineers directly on coding, often putting resources in architecture and security process to try to help them help themselves by giving them the tools they need to improve security outcomes. We're funding the development of new security testing tools. We're providing tools to help projects assess themselves against well-understood security practices that'll help give better outcomes. Then, when they don't meet all the criteria, help them achieve those criteria so that they can get better security outcomes.

The CII has continued this work, and while hardening critical infrastructure is a task that's never finished, many of the most problematic areas uncovered by Heartbleed have since been fixed.

Thinking Differently About Risk

The best that we can probably say is that software being open source is neither a hazard nor a particular panacea. And it's probably not a very useful debate.

Patrick Heim, CISO, ClearSky Security, argued at the 2018 Open Source Leadership Summit that "Maybe [we] need to move beyond the argument of which is better. How do we live in this new world where there is more open source? We have to think slightly differently about how we manage risk."

Identify	Protect	Detect	Respond	Recover
Risk management strategy	Access control	Continuous monitoring	Incident Response Plan	Develop & implement improvements
Regulatory compliance	Data security Information protection Process & Procedures	Detection process	Communication Mitigation activities	Communication
Asset management	Protective technology			

Figure 2-2. *The National Institute of Standards and Technology (NIST) cybersecurity framework focuses on using business drivers to guide cybersecurity activities and considering cybersecurity risks as part of the organization's risk management processes*

This includes a lot more automation. A lot more monitoring. And a lot more understanding of a software supply chain that increasingly will include open source components.

And, ultimately, it's about making risk-based decisions. That means having an honest conversation with the business about priorities and risk management which includes the many aspects of a cybersecurity plan such as those shown in a framework like the one in Figure 2-2.

Securing the Supply Chain

Before wrapping up though, let's consider that software supply chain in more detail. First, some background.

With the increased use of open source software generally, open source code is finding its way into more and more applications—proprietary as well as open source. For example, for its "2020 Open Source Security and Risk Analysis Report," Synopsys audited 1,253 applications and found that 99% of them included open source components and that, overall, 70% of the total code was open source.

That's good, right? Open source really is eating software.

However, there's a flip side to that reality. Synopsys also found that 82% of codebases had components more than four years out of date and 88% of the codebases had components with no development activity during the last two years.

The issue isn't that companies (and individuals) are making use of open source components. It's that, in many cases, they're not managing that use. We see similar patterns for container images downloaded from public repositories and for applications that are simply no longer maintained.

Open source code can be a source of security vulnerabilities if you use unsigned software or deploy open source code in an insecure manner. Using unvetted open source software directly from upstream communities can leave you open to security vulnerabilities and supply chain attacks, which exploit weaknesses in third-party services and software to compromise a final target. These attacks take many forms, including hijacking software updates and injecting malicious code into legitimate software. Supply chain attacks increased by 78% in 2018 according to the Symantec "Internet Security Threat Report, Volume 24."

The lesson though shouldn't be not to use open source software. The same problem exists with proprietary libraries that haven't been updated.

Rather, one lesson should be to know the answer to questions such as whether a software component is being maintained, who is maintaining it at what level of activity, and who is vetting it for trustworthiness. Another is to obtain software directly from trustworthy sources. And still another is to actively scan your software throughout its life cycle with automated tools that can detect unpatched known vulnerabilities, insecure configurations, or other factors that an attacker could take advantage of.

Enter DevSecOps

I'll cover the iterative development and operational approach known as DevOps later in this book, but here I want to highlight the security aspect in particular.

The DevOps term was supposed to connote breaking down the wall between developers and operations teams. But quite a few people started arguing that security should be explicitly in the term too; after all, no team was more siloed historically than security specialists.

Others pushed back. Why not DevBizOps (developers and operations working together with business stakeholders)? Or the many other variations of functional groups within an organization who should talk to each other? DevOps, they argued, always assumed broadly cross-functional coordination.

But the security drumbeat kept on. Eventually, even some of the influential practitioners who were most resistant to the DevSecOps term conceded that security often still *didn't* get the attention it deserved. Maybe DevSecOps served as a useful reminder after all.

What Is DevSecOps?

DevSecOps is a way for organizations to extend some of the practices and processes from DevOps to continue rapid development and release cycles while simultaneously addressing security concerns. And doing so without the overhead and delays for which security has often been blamed.

It's an area of widespread interest. According to market researchers Gartner, "Throughout 2019, integrating security into DevOps—i.e., delivering DevSecOps—has been one of the fastest-growing areas of client interest, with discussions of the topic at Gartner increasing by more than 200%, compared with 2018."

Specifically, the goal of DevSecOps is to take DevOps and secure every aspect of the application development pipeline, delivery, and operations. This includes integrating and automating appropriate security tools, methods, and culture throughout the entire application life cycle. It also requires combining DevOps expertise with security expertise with a common goal of providing the optimal balance of security, speed to market, and stable, reliable applications in production.

DevSecOps is also part of an effort to improve speed by systematically introducing security earlier ("shifted left") in the development process, so the security people don't just get notified at the end, when the software is ready to deploy, forcing the security team to start their evaluation of everything that was missed throughout the entire process. This workflow positions the security team as the team that always says "no" as the final gatekeeper prior to deployment. It also makes for expensive rework, especially if it turns out there are fundamental security design flaws in the software.

One ongoing challenge for DevSecOps with respect to both applications in general and cloud-native applications in particular is that, as noted earlier, security is a multifaceted problem. There's scanning for known vulnerabilities in source code. There's confirming that current versions of application dependencies like libraries used to build the application. There's checking that applications running in production remain up to date. There's searching for vulnerabilities in containers that encapsulate applications together with other components they need. There's making sure that the application platform, toolchain, and developer clients are themselves secure.

The list goes on. One result is that it's usually not possible to have a single comprehensive security platform that handles everything end to end. On the other hand, with both technologies and threats evolving rapidly, the many open source and open source–adjacent tools in this space mean that a great deal of innovation is going on. Furthermore, there are integration points between many of the cloud-native security tools in particular, and more are being added all the time.

A number of companies have the goal of putting together offerings that handle a bigger slice of the security pie with one integrated tool, and they're making some progress. That said, security products have tended to be point products that mostly did one thing more or less forever, and that's unlikely to radically shift in the near future.

Trusting the Cloud

A relative recent security wrinkle is that workloads increasingly run, in whole or in part, on systems which are under the control of a third-party public cloud provider to greater or lesser degrees.

Relying on third-party infrastructure isn't new of course. Web hosting dates back to the 1990s, and timesharing is even older. But the advent of another whole abstraction layer in the form of containers, the increased use of services provided by multiple providers, and a generally scarier threat landscape overall have provided the impetus to better protect applications and data from vulnerabilities in underlying layers of the stack. (See Figure 2-3.)

Red Hat chief security architect Mike Bursell writes that

The reason we care is not just the different versions and the different layers, but the number of different things—and different entities—that we need to trust if we're going to be happy running any sort of sensitive workload on these types of stacks. I need to trust every single layer, and the owner of every single layer, not only to do what they say they will do, but also not to be compromised. This is a big stretch when it comes to running my sensitive workloads.

Figure 2-3. *Layers of the stack in a containerized environment. Source: Opensource.com CC-BY-SA 4.0*

One approach to dealing with this problem is trusted execution environments (TEEs), which work in conjunction with the secure enclave technologies built into many modern microprocessors. TEEs can eliminate the need to trust much of the underlying software. They don't completely eliminate the need to trust underlying layers, but they can much reduce the attack surface. There's still the processor and its firmware. And you need to trust the TEE middleware itself. (But that's open source and available for inspection.)

Enarx is one open source project that provides hardware independence for securing applications using TEEs. Enarx lets you securely deliver an application compiled into WebAssembly all the way into a cloud provider and execute it remotely. As Red Hat security engineer Nathaniel McCallum puts it:

> *The way that we do this is, we take your application as inputs, and we perform an attestation process with the remote hardware. We validate that the remote hardware is, in fact, the hardware that it claims to be, using cryptographic techniques. The end result of that is not only an increased level of trust in the hardware that we're speaking to; it's also a session key, which we can then use to deliver encrypted code and data into this environment that we have just asked for cryptographic attestation on.*

The Promise of Machine Learning

Another promising new set of technologies related to security is machine learning, which can potentially identify issues that haven't yet been manually identified and added to a database. For example, by aggregating security metrics, such as from secure code scanning or the frequency of vulnerabilities raised against a project or community response times, machine learning can assess a project's dependency list and make real-time recommendations for improving the security posture of the monitored software project.

Machine learning also shows a lot of promise in the area of "Configuration as Code" (CaC) and "Infrastructure as Code" (IaC). Both forms of configuration management often contain datasets that enforce separation of security boundaries via network policy or access control, often expressed as human-readable text in a configuration file. (YAML and JSON are common formats.) As software evolves over time to introduce new features, machine learning models can monitor these configurations for possible security risks introduced and make recommended changes to the user, ideally as a "pull request" that can be reviewed and merged by the user.

How Do You Get Started?

Our journey so far has taken us from the earliest days of free software through initial commercialization to the products that derive from open source projects. It will soon be time to roll our sleeves up and dive into what it means to develop open source software and how to participate in open source communities. But, first, there's the matter of the law. What's the legal status of open source, and what are some of the important basics you should know?

CHAPTER 3

What's the Law?

Turn the clock back to the late 1990s, and a common, if often self-interested, criticism of free software was that it subverted intellectual property (IP) law by giving away creative works. Even worse, it allowed others to profit from those works without any of that profit finding its way back to the original creator. Furthermore, it made it more difficult for companies and individuals who wrote and controlled the sale and distribution of their software in the traditional and proprietary way to profit from *their* creative endeavors.

For example, Sun Microsystems' eventual demise as an independent company can be traced in no small part to Linux cutting into the sales of Sun's proprietary Solaris Unix operating system (and the associated expensive systems that ran it). Sun did eventually open source a version of Solaris as OpenSolaris, but it was too little, too late. Microsoft famously attacked Windows competitor Linux for being what then-CEO Steve Ballmer called "a cancer."

In fact, free and open source software is very much entwined with IP law in three main areas: copyright and licensing, trademarks, and patents. This chapter only scratches the surface of a specialized area of law, but it should provide you with the basics to at least know the right questions to ask when discussing these matters with a lawyer, which you should generally do if you have important questions related to a specific situation.

In this chapter, I've tried to present a balanced view of mainstream legal opinion concerning these areas of law. However, be aware that not all the questions covered in this chapter are the subject of substantial bodies of legislation and case law, and, partly for this reason, experts may disagree on some of the nuances.

How Copyright Works

I start with copyright because much else rests on owning the copyright in a software work.

The first statute to provide for a government-enforced copyright for publishers was the Statute of Anne, an act of the Parliament of Great Britain passed in 1710.

47

© Gordon Haff 2021
G. Haff, *How Open Source Ate Software*, https://doi.org/10.1007/978-1-4842-6800-1_3

It was, among other things, a rather belated attempt to address the fact that anyone could buy or rent a printing press and print any text that they wanted, whether they had written the work or not. In 1886, the Berne Convention first established the recognition of copyrights among sovereign nations, and the Berne Convention as modified over the years still largely governs copyright internationally today.

There are many intricacies to copyright. But, for our purposes here, it covers most original expressions of creative, intellectual, or artistic forms. It does not cover ideas or, in general, facts. It exists from the moment of creation, such as the act of writing a letter. Registration is not required, although in the United States doing so may be useful if the need arises to pursue damages for copyright infringement. Copyright grants its holder, whether the creator or someone who has commissioned the work for hire, exclusive rights to publication, performance, and other uses for, in most of the world, 50–70 years after the author's death.

There are some exceptions. The first-sale doctrine in the United States, often called exhaustion of rights elsewhere, allows for the reselling of a book or other physical object. Fair use permits some limited copying and distribution without permission of the copyright holder, for example, to excerpt a paragraph from a book in order to critique it. US government works are generally not subject to copyright at all (at least within the United States itself).

Can Software Be Copyrighted?

Copyright law came about once it became economical to inexpensively reproduce a creative work. The printing press was the initial impetus, but similar logic carried over fairly naturally to audio and, eventually, film recordings.

But what of software? Certainly it can be easily reproduced, but, coming from a historical mindset where copyright covered mostly artistic works, is a set of step-by-step instructions—which, after all, is all a program is—deserving of copyright protection?

This wasn't even a very interesting question for a long time. As we've seen, early-on software existed to sell hardware, and both companies and users were pretty casual about passing that software around.

As Red Hat IP lawyer Richard Fontana puts it:

> *Software as a kind of product of human ingenuity got going during a time period when the legal status of software was very unclear. If there was any sort of consensus, it was that software was a thing that wasn't susceptible to*

being owned. It wasn't a form of property. Although the reality is, almost from the beginning, the situation was more confusing than that may sound. It was just not very clear. There were differing viewpoints about the legal situation and about whether it would be good policy or not for the legal system to allow software to be something that you can own. And, for business related reasons, the question was, for a long time, not super critical because there wasn't a software industry as such.

Copyright Comes to Software

But this state of affairs began to change in the 1970s.

In 1974, the Commission on New Technological Uses of Copyrighted Works (CONTU) was established in the United States. It decided that "computer programs, to the extent that they embody an author's original creation, are proper subject matter of copyright." In 1980, the US Congress enshrined this decision in copyright law. Fontana adds

By 1980, it's clear in the United States and other countries that software source code at least[1] is something that you can have copyright on. And therefore, if you develop software, it's something you can own and if you can own it, then you can license it and if you could license it, you can make money from controlling the scarcity.

Open Source Software Is Copyrighted Too

At this point, it's worth highlighting an important fact. Open source software *is* copyrighted software that just happens to be released under an open source license (of which more in a bit).

---

[1]It was still not necessarily clear at the time whether the machine-readable output of that source code, that is, the program a computer actually runs, was also covered by copyright. However, this protection became established over time as well. (In the United States, this protection is associated with the Apple v. Franklin 3rd Circuit case in 1983. `https://en.wikipedia.org/wiki/Apple_Computer,_Inc._v._Franklin_Computer_Corp.`)

Generally speaking.

An exception is software that has been put into the public domain. Public domain is a bit of a muddle, and the term is also widely misused, so it's worth touching on briefly.

No one owns a work in the public domain. Anyone can modify, distribute, or sell a book, a musical composition, or software in the public domain without any attribution. They can even claim they wrote it (which could be plagiarism, but that's not a concern of copyright law nor, in general, of the legal system).

Public domain does *not* simply mean that something is publicly available. The website that you're reading for free is probably still copyrighted even though its contents can be read by anyone. You can't legally copy those contents and republish them on your own site.

How Do Works Get into the Public Domain?

Prior to some US copyright law changes in the late 1970s and 1980s, copyrighting something in the United States required an explicit copyright notice. Absent such a notice, whether left off deliberately or accidentally, a work automatically fell into the public domain. (This was often not the case in other countries which had generally shifted away from pre–Berne Convention copyright notice formalities.) However, once copyright was made automatic, it became necessary to actively give the work into the public domain by a waiver statement—though there's no generally accepted form that such a statement takes.

As noted earlier, many government documents are also never copyrighted. Copyright terms also eventually expire, although the long terms of current copyright mean that likely no software has entered the public domain in this manner.

Some consider public domain software to be a form of free or open source software. For example, the FSF says that "if a work is in the public domain, it might as well have an all-permissive non-copyleft free software license."

However, this is a contentious topic. The usual argument against public domain is that there is no mechanism to dedicate something to the public domain in most countries. There isn't a recognized way in the United States either although the United States does have the concept of "copyright abandonment" which is probably what's being exercised from a legal perspective when software says it's dedicated to the public domain. Furthermore, some countries also have the concept of moral rights that relate to things like attribution and preserving the integrity of a work which are not generally recognized in common law countries like the United Kingdom and United States but are seen as rights that one can't disclaim to varying degrees elsewhere, including parts of continental Europe.

Public Domain Alternatives

While most of these issues mostly don't affect individuals *using* software (which was the FSF's historical concern), they're problematic for open source software projects in other respects. As we'll discuss in the next chapter, "FOSS isn't just a license, it's a way of organizing to make software. Public domain sidesteps both the license and the community aspects, and it's the latter that usually makes FOSS valuable," as James Vasile, a partner at Open Tech Strategies, puts it.

The fact that public domain doesn't have a clear legal status in some countries makes it hard to collaborate given the uncertainty.

In fact, one of the early open source licenses grew out of questions about public domain software.

According to Jim Gettys, "Distributing X [Window System, a windowing system for Project Athena at MIT in the mid-1980s] under license became enough of a pain that I argued we should just give it away." However, it turned out that just placing it into the public domain wasn't an option. "IBM would not touch public domain code (anything without a specific license). We went to the MIT lawyers to craft text to explicitly make it available for any purpose. I think Jerry Saltzer probably did the text with them. I remember approving of the result," Gettys added. This became the original MIT License, also called the X Consortium or X11 License at the time.[2]

Various licenses have been created to address the shortcomings of copyright waivers. CC0 from Creative Commons is probably the best known, but it's not on the set of approved licenses maintained by the Open Source Initiative (OSI) whose approval of licenses serves as a generally accepted standard for what constitutes an open source software license. Creative Commons did submit it for approval at one point but withdrew it over OSI concerns related to patent language in the license.

However, other licenses have since been approved by the OSI. The MIT-0 (sometimes referred to as MIT-Zero) license simply strips the attribution requirement ("The above copyright notice and this permission notice shall be included in all copies

---

[2]https://opensource.com/article/19/4/history-mit-license gives a more in-depth account of the slightly mysterious history of the MIT License.

or substantial portions of the Software") from the already minimalist MIT License. The Unlicense takes a more explicitly anti-copyright stance.

In practice, choosing an OSI-approved license is the sensible approach for most projects. Many organizations only allow the use of open source software that is licensed under the terms of some subset of OSI-approved licenses. It's worth noting that subset may be fairly small at many companies. Therefore, even given the existence of MIT-0 and the Unlicense, it may still make sense to use one of the common permissive licenses for your project—even if you prefer the idea of a more public domain–like license.

What Is This Licensing Stuff Anyway?

So far, this chapter has gone back and forth between discussions of copyright and licensing without actually explaining what licensing is. Before getting to open source licensing in particular, let's briefly look at licensing in general. Specifically, why do you often need a license to run software? After all, if I buy a book and read it, I don't need to agree to a license in order to do so.

Licensing (Probably) Isn't Necessary

One common rationale for licensing goes something like this. When I read a book, I look at the pages with my eyes and my brain comprehends the content. There's no copying going on, at least not in a literal mechanical way.

However, if I buy a computer program on some media, running that program typically requires copying it to a disk drive, and, subsequently, at least parts of the program need to be copied into various components of a computer's memory system in order to run. Therefore, one line of thinking goes, you need a license to do all that copying.

But copyright law allows for incidental copying needed to use a product. And, in fact, the law has been amended over time to explicitly allow certain types of reproduction for functional purposes. One could argue that with today's digital distribution, the situation is murkier but it really doesn't matter because software that's sold or broadly distributed typically *is* licensed.

So Why Licensing?

So if licensing likely isn't *needed* just to use software, why is it so commonplace?

The exact origins of software licensing are unclear, but the practice became institutionalized after IBM introduced its System/360 mainframe in 1966. Prior to the System/360, IBM's multiple products were all incompatible with each other. By contrast, the new compatible System/360 line let customers upgrade to larger systems without replacing or modifying their application programs. In fact, those programs can still mostly run on IBM's current IBM Z mainframe models.

Historically, IBM like many other computer companies "bundled" its hardware and software together; you couldn't buy one without the other, and the customer only saw the bundled price. However, as the System/360 was starting to roll out, IBM made the decision to unbundle some of its software from its hardware.

The impetus for IBM's decision seems to have been RCA's introduction of a "plug-compatible" competitor to the System/360, which is to say a computer that could, in principle, run the same software and attach to the same hardware peripherals. The RCA system was ultimately unsuccessful for a variety of reasons, but IBM was nonetheless concerned that refusing to sell its software to run elsewhere could raise antitrust concerns. And, if it priced and sold software to RCA's customers, it needed to sell software to its own customers as well.[3]

In December 1966, IBM established an unbundling task force led by Howard Figueroa, the IBM director of policy development on the corporate staff.

The task force looked at options to control the use of their software. In the words of task force member Watts S. Humphrey:

> *We debated a family of asset protection alternatives, including patenting, trade secrets, and copyright. We quickly dismissed patenting. It was not clear that software could be patented, and the volume of software products and versions would quickly overwhelm the patent process... That left copyright as the only viable alternative.*[4]

---

[3]Bundling and tying have been an antitrust focus in quite a few cases, including an earlier IBM case involving the bundling of hardware and maintenance services. In the mid-1980s, Data General would lose in court for refusing to sell the RDOS operating system used by its NOVA minicomputer to Digidyne, a maker of NOVA-compatible hardware.

[4]Watts S. Humphrey, "Software Unbundling: A Personal Perspective," *IEEE Annals of the History of Computing*, 2002.

Yet, IBM viewed copyright as weak protection. In part, this was likely because the status of software copyrightability was still an open question in the 1960s. In any case, Humphrey went on to write that "To improve the level of protection, we coupled the copyright with a license and counted on the license to provide the real protection."

The practice has remained popular with vendors in part because companies have been trying to find ways around the first-sale doctrine provided by copyright law for a long time. First-sale basically allows you to sell a book or chair you own to someone else without either getting the permission of the original manufacturer or retailer or giving them any additional money. But if you sell widgets, you don't want Joe to buy your used widget (for which you don't get any money); you want Joe to buy a new widget from you.

Licensing is one way of sidestepping first-sale; if you don't actually own a product, you can't resell it. This is a major reason why we see the widespread use of licensing with respect to digital products of all kinds today.

How Open Source Licensing Works

This brings us to open source licensing specifically.

In some respects, the choice of open source licenses is a less contentious topic than it used to be. However, 2019 in particular saw rekindled debate on a couple of separate but related fronts, which I'll get to in a bit.

Licenses as a legal concept remain an important part of open source software's foundations. As a result, it's useful to broadly understand their role and some of the key distinctions among them that can affect how open source development works.

Do You Have to Give Back or Not?

There are two broad categories of open source licenses. One includes "copyleft" licenses, of which the GNU General Public License (GPL) is the best known and is the one used by Linux. The other includes "permissive" licenses, most notably the Apache, BSD, and MIT licenses.

There are a variety of other licenses as well. Some are essentially legacy licenses that have just never been retired. Others are designed to be more suitable for other copyrighted material such as books or photographs. For example, the CC BY-SA Creative

Commons license variant requires attribution but does not prohibit noncommercial use or remixing.[5]

Other licenses impose more, fewer, or different types of restrictions within that general framework. But copyleft and permissive capture the core distinction.

Protecting the Commons

A copyleft license requires that if changes are made to a program's code and the changed program is distributed outside an organization, the source code containing the changes must likewise be distributed. Permissive licenses don't include that requirement.

Essentially, copyleft says that you can't take someone's code, change it or mix it up with other code, and then ship the resulting program in machine-readable form without also making it available in human-readable source code form. There's a philosophical point here. If you take from the commons—that is, use open source software someone else has created—you also have to give back to the commons if you distribute it.

This reciprocity requirement also had roots in the practical. In a software world that seemed to be becoming increasingly proprietary and profit-seeking in the 1980s, why *wouldn't* corporations naturally vacuum up code from the commons, give little in exchange, and effectively become free riders? After all, the "tragedy of the commons" was a social science phenomenon articulated way back in 1833 by the British economist William Forster Lloyd, from the hypothetical example of unregulated grazing on common land in the British Isles. Better to require reciprocal contributions, especially given that the advantages of open source as a development model mostly hadn't yet been articulated and proven. (And any *disadvantages* of a copyleft approach for collaboration hadn't really been thought through.)

But it was also just a reflection of a software movement that was as much about philosophical principles as it was practical results.

A couple of things that cause confusion are worth highlighting.

---

[5]Other Creative Commons license variants impose restrictions such as NC (noncommercial use only) which do not conform to commonly accepted open source software license standards.

Seeing Through the Copyright Mire

The first is that precisely defining "mix it up" gets into technical and legal details that, absent substantial case law, remain a matter of some debate. For example, some argue that the manner in which two programs are combined together—that is, whether they're dynamically or statically linked in Unix parlance—makes a difference. Others say it doesn't. However, to the degree that there's a risk, it's usually not so much that it's hard to determine whether code is actually being mixed. Rather, it's that code under a copyleft license is deliberately but carelessly used in projects inappropriately or against company policies.

The other point is that copyleft licenses are specifically about *distribution*. Again, there are some nuances, but, essentially, if you distribute software, for profit or otherwise, by itself or as part of a hardware product, you must make the source code for the work that incorporates the copyleft code available. In other words, so long as software is used internally, there's no requirement to distribute the code. (Historically, distribution was about electronically or physically delivering a program outside your organization; as we'll see, there are some more recent wrinkles.)

Permissive Licenses Gain

There's also long been a parallel thread of licenses lacking the copyleft reciprocity requirement. Formal licenses in this vein written by lawyers date to about the same mid-1980s era as the GPL with the BSD and MIT licenses. What obligations they imposed were originally mostly about attribution in various forms.

A lot of other code published at the time in places like computer magazines didn't have a license at all. But the general understanding was you could use it and modify it. Giving credit to the author was a social expectation if not a legal requirement. And it was under a publisher's copyright if you tried to sell it in a competing book or magazine. In general though, from a user's perspective, such code was effectively under a permissive license for most purposes.

We're seeing an ongoing shift to more permissive licenses.

Going back a decade, Matthew Aslett, market researcher at 451 Group, wrote that "2010 was the first year in which there were more companies formed around projects with non-copyleft licenses than with strong copyleft licenses." More recent data shows a continuing trend, as do the anecdotal observations of industry observers. Black Duck (now part of Synopsys), which automates security and open source license compliance, maintains a knowledge base of over two million open source projects. As of 2018, among projects using the top five licenses accounting for 77% of the total projects, about two-thirds used a permissive license (MIT, Apache 2.0, or BSD).

There are some differences among these permissive licenses, primarily with respect to the types of copyright and other notices that must be retained and displayed. Patent language, both explicit and implied, also differs; newer licenses are more likely to call out patents specifically in the text of the license. These differences will be important to many organizations shipping products that make use of open source code. However, we can mostly think of these permissive licenses as giving permission to use code covered by such licenses without significant restriction.

In general, this shift reflects a lessening concern about preventing free riders and an increased focus on growing communities.

Driving Participation Is the Key

While individuals and organizations widely participate in and collaborate on projects licensed under the GPL, most famously the Linux kernel, permissive licenses have come to be viewed as the better choice for at least some purposes. In part, this is because companies developing with a combination of open source and closed source code want to maintain the flexibility to decide what code to contribute and when based on their own desires rather than the demands of a license. Permissive licenses also reduce license incompatibility issues; software licensed under major permissive licenses can generally[6] be added to GPL-licensed code, but the reverse doesn't apply because the GPL is more restrictive than a license like MIT.

Whatever the reason in an individual case, it's often related to maximizing participation in projects. The Eclipse Foundation's Ian Skerrett argues that

> *...projects use a permissive license to get as many users and adopters, to encourage potential contributions. They aren't worried about trying to force anyone. You can't force anyone to contribute to your project; you can only limit your community through a restrictive license.*

---

[6]There are some exceptions related to language around patents, for example.

Enter the Cloud

Furthermore, in a cloud services world, the GPL doesn't even protect against free riding especially well. If you sell me a service delivered through a web page rather than software I download, that's generally not distribution from the perspective of the GPL.[7] Yet, this is the increasingly dominant way through which you use many types of software. Salesforce.com. Amazon Web Services. Microsoft Azure. Google Cloud Platform. All you need is a web browser to use any of them. You don't need software that is distributed in the traditional sense of shipping bits on disk or making them available for download.

To some, this is simply a loophole that came about because of the changing nature of software distribution. The Affero General Public License (AGPL), which in effect redefines the meaning of distribution to include software delivered as a service, was created to close it. (Strictly speaking, the AGPL makes source code availability to the service user a condition of modification in a SaaS (software-as-a-service) setting unlike some older obscure licenses that did literally redefine distribution.) But it hasn't been widely adopted since it was introduced in conjunction with GPL v3 in 2007.

Who Can Use It?

A software license fundamentally tells you the manner in which you are allowed to use a software work. For example, historically, many licenses allowed free or low-cost usage of a program so long as it was for educational or noncommercial purposes only.

However, although free and open source software licenses impose more or fewer restrictions of their own, the mainstream licenses do *not* impose restrictions on who can or cannot use the software or, with minor exceptions, how it can be used. In fact, "No Discrimination Against Persons or Groups" and "No Discrimination Against Fields of Endeavor" were written into the Open Source Definition (OSD) which is widely regarded as the authoritative definition of what constitutes open source software.

The OSD was drafted and adopted by the OSI shortly after the organization was founded in 1998. It was essentially a rebranding of the existing Debian Free Software Guidelines with relatively minor changes, and it has changed little since.

---

[7]While generally true, some services involve distribution of JavaScript and JSON (and HTML) and so forth to the browser or other client program. With JavaScript, at least, this may lead to open source license compliance concerns if a copyleft license is used.

Of late, we've seen pushback against one or both of these elements of the OSD for two distinct reasons.

Open Source That Isn't

The first is licensing-led attempts to forestall direct competition from cloud vendors. For example, a vendor with an open source database project may want to prevent Amazon Web Services from taking the project and providing a competing database-as-a-service offering using the open source code. (Increasingly, even traditionally on-prem open source vendors face increased market demand to also provide their own service offerings.)

An example is the Redis Source Available License (RSAL). Redis Labs allows you to "Freely use the RSAL-protected software, as long as it is not part of a 'database product' offered by a third party other than yourself or Redis Labs."

I'll return to this topic when I discuss both business models and the impact of public cloud providers on open source. For now, suffice it to say that licenses in this vein have been controversial in that they attempt to benefit by implied association with open source without being, well, actually open source. Many are also just skeptical that they will work.

RedMonk analyst Stephen O'Grady wrote in 2019:

> *The benefits, therefore, at best come with caveats. The costs, however, are clear. Non-open source licenses necessarily come with collateral damage. Developers suddenly need approval where none was needed before; competitors spread fear, uncertainty and doubt and ask your customers questions like 'if they changed the license once, what makes you think they won't do it again?'; partners are faced with the prospect of having your new license (and that of everyone else pursuing a similar course) processed by legal; once friendly open source communities become enemies due to the risks hybrid approaches pose to the clean definitions and related acceptance of open source software. And so on.*

Ethical Licenses

This next group of licenses is interesting in part because it highlights how licensing has arguably assumed an outsized centrality in open source discussions. Open source lawyer and co-founder of Tidelift Luis Villa argues that

We have really lashed ourselves to the mast of licensing. And maybe we wouldn't be having so many of these discussions today if we said "Hey, codes of conduct are also important and how we behave with each other as peers and friends and human beings." If we'd extracted that from the licenses earlier, maybe we wouldn't be having some of the arguments that we're having today.

Licenses that prohibit certain groups from using a developer's software are nothing new. Bruce Perens, who largely wrote the OSD, cites the license used by the Berkeley SPICE software by the University of California, which prevented the use of the software by the police of South Africa during the apartheid era.

There's no record of this approach having any particular effect; in this case, the South African police likely had little need for electronic design software. But the political polarization of the late 2010s has nonetheless led to calls for open source licenses that prohibit their use by certain government agencies in particular. US Immigration and Customs Enforcement (ICE) has been one particular target.

The Hippocratic License created by Coraline Ada Ehmke has received the most attention. The license prohibits software from being used "by any person or entity for any systems, activities, or other uses that violate any Human Rights Laws."

The License Isn't the Goal

However, outside of somewhat limited examples, licensing is less of a major focus for creating successful communities, projects, and businesses than it once was. As Chris Aniszczyk of the Cloud Native Computing Foundation (CNCF) puts it, "Licensing and all that is table stakes. That's a requirement to get the gears going for collaboration, but there are [other] aspects around values, coordination, governance."

This touches on an important point.

When you close off avenues of competition or make it harder for others to profit from your code, there's an implicit assumption that your code has value and adoption. Yet, the biggest problem open source projects (and, indeed, many forms of intellectual property generally) face is obscurity. If you keep competitors from using your code at the cost of reducing usage and collaboration with others, you may not have made a good trade-off.

Furthermore, if your priority truly is control, perhaps an open source license just isn't the right choice. Going the open source route has many benefits, but it can introduce some potential challenges when it comes to commercialization. If you don't want to live with that trade-off, maybe you should consider a proprietary license given that "open source" isn't just a feel-good marketing slogan.

Maintaining Open Source Compliance

Maintaining compliance with these different types of open source licenses can sometimes seem intimidating, but it's mostly about having established processes and following them with reasonable care.

Putting Controls in Place

The Linux Foundation recommends having a designated open source compliance team that's tasked with ensuring open source compliance.[8] Such a team would be responsible for open source compliance strategy and processes to determine how a company will implement these rules. The strategy establishes what must be done to ensure compliance and offers a governing set of principles for how employees interact with open source software. It includes a formal process for the approval, acquisition, and use of open source, and a method for releasing software that contains open source or that's licensed under an open source license.

As open source becomes more widely used within many companies, it's increasingly important to have these kinds of controls in place anyway for reasons that aren't directly related to license compliance. Unvetted code from public repositories may not be current with security patches or may otherwise not meet a company's standards for production code.

What Are Your Policies?

A first step is to establish a process and appropriate policies. Often this includes a list of acceptable licenses for software components used for different purposes and in different roles. For example, companies widely use commercial enterprise software that includes programs licensed under the GPL like Linux. However, they may choose to only incorporate open source software components that use permissive licenses into their

---

[8]www.linuxfoundation.org/using-open-source-code/. Excerpts under Creative Commons Attribution-ShareAlike 4.0 International License.

own software. Or they may be fine with GPL components for their internal software but not in products that they ship or otherwise expose to partners and customers.

In any case, these are matters of policy for management, including the legal staff. One important general recommendation, however, is to not make things too complicated. As Ibrahim Haddad, formerly vice president of R&D and head of the Open Source Group at Samsung Research America and now at the Linux Foundation, puts it, "If your code review process is overly burdensome, you'll slow innovation or provide a good excuse for developers to circumvent the process completely."

An Ongoing Process

The ongoing process then uses scanning tools—whether proprietary or open source—to determine the software components in use, the licenses of those components, potential license conflicts, and any dependencies. Related tools can be used to identify known security vulnerabilities. Problems can then be identified and resolved. For example, a proprietary software component linking to a GPL-licensed component might be in compliance with policy for an internal tool but should raise a flag if it's going to be shipped externally.

Trademarks

As we've seen, licenses and copyright have been widely used, perhaps to a fault, to control the distribution and use of open source software. Trademarks (and branding more generally) have often been an afterthought for open source projects with casual early project decisions leading to problems down the road. However, RedMonk's O'Grady points to "the potential for trademark to usurp copyright as the legal fulcrum on which commercialization hangs."

Fundamentally, a trademark is any word, name, symbol, or design, or any combination of those items, that's used to indicate the source of goods or services and to distinguish them from those supplied by others.

Trademark legislation was first passed in 1266 under the reign of the English king Henry III, requiring all bakers to use a distinctive mark for the bread they sold. Modern trademark laws emerged beginning in the late 19th century.

What's in a Name?

As described in fossmarks.org:

> *The goal is to pick a name that won't be confused with anyone else's name for their software or related goods and services: that is, you want to pick a name that won't infringe the existing rights of others. It isn't as simple as letter string identicality—instead, the legal concept of confusion considers the sound, spelling and connotation of the words or designs, whether they incorporate terms that are commonplace or unique, and how similar the goods and services are from the intended consumer's perspective.[9]*

I've been on teams chartered to come up with product or product line names several times in my career, and the process can be difficult. Most people don't want to just grab some output from a name generator and call it a day. But you can be sure that most names from mythological pantheons, obvious computer-related wordplay, and any synonym for cloud are being used by someone.

Your name doesn't have to be unique if it's being used in an unrelated industry. That said, lawyers tend to be conservative about even fairly distant relationships, and, today, you also have to be concerned about how something that is well known in even a very different market can overwhelm your search results. The same can be the case when using common words. (There are some other limitations to using common words as well.) In general, you want the name to be unusual so that it is likely to appear at the top of search results when people look for it.

People use a variety of techniques to come up with names.

You can concatenate two words. Red Hat's Kubernetes-based container platform is called OpenShift—the Open from open source, the Shift as in automobile gear shift. The name fit in with a set of auto-related nomenclature and imagery used at one time with the product.

Acronyms or words derived from acronyms can work. The Samba suite of Windows interoperability programs is from SMB, "server message block." In this case, samba is also a form of Brazilian dance, which might have been an issue for a lesser-known project. (Samba was initially released in 1992, so search wasn't a consideration at the time.)

---

[9]The fossmarks.org guide was written by Pamela S. Chestek, Weston Davis, Anthonia Ghalamkarizadeh, and Rafal Malujda. It is licensed under the Creative Commons Attribution 4.0 International License.

You can use wordplay. "Rules" for a business rules management system can't be trademarked because it's not distinctive. But transform it into "Drools" and you have the name of an open source rules engine.

Finally, FOSSmarks provides an example of a made-up word that cleverly refers to an aspect of the project. "Qpid is a Java message broker that implements the Advanced Message Queuing Protocol (AMQP). It uses 'QP,' and is a homophone for 'cupid,' successfully making a non-infringing reference to AMQP in a memorable way."

It's probably the case that a lot of the cleverness that goes into naming projects and products is wasted on most audiences. Nonetheless, it's hard to resist a name that has some sort of story or significance attached.

Project or Product

In the last section, I deliberately used project and product fairly interchangeably because it mostly doesn't make much difference from a naming perspective. That said, the names of larger projects and certainly commercial products should generally be more carefully vetted by legal counsel and trademark searches than in the case of a small project. Occasionally, projects do need to change their names for trademark reasons, and the higher their brand awareness and the further down the commercialization path they are, the more costly the change will be.

But even smaller projects should generally do at least some minimal legwork using free online resources before finalizing a name. In "How to choose a brand name for your open source project," Chris Grams wrote in 2016 that

> *One mistake I've seen made regularly in the open source world is people picking a name for their open source project they have no hope of successfully protecting with a registered trademark. Usually the name is already in use by another project or organization, or it is a common word that will be difficult or impossible to protect.*

However, there's another point worth discussing here. That is whether the project and the product should have the same name. And, for that matter, should a company established to sell the commercial product *also* use the same name?

A project on the cusp of commercialization has presumably achieved some degree of name recognition and brand equity, so it's natural to want to carry that over to the product. And since you're thinking that product or closely related ones will be your company's exclusive focus for the foreseeable future, maybe you should draw on that name recognition for the company as a whole as well.

Certainly it's not unusual to see products and their upstream projects with the same names given that this is probably the path of least resistance. And it's not *necessarily* a recipe for disaster. But using the same name for a community project, a commercial product, and a company does conflate three things that are fundamentally different.

Chris Aniszczyk argues

> *...there's a common pattern where people will start a project, it could be within a company or yourself or you have a startup and you'll call it, let's say, Docker. And then you have Docker the project, then you have Docker, the company. And then you also have Docker the product or Docker Enterprise product, and all those things serve different audiences. And it just leads to confusion. I have an inherent belief that the name of something has a value proposition attached to it. And so I think the common anti-pattern I see is it could be attractive to name everything the same thing because you're like, "Oh, it's super popular," but it actually leads to confusion. It could be harder for you to distinctly target to either sell to people that want to buy your product or sell to developers you want to have contribute to your project.*

At the very least, think the matter through and make a deliberate decision rather than just going with the flow.

Trademark Ownership and Registration

In general, unless copyright is assigned to a project's owner or they're doing a "work for hire" under their employment terms, the person who created a subroutine in a program, wrote a documentation file, or drew artwork for a project has copyright on the part of the work created by them. Fontana writes that "the general view in open source is that the developers contributing to a project do not jointly own the copyright, but rather that each contributor owns copyright in their 'sliver.'"

Trademark is generally different.

It's typically owned by a legal entity (whether a person or an organization capable of owning property). It *can* also be owned by an "unincorporated association," and it might be possible in some cases for an informal group of developers to be characterized as such an association. However, on the trademark side, this often leads to problems typified by "band name cases" as IP lawyer Pamela Chestek calls them. "Usually band name cases are pretty ugly, about a bunch of people getting together without any legal formalities," she writes.

The original creator of the name can just hold onto trademark rights themselves, even if the project later goes under a foundation or some other governance structure. Linus Torvalds is that person in the case of Linux. Or the name's creator may just not do anything formal about trademarks at all which can lead to legal issues down the road. Trademark rights can also be legally transferred to another person.

In general though, open source practitioners recommend governance structures that aren't built around a single individual and that formally establish ownership.

Therefore, the person who created the name should generally transfer it to some organization at least for projects of any size. This might be the project's own community as represented by some umbrella organization, a company that sponsors the project, or a separate entity that maintains arm's distance from a company.

However, the best practice is often to transfer rights to a neutral organization like a foundation, especially as a project grows. Trademark is really just one part of open governance that includes the ownership of trademarks, domains, project assets, and even decisions about how maintainers are added and removed. We'll return to governance in more detail in the next chapter.

A short sidebar here goes to Google launching the Open Usage Commons (OUC) foundation to offer open source projects "support specific to trademark protection and management, usage guidelines, and conformance testing" in July 2020. It is thus an attempt to decouple trademarks from other governance concerns. In the words of OUC board member (and former Googler) Miles Ward, "Utility comes either in bundling or unbundling. We endeavor to decouple the trademark part from some of the other parts of a more typical foundation bundle, and see if that smaller unit is useful."

Through one lens this is just a simple experiment. Matt Asay writes, "It's quite possible, as John Mark Walker has noted, 'there's a large number of individuals with GitHub projects who have no desire to officially join a foundation,' but who would benefit from low-touch trademark protection."

The catch though is that Google created the OUC right in the middle of something of a tempest around the governance of a Google-dominated project, Istio, which would shortly become one of the first projects to park their trademark there. Some of the condemnation has been impassioned such as that from the CNCF's Chris Aniszczyk arguing it's

...really about one company lying to their community partners and dragging their feet for a couple years. [Let's] focus on the loss of trust here... and why a new gerrymandered org was necessary vs. ASF [Apache Software Foundation], EF [Eclipse Foundation], SPI [Software in the Public Interest], etc.

Thus, it's hard to separate the immediate political situation from questions of whether a separate organization holding solely trademarks might make sense as part of an open governance scheme.

So far, we've been discussing unregistered trademarks which derive their rights from active use. You can also register a trademark by which the government grants you rights or officially recognizes your rights in the trademark. Registration isn't strictly necessary, but, outside the United States, it's effectively required to have enforceable trademark rights in most countries. The ® symbol denotes a registered trademark; ™ or simply a written notice indicates an unregistered trademark. Most trademark registrations are for a specific country, although a few registration schemes cover multiple countries.

The Power of Trademark

It's probably clear, in a general sense, why you don't want your product or service to be confused with inferior knockoffs—or even just with a competitor's offering after you've invested to make your own product well-known. But what does this have to do with open source specifically?

Let's imagine the following scenario. You start an open source database project. Let's call it TransduceDB. You select an OSI-approved license. You build a community. You gain lots of users. Perhaps it helped that you didn't pick a license that got in the way of both community and usage. And you start selling a commercial product based on this project, initially as on-prem software and later as a managed service. Money starts coming in. Life is good.

But others gaze upon your success with envious eyes. One public cloud provider in particular—let's call them AGM—considers standing up their own TransduceDB service. After all, the code is just sitting there ready for use.

AGM can, in fact, do exactly what they want to do given that your software is under an open source license (so long as they comply with the license's requirements for making source code available). What they *can't* do is call their service TransduceDB if you have a valid trademark.

This is no small protection. While people certainly buy clones of products and services because they're cheaper or perhaps even better than the original, all things being equal, most will go with the branded product.

Concerns about incompatibilities in a clone are probably less with open source software than when someone is trying to reverse engineer closed source. Nonetheless, the brand of the original project and company, as represented in part by its trademark, carries a presumption of quality, expertise, and compatibility that a competitor would need to earn.

Patents

A patent is essentially a government-granted monopoly that gives someone exclusive rights to make, use, or sell an invention for a limited number of years, typically 20, in exchange for publicly disclosing the invention. The patent holder can also provide a license to others who want to use their work. Patents were originally intended to promote the invention of useful mechanical devices—say, a more efficient steam engine—but, over time, this means of protecting intellectual property has been (sometimes controversially) extended to cover more abstract inventions such as software, designs, and even business methods.

The first pure software patents seem to date to the 1960s, but different agencies and branches of the US government gave confusing and conflicting guidance on the topic. It wasn't until about the mid-1990s that the situation began to clearly resolve in favor of software patents.

Patent Claims

Patents are a complex topic, and details vary from country to country. Here I will just cover some of the basics that you should know if you are writing and distributing nontrivial software even if you have no plans to yourself patent software. You can find more detailed information in "A Legal Issues Primer for Open Source and Free Software Projects" from the Software Freedom Law Center (SFLC).[10] However, as noted earlier, questions specific to a particular situation should be taken to a lawyer versed in this area of law.

In the United States, patents are issued by the US Patent and Trademark Office (USPTO) and grant the aforementioned monopoly. The heart of a patent is the claims, which define what the patent actually covers. There are a number of different types of claims including, in the case of software patents, "system" or "apparatus" claims, "method" claims, and "computer program product" or "computer-readable medium" claims. Claims must meet various patentability requirements, which generally include novelty (lack of prior art), usefulness, and nonobviousness.

However, it can be difficult for nonspecialists to understand the scope of what is being claimed. As the SFLC notes:

> *If you have become aware of a patent that you believe may threaten your project, your first step should be to ascertain the meaning of the claims. This is not a simple task, because patent claims are drafted artfully, using jargon unique to patent attorneys, and are often deliberately drafted in an obscure manner. You should first try to determine the "plain meaning" of the claims. Terms in patent claims are presumed to have their ordinary and customary meanings, which include definitions in use in the relevant technical field.*

Are You Infringing?

Copyright has its own complexities. Does a use exceed the limits of fair use? And, periodically, a fracas breaks out over whether some type of expression is covered by copyright or not. (APIs play a big role in a dispute between Google and Oracle that is in front of the US Supreme Court as this is being written.) But, as a software developer, the issues are pretty straightforward so long as you don't try to make use of code to which you don't hold an appropriate license. Except in trivial cases, you're unlikely to write a program that looks substantially identical to someone else's.

Patents work differently.

---

[10]www.softwarefreedom.org/resources/2008/foss-primer.html. There have been some important court cases in the United States relating to software patents since that primer was written, most notably Alice v. CLS Bank. Alice held that implementing abstract claims on a computer was not enough to transform them into patentable subject matter, an approach taken by a number of software patents in an attempt to get around the fact that ideas are not generally patentable. https://en.wikipedia.org/wiki/Alice_Corp._v._CLS_Bank_International

Lack of prior knowledge of a patent is not a defense to patent infringement. It is also no excuse that you independently came up with a novel technique implemented in your software. In general, all that matters is that the software implements everything recited in one of the patent's claims. Infringement is based directly on the claims of the patent.

How big a problem is this for open source developers? For small projects, probably not so much. But it is certainly a general concern for companies selling commercial open source products. As the SFLC puts it:

> *There is a tendency both to overestimate and underestimate the threat that patents pose to FOSS. Patent holders are unlikely to sue individual developers or nonprofit organizations associated with FOSS projects, since they do not hold substantial assets or enjoy a revenue stream from which substantial patent royalties could be extracted. Nevertheless, such lawsuits are not without precedent and might be a tactic employed by proprietary software companies competing unsuccessfully with FOSS projects. Moreover, commercial distributors and users of a FOSS project are a likely target for litigious patent holders, and suits against such parties may adversely affect the entire community surrounding the project, including the developers producing the software.*

Creating Patent Pools

Because of increased software patent litigation—often by patent assertion entities (PAEs) or, as they're popularly called, patent trolls—in recent years, companies working in the open source software space have taken steps to defend themselves. A PAE, in general, refers to an organization with a portfolio of patents they often did not themselves develop but which they use to pursue patent lawsuits through aggressive legal tactics.

Many companies have accumulated large patent portfolios over time for defensive purposes even if they don't intend to require licensing or other payments for the use of those patents. Obtaining a patent in this way prevents someone else from getting a patent for the same thing. A large patent portfolio can also serve to discourage competitors from suing you for patent infringement given that they themselves are potentially infringing on some of your patents.

Companies and other organizations have also come together to create even larger defensive patent pools. One example is the Open Invention Network (OIN). Created in 2005 by Red Hat, IBM, Novell, NEC, Philips, and Sony, OIN takes a twofold approach. First, OIN establishes a shared defensive patent pool to protect innovation in the Linux environment. Second, OIN creates a royalty-free patent cross-license arrangement among its members—effectively a zone of protected open source technologies where developers can collaborate without fear of patent claims by OIN's participants. Today, it has 3,300 members in total, and the community owns more than two million patents and patent applications, of which about 1,300 are global with broad scope.

A related entity is the LOT Network started in 2014. LOT members can still sell patents and sue other members. But if a patent passes to a PAE, such as through a sale, that event triggers the cross-licensing of that patent to all members—effectively foreclosing litigation by the PAE.

Patents and Licensing

The foundations of open source software predate software patents as a major source of concern and contention.

At least mostly for this reason, the OSD, which serves as the canonical set of underlying rules that licenses must follow to be approved by the OSI, does not mention patents at all. That hasn't kept some licenses from tackling patents over time. A number of more modern licenses grant patent rights using various volumes of legalese.

However, in general, the OSI has taken the position that patent grants are implicit even when not explicit and that "copyright-only" licenses that do not otherwise convey the rights needed to run the software are not open source. The organization also objected to a clause in the submitted (later withdrawn) CC0 license that explicitly did *not* grant patent rights.

Richard Fontana argues that "It would be challenging to satisfactorily address the patent question through a revision to the OSD, but the resulting certainty could be very beneficial."[11]

Lawyers will generally argue that modern licenses that are specific about associated patent grants are to be preferred. In practice, though, many developers—if they think about the matter at all—lean toward simple licenses like MIT that sidestep the issue and the legal language that comes with it. This is not to say that MIT is *necessarily* ambiguous with respect to patents even though it doesn't mention patents explicitly; Red Hat IP lawyer Scott Peterson argues that MIT

---

[11]Fontana asks more broadly, "Is it time to revise the Open Source Definition?" https://opensource.com/article/20/9/open-source-definition explores some of the issues covered in this chapter.

...is an express license. Does that express license grant patent rights? Indeed, with permission granted "to deal in the Software without restriction," it does. And there is no need to arrive at that conclusion via anything more than a direct reading of the words that grant the license.[12]

Trade Secrets

In the interest of completeness, I round out this chapter with a brief discussion of trade secrets.

Trade secrets are basically any information that has value because it's not generally known by others and which the owner takes reasonable measures to keep secret. The formula for making Coca-Cola is a canonical example.

Trade secrets wouldn't seem to have much to do with open source. After all, the very nature of open source requires that source code be available for all to see. Furthermore, the best practice for open source communities is to keep discussions and decisions in the open as much as possible. Such transparency is mostly in opposition to trade secrets.

That said, commercialized open source, which is to say open source products, comes from companies that typically do have trade secrets. These can be of a technical nature such as the details of software build systems, software and processes used internally for delivering software-as-a-service, or internal engineering metrics. Perhaps more obviously, companies consider a great deal of information such as customer lists proprietary—and indeed they may be required to keep a great deal of that information confidential for contractual and other reasons. Working transparently in open source communities doesn't mean that everything about your business is available for outside inspection—although the work you do within the community should be as open as possible.

When Does It Matter?

This chapter has covered a number of matters related to open source software and intellectual property law.

---

[12]https://opensource.com/article/18/3/patent-grant-mit-license

Licensing is the topic that's been most highlighted historically, in part because it's often been so intertwined with what conditions must be present for software to be considered open source in the first place. Licensing has also historically served as the instrument seen as distinguishing the free and open source camps of FOSS (even if that's a simplistic and not really accurate way of framing the copyleft and permissive license dichotomy).

Licensing continues to sometimes be a point of contention given that it's intimately connected to the Open Source Definition and therefore to allowable restrictions on who can be restricted from using or competing with open source software.

However, in general, licensing has simultaneously receded in overall importance and come to be viewed as an instrument that enables cooperative software development as much as it protects user freedoms. Furthermore, it's come to be seen as just one of the legal instruments that matter for open source projects and products; trademarks can also be important as can patents, especially from a defensive perspective.

For individual developers, two points are probably of greatest importance.

You should choose *some* license for your project. GitHub provides a handy license picker[13] because, as they note, "Public repositories on GitHub are often used to share open source software. For your repository to truly be open source, you'll need to license it so that others are free to use, change, and distribute the software." (Initially, a great deal of code on GitHub was not licensed, a fact that became a point of some criticism.)

To the degree that you incorporate other open source code into your project, it's also important that the license for that code be compatible with the license you have chosen. If the code that you are using is permissively licensed, that is not usually a problem. But there are often incompatibilities between different copyleft licenses. The FSF provides a basic summary of license compatibility and relicensing.[14]

All of this matters, in part, because you may want to commercialize your work some day in whole or in part. But it also matters because decisions made with respect to intellectual property may encourage or discourage collaboration around your project and its code. And, as we'll see in the next chapter, it's the collaborative open source development model that's perhaps the greatest strength of open source software.

---

[13]https://docs.github.com/en/free-pro-team@latest/github/creating-cloning-and-archiving-repositories/licensing-a-repository

[14]www.gnu.org/licenses/license-compatibility.en.html

CHAPTER 4

Open Source Development Model

We've seen some of the ways in which the thinking around free and open source software has evolved over time. Perhaps the biggest change is the realization that it can be such an effective development model as opposed to just a source of user freedoms. As a result, understanding modern open source has to include understanding how it's developed. And more specifically, how it's developed when multiple individuals and organizations participate and collaborate.

This chapter delves into the open source development model, which is best thought of as a toolbox of practices that need to be tailored to the requirements of a given community and project. There's no single governance model. Projects have different goals and missions. Communities develop across a variety of lines based on their membership and what they're trying to accomplish.

Open Source Is Also About Development

Although it's not necessarily the best lens through which to view modern open source development, Eric Raymond's *The Cathedral and the Bazaar: Musings on Linux and Open Source by an Accidental Revolutionary* (O'Reilly Media, 2001), an essay and later book, gets frequently cited. First published in 1997—about the same time that the "open source" term was finding its way into the wild—it contrasted code developed by an exclusive group of developers with code developed in public over the Internet. This was also around the earliest point in time at which you could really talk about the "public" having access to the Internet rather than the employees of a fairly small number of companies or researchers at elite universities.

© Gordon Haff 2021

G. Haff, *How Open Source Ate Software*, https://doi.org/10.1007/978-1-4842-6800-1_4

Central vs. Distributed Control

Raymond took Linux as his model for the bazaar. He writes that

> *Linus's innovation wasn't so much in doing quick-turnaround releases incorporating lots of user feedback (something like this had been Unix-world tradition for a long time), but in scaling it up to a level of intensity that matched the complexity of what he was developing. In those early times (around 1991) it wasn't unknown for him to release a new kernel more than once a day! Because he cultivated his base of co-developers and leveraged the Internet for collaboration harder than anyone else, this worked.*

Today, *The Cathedral and the Bazaar* is often recalled as a commentary on proprietary vs. open source software.

The cathedral is the architected and carefully constructed creation of an insular group of specialist trades. Its design the result of singular vision and skilled craft. A tidy and managed process leading to an inexorable endpoint. The result may or may not be beautiful, but it will be deliberate.

By contrast, the bazaar is messy. Anyone can participate. There's duplication. It's not efficient. Some of the stalls will have higher-quality goods than others. The whole evolves organically. The bazaar encourages broad participation and experimentation, which may be ultimately effective for the customers. But you need to accept that it won't be neat and organized and that no one is necessarily going to be able to step in and exert ultimate control.

Raymond was indeed writing about two different software development approaches, but he was actually contrasting two different types of *free software* development practices. Specifically, he was comparing the cathedral-like development of programs like Stallman's GCC (the GNU Project's C language compiler)—which he argued was stagnating—with the more bazaar-like development of Linux with its diverse population of contributors.

That said, looking back at *The Cathedral and the Bazaar* with the advantage of 20 years of hindsight, the bazaar remains a useful lens through which to view the often unruly open source development landscape.

Differing Open Source Approaches

Open source software development does tend toward the bazaar rather than the cathedral. However, as even Raymond acknowledged at the time:

> ... *There is a more fundamental error in the implicit assumption that the cathedral model (or the bazaar model, or any other kind of management structure) can somehow make innovation happen reliably. This is non-sense. Gangs don't have breakthrough insights—even volunteer groups of bazaar anarchists are usually incapable of genuine originality, let alone corporate committees of people with a survival stake in some status quo ante. Insight comes from individuals. The most their surrounding social machinery can ever hope to do is to be responsive to breakthrough insights—to nourish and reward and rigorously test them instead of squashing them.*

As we consider the open source development model and the communities associated with it, these points about insights, and hence innovation, are the ones we should most take away from Raymond's essay. Successful projects and communities have a bit of cathedral *and* a bit of bazaar in them.

A Caveat

At this point, it's worth noting that not all open source software really uses an open source development model.

Many of the projects in a public repository like GitHub are occasional hobbies or just something that a developer threw together to solve some narrow problem. Even significant projects don't always have broad participation. This can be a problem when many users depend on a project but it doesn't have sufficient funding—as we saw in the case of OpenSSL.

One company may also drive a project that never attracts significant outside participation for whatever reason. Such projects may be successful by reasonable metrics. They may serve as upstream projects for successful commercial products. They just don't really benefit from the open source development process and probably don't operate in a way that looks much like an open source project with a diverse set of participants. They therefore aren't a good study point for how open source software development is different.

But when open source serves as a strategic approach to software development, it follows certain models and takes certain approaches, and that's the topic for this chapter.

Participating in Open Source Projects

Before moving onto how the open source software development process works in more detail—how communities work, how they're governed, what the process looks like—let's consider what getting involved in open source looks like.

We can approach the question of participation from a number of different angles. Here are three:

- Starting an open source project associated with a current or planned software product

- Doubling down on an existing open source project

- Creating an open source program office (OSPO) to manage internal open source use and external contributions—including creating new projects

There are common themes to these. One of those is that participating in open source is not a philanthropic endeavor or certainly doesn't need to be. Rather, as the Linux Foundation's Jim Zemlin put it to me in 2018:

> *The epiphany that many companies have had over the last three to four years, in particular, has been, "Wow. If I have processes where I can bring code in, modify it for my purposes, and then, most importantly, share those changes back, those changes will be maintained over time. When I build my next project or a product, that project will be in line with, in a much more effective way, the products that I'm building. To get the value, it's not just consumed, it is to share back and that there's not some moral obligation (although I would argue that that's also important), there's an actual incredibly large business benefit to that as well." The industry has gotten that, and that's a big change.*

Another theme is that there's no template. There are principles and practices that recur over and over in most successful open source projects, many of which should be regarded as more than guidelines but less than an absolute set of rules. However, while many open source projects fall into certain recurring patterns, there's no singular correct approach. Chris Aniszczyk calls it the Tolstoy principle for open source, "Each project is unhappy in its unique own way." (By "unhappy," read has singular concerns, needs, and challenges.)

Starting an Open Source Project

The lines between the developers of software and the consumers of software are increasingly blurred. So is the demarcation between those who make money from software and those who make money from doing other things like building widgets; companies increasingly deliver software services and experiences as well as physical things. (And physical things increasingly have a software component, even if that's sometimes taken to unnecessary extremes as in the case of overly complex appliances.)

But it's still useful to treat open source projects that are directly tied, now or in the future, to commercial software products as distinct from projects created by organizations with other purposes in mind.

One of the first questions to ask, though, is one of the most important. Do you need to start a new project? In some cases, yes. Many commercial software products start life as a new open source project. In other cases, there's an existing commercial software product, and the company or an acquirer of the company wants to start a project based on the product's code. At Red Hat, for example, when we acquire companies and products, we routinely go through a process to make the software products that we sell open source. In still other cases, a software company has a new engineering initiative that it wants to develop in open source, but there's no existing project that's a natural fit. In yet other cases, it's a project a company—whether a vendor or an end user—created for some internal purpose, and now the company wants to open up the code to a broader community.

By contrast, some of the most successful open source projects have gotten that way because companies and individuals decided to rally around an existing project rather than going off and doing their own thing. This sort of behavior is, after all, central to the open source development model, and a fragmented landscape of projects that do similar things tends to dilute developer attention. But let's assume that you have good reasons to create a new project. What are some of the things you'll want to think about next?

What Does Success Look Like?

Deciding what success looks like for the community project is a good place to start. This should correlate with the reasons you have for creating a new project. What are you trying to accomplish? What are your business objectives?

The project might support the success of a product offering based on the project—or otherwise support commercial objectives such as creating brand association for the sponsoring company. If, on the other hand, it's a pure community project that's not associated with a commercial product, it should be able to stand on its own as a viable open source community project.

From there, you can move on to considering project-specific needs for a community launch. These can include

- Existing closed source code that you plan to open source

- Source code licensing as discussed in the last chapter

- The governance structure of the project

- How the project will be positioned relative to downstream products from marketing, trademark, naming, and other perspectives

Doubling Down an Existing Open Source Project

However, organizations can often most effectively participate in open source development by joining an already existing community. Doing so can come with its own set of challenges if the community is dominated by companies or individuals with interests that run counter to your own. Nonetheless, connecting to an existing project is often easier, quicker, and more certain than trying to kickstart a new initiative.

Participation in open source communities doesn't need to be about coding. For example, companies can help with testing in their specific environments, which will often be at higher scale points or otherwise different from configurations that can easily be tested in a lab. This sort of participation in software development by end users was commonplace even before open source software became so widespread. We typically referred to it as alpha or beta testing depending upon how early in the process you were involved.

Writing documentation and providing funding are also ways to get involved.

However, as longtime IBM Software Group head Steve Mills put it, "Code talks." The Linux Foundation also argues that the greatest influence in open source projects is through the quality, quantity, and consistency of code contributions.[1]

Stormy Peters, the director of Microsoft's Open Source Programs Office, has observed that

> *For many larger projects, we know that most of our contributors are going to be people who work at companies that need to use projects like Ceph and Gluster. We have customers, and customers often contribute to software because they're using it. We consider both the individual participation and the company participation as success stories.*

Some companies may participate in open source software development as a way to give back to the community. However, there are plenty of business justifications as well.

A big reason is to take advantage of the open source development process. While it's often possible to use and modify open source code without making contributions, "forking" a project in this way "defeats the whole purpose in terms of collective value" in Jim Zemlin's words. He adds that "You're now, basically, supporting your own proprietary fork. Whether or not it's open source, it doesn't matter at that point. No one understands it but you." Microsoft's Stephen Walli describes it as being "very expensive to live on a fork."

To be clear, the right to fork is a fundamental characteristic of open source licenses. But that doesn't mean you should take such a step casually without due consideration of your other options.

Stormy Peters and Nithya Ruff, Executive Director, Open Source Program Office at Comcast, add that

> *Companies that start fixing bugs or adding new features and functionality to an open source project without contributing them back into the upstream project quickly learn that upgrading later to add new features or apply security fixes can be a nightmare that drives maintenance costs through the roof. Contributing your changes back into the upstream project means that they will automatically be included in future updates without incurring additional maintenance costs.[2]*

---

[1] www.linuxfoundation.org/resources/open-source-guides/improving-your-open-source-development-impact/

[2] www.linuxfoundation.org/participating-open-source-communities/

Furthermore, coming back to Mills' talking code, new features and functionality come from code contributions, and those contributions can influence the direction of the project. If you want the project to have specific functionality that you need, it may be up to you to implement those changes.

That said, working with open source projects requires awareness of and sensitivity to the norms, expectations, and processes associated with the specific community. While your contributions, of whatever form, will often be welcomed, that doesn't mean just showing up and throwing weight around. You need to be aligned with both the overall direction of the project and the way that the project and its associated community operate. A good approach is to have someone join the community and spend some time observing. Alternatively, you can hire someone who already has a proven track record of participation in the community.

Communities have different characters, ways of participating, and channels for communication—which include mailing lists, forums, IRC, Slack, bug trackers, source code repositories, and more. These are useful both for ongoing communications and to understand how a community works before jumping in. "Lurk first" is what Peters and Ruff advise because "the more time you spend reading and listening, the more likely it is that your first contribution will be well received."

They also counsel reading up on the project governance and leadership before contributing. Who makes the decisions for various types of contributions? Is there a contributor licensing agreement? What's the process for contributing? What classes of contributors are there? It's important to appreciate that the rules of the road—both formal and informal—in one community may not apply to another.

Peters and Ruff also suggest starting small. For example, tackle a simple bug or documentation fix to start. It will be easier to learn the process and correct mistakes on a small contribution that isn't critical to your organization's needs. Companies can and do become major contributors to projects that they didn't themselves start all the time, but ramping up participation is a process that owes as much to building up relationships at both the individual and overall community levels as it does to cranking out code.

Creating an Open Source Program Office

Increasingly, the logical next step for many organizations is to formalize their participation in open source by establishing an open source program office (OSPO).

Nithya Ruff and Duane O'Brien identify a number of common problems that tend to indicate establishing an OSPO could be useful.[3] Several have to do with a general lack of institutional knowledge about participating in open source. Or maybe there's some knowledge, but it's in isolated pockets; no one is quite sure where to go to get their questions answered. The legal team is getting overwhelmed with ad hoc requests, and it's hard to get definitive answers about open source "compliance"—or indeed to fully understand what the pertinent issues even are.

More broadly, there may just be a lack of overall strategy. What projects should be of interest? What events or organizations would it benefit the company to sponsor? How do you establish a reputation in open source communities so you can better attract developers? (Participating in open source as a way to attract talent is a motivation that I hear more and more often.)

As with open source communities themselves, there's a lot of variation in OSPOs. Ruff and O'Brien identify "6 Cs": communicate, consume, contribute, collaborate, create competency, and comply. However, they go on to note that some offices will be of narrower scope than others.

For example, one office might be primarily focused on reducing risk to the company by ensuring that the use of open source code doesn't create any compliance issues from a legal perspective. A different office might be seeking to improve collaboration within the company by using techniques and workflows inspired by open source projects. Tim O'Reilly is credited with coining the term "inner sourcing" to describe this use of open source development techniques within the corporation.

John Mark Walker, who directs Capital One's OSPO, emphasizes the importance of building relationships with nontechnical risk and legal partners within the company. As you can imagine, this is particularly important with a regulated bank like Capital One, but it really applies everywhere. Walker also highlights the importance of establishing an easy process for contributing to open source projects; it should generally involve pushing code contributions directly to the upstream project. "By getting involved upstream, you increase the quality of code produced," which, in turn, improves the quality of your own code when you make use of software from upstream, Walker adds.

In a pattern that's probably becoming familiar in the context of open source communities and projects, the authors of the Linux Foundation's "Creating an Open Source Program" write that

---

[3]https://osls18.sched.com/event/DjtZ/so-youve-decided-you-need-an-open-source-program-office-duane-obrien-indeedcom-nithya-ruff-comcast

For every company, the role of the open source program office will likely be custom-configured, based on its business, products, and goals. There is no broad template for building an open source program that applies across all industries—or even across all companies in a single industry. That can make its creation a challenge, but you can learn lessons from other companies and bring them together to fit your own organization's requirements.[4]

The purpose will also influence where the office is hosted within a company. If there's a strong focus on mitigating legal risk, the legal department might be a logical fit. If, on the other hand, the emphasis is more on participating in open source communities, that seems a better match with the CTO's office or elsewhere in the engineering organization.

The leadership of the OSPO can be influenced by these considerations as well. If the motivations are largely driven by internal aspects such as improving collaboration, then it may be important to pick someone who knows how to navigate the twisty byways of a typical enterprise organization. If it's more outwardly facing—perhaps you want to get involved in some existing open source projects that relate to your company's strategic interest—you may be better off with someone who has experience and skills in open source communities and practices.

Ruff and O'Brien identify good traits to have as including the following: consensus building, some technical skills, project management, community roots, and presentation chops. It's probably obvious from that list that OSPO leadership is heavily weighted to connecting, influencing, and persuading.

That because, as Jeff McAffer, former director of the Open Source Programs Office at Microsoft, wrote

This is a culture change endeavor. The code is obviously a big part of it, but the community and the engagement is a people-to-people thing. If you're going to start an open source program office and you're going to try to make it a real thing, you're going to need to understand the culture and get somebody in place who can help drive that culture to a new level. Your head of open source is really a change agent.

---

[4]www.linuxfoundation.org/creating-an-open-source-program/

Models for Governing Projects

As we saw in the last chapter, licenses have historically assumed an outsized importance when it comes to the rules put in place around an open source project.

However, licenses don't speak to how decisions are made, how members will interact, what processes the community will follow, and how it will be structured. These fall into the domain of governance. You can think of governance as a social and decision-making framework for a project.

The word "framework" is important. An explicit project and community governance model can help to provide a general approach to moving a project forward. It makes key assumptions explicit. (However, as I'll discuss later, there's much more to encouraging new contributors, maintaining an existing community, and dealing with conflicts than just putting a governance model in place.)

The answers will differ from project to project, but setting up governance involves answering questions such as the following[5]:

- Who makes the decisions?

- How are maintainers added?

- Who owns the rights to the domain?

- Who owns the rights to the trademarks?

- How are those things governed?

- Who owns how the build system works?

Scott Nicholas, senior director of Strategic Programs at the Linux Foundation, advises that certain decisions are best addressed up front. In particular, he highlights license and IP decisions, mission and scope, and initial technical roles. At the same time, he also recommends that less is more, and it's often best to "empower decision making by the various project bodies as opposed to attempting to address all potential decisions up front." For example, oversight bodies can set their own rules for voting procedures and elections, while technical bodies can likewise make independent decisions about technical roles and project life cycle guidelines and procedures.

---

[5]https://opensource.com/article/20/2/open-source-projects-governance

Who Decides?

If you've ever been involved in setting up an organization with any sort of formal structure—or even just tried to get a large group to decide on where to go for lunch—you know how difficult decision making can be absent a process.

But it's not even so much that making routine decisions is hard. Dining choices notwithstanding, convivial groups can usually reach consensus without *too* much difficulty when the stakes are low and there's broad agreement on facts and criteria. Then the day comes when something polarizing comes along and there's no playbook to make the controversial call. My own experience on boards is that a casual approach to decision making works well. Until the day it doesn't.

This isn't much different from decision making in many healthy organizations. When there are irreconcilable differences, it matters how the logjam gets broken. Some projects do indeed have stricter hierarchies than others. But many of the same principles apply to making decisions in open source communities as elsewhere.

There are many ways to think about differences among open source communities. One can distinguish among single vendor open source projects, development communities, user communities, and open source competence centers—although the lines between these aren't hard and fast.

For example, single vendor open source projects suggest projects that remain under the control of a single software company. However, these can range from projects that are really open source in name only to projects that, at least in principle, welcome outside contributors, but a company retains ultimate decision-making authority over the core project.

Communities of developers and communities of users often blend together. In fact, it's been something of a trend for major open source foundations and communities like OpenShift Commons to increasingly be as much about bringing together end users with each other and with developers as more traditional communities that were mostly focused on writing code.

The lines between who is a software company and who isn't blur.

Though governance of open source projects is important, it's not always explicit. Researcher Javier Canovas studies how software is developed. He queried the widely used GitHub software repository in 2018 to collect the 25 most starred—think of this as roughly equivalent to most popular—open source projects on the platform.[6] He found

---

[6]https://opensource.com/open-organization/18/4/new-governance-model-research

that about three-quarters didn't provide any information about the governance model used by the project.

There were exceptions. For example, he found that "the Node.JS project provides a detailed description of the main developer roles of the project, their responsibilities, and how they are elected." (It's perhaps worth noting that this project is part of a foundation, the Node.js Foundation, which tends to be associated with more formal governance structures.) But, although the situation was better than it was when he last looked at the numbers two years previously, a lot of significant projects still weren't explicit about how they were run. Lack of license information on GitHub has also been an issue in the past although it now takes more of a deliberate effort to avoid choosing a license and the percentage of projects with a license has risen correspondingly.

Community projects generally fall into three broad buckets with respect to basic decision-making approaches.

Benevolent Dictator for Life

There's the BDFL (benevolent dictator for life). One person, who is usually the project's founder, generally has final say on major project decisions. This is the norm for smaller projects, which may not even have a formal governance process. However, many major open source programming languages also take this approach. And, notably, Linux— while having well-established development processes and formal structure—also has Linus Torvalds as a BDFL by most reasonable definitions.

Projects that are under the direct control of a single organization often use a process that looks similar in practice. Outside contributions may be encouraged and decision making delegated to proven contributors. However, the right to make decisions about fundamental project direction and similarly important matters is often retained by the commercial entity in ultimate control.

My Red Hat colleague, Dave Neary, notes that BDFL control is often *de facto* rather than structured in a formal manner.

He adds that

> *...there are a number of reasons why it's hard for companies to get involved when one vendor is dominant; it is like jumping on a train that is speeding through a station. The learning curve is steep and the community is not set up to onboard new "outside" contributors. Another reason is an organizational fear of being a second class citizen; until you have a 2nd company engaging, and can see how they are treated, decision makers figuring out whether to engage or not assume the worst.*

I include a benevolent dictator model because many projects end up here by default. However, as another colleague, Joe Brockmeier, observed to me, it's mostly considered an anti-pattern at this point. "While a few BDFL-driven projects have succeeded and continue to do well, others have stumbled with that approach," he says. On the one hand, the BDFL model means that there is a clear, unambiguous decision maker. On the other hand, ego and conflicts of interest between a project and commercial ambitions can easily drive a wedge between the community and an increasingly malevolent dictator—causing the project to flounder or fork.

Meritocracy

Meritocracy as a formal approach is most associated with the Apache Software Foundation. Unlike Linux, Apache's original project, the Apache web server, was started by a diverse group of people with common interests rather than by a single developer. As the project developed, in the words of the Apache Software Foundation:

> ...when the group felt that the person had "earned" the merit to be part of the development community, they [were] granted direct access to the code repository, thus increasing the group and increasing the ability of the group to develop the program, and to maintain and develop it more effectively. We call this basic principle "meritocracy": literally, government by merit.

Apache has a formal structure built on these principles, which go so far as to require that contributions be only made by individuals representing themselves rather than their employer. While projects outside the Apache Software Foundation may not have such a formal structure and approach to meritocracy, the basic idea of meritocracy is a common principle and practice.

As a sidenote, the "meritocracy" term has a controversial, if somewhat obscure, history. British sociologist and politician Michael Young published *The Rise of the Meritocracy* (Thames and Hudson) in 1958. In this book, he described a future dystopian society stratified between an intelligent and merited power holding elite and a disenfranchised underclass of the less merited. However, in the tech industry, meritocracy is mostly used in a positive way to connote decisions ostensibly made on the basis of knowledge and experience rather than rank or financial contribution.

Consensus

Under a consensus, sometimes called a liberal contribution, model, Open Source Guides writes that

> ...the people who do the most work are recognized as most influential, but this is based on current work and not historic contributions. Major project decisions are made based on a consensus seeking process (discuss major grievances) rather than pure vote, and strive to include as many community perspectives as possible.[7]

In practice, there are fewer differences in how decisions get made in healthy communities than the categories may indicate. For example, the meritocratic Apache Software Foundation writes about how the process to resolve negative votes on proposals "is called 'consensus gathering' and we consider it a very important indication of a healthy community." Conversely, even if decisions are always made by consensus, this inherently suggests a fallback to some sort of majority rules mechanism for the times when everyone can't come to an agreement.

What Are Some Principles?

Some of the foundational principles common to many open source projects are fairly straightforward. Projects should generally use an approved OSI license. Projects should also have a clear statement around intellectual property. For example, all contributions to projects under the Eclipse Foundation's top-level project charter must adhere to the Eclipse Foundation Intellectual Property Policy.

Separating Technical and Business Decisions

One core principle for many projects is the separation of business and technical governance.

---

[7]https://opensource.guide/

As Red Hat's Jason Baker wrote in the case of OpenStack:

The OpenStack Foundation has roles for many different types of contributors in their structure. The Board of Directors oversees financial decisions and long-term strategy, while the technical committee—not surprisingly—gives technical direction, and the user committee helps ensure the project is meeting the needs of organizations working with the software on the ground.[8]

This gets to the ideal, which finds its way into practice to greater or lesser degrees, that open source projects should be steered, at least in part, by those contributing the code. This is a fundamentally different approach from the marketing textbook view of product development in which product requirements are gathered, business priorities assessed, and, only then, development priorities established. There is a broader and more diverse set of stakeholders in open source software development than with proprietary software, which is certainly a contributor to open source's often bazaar-like atmosphere.

Or take the Fedora Project, which creates Fedora—a Linux distribution intended to focus on innovation and integrate new technologies early on—and also serves as a community upstream project for Red Hat Enterprise Linux. Its top-level community leadership and governance body, the Fedora Council, is composed of a mix of representatives from different areas of the project, named roles appointed by Red Hat, and a variable number of seats connected to medium-term project goals. Most of the project is then roughly organized under the FESCo (the Fedora Engineering Steering Committee) or the Mindshare Committee.

Open First

Less obvious for companies accustomed to developing more traditional software is the need to work in the open. Take the example of Kubernetes. It started out as an internal Google project that can be traced back to Borg, Google's internal container cluster management system. Launched in 2014, Kubernetes emerged as the leading technology to deploy and orchestrate containers for cloud-native workloads.

In 2016, Google turned Kubernetes over to the Cloud Native Computing Foundation (CNCF). As then–CNCF executive director Dan Kohn told me, "one of the things they

---

[8]https://opensource.com/business/14/4/governance-openstack

realized very early on is that a project with a neutral home is always going to achieve a higher level of collaboration. They really wanted to find a home for it where a number of different companies could participate."

However, when Sarah Novotny took over as program manager of the Kubernetes community at Google, she found shifting the company mindset toward open participation took work.

In 2017, she said that

> ...giving up control isn't always easy even when people buy into doing what is best for a project. Defaulting to public may not be either natural or comfortable. Early on, my first six, eight, or 12 weeks at Google, I think half my electrons in email were spent on: "Why is this discussion not happening on a public mailing list? Is there a reason that this is specific to GKE [Google Container Engine]? No, there's not a reason." There were lots and lots of conversations that looked like that initially just to remind the Googlers that by default they should be discussing this publicly if they wanted the transparency, the openness, and the engagement from the community that intellectually they did.

Open Governance

Another area of openness that's attracted recent attention is open governance. This essentially means that a project's original creator, for example, can't unilaterally change the rules for participating in a project and unfairly advantage themselves relative to other contributors.

Chris Aniszczyk points to the role of open governance in building trust and confidence that a company can't just take over a project unilaterally for its own ends. "Trust is table stakes in order to build strong communities because, without openly governed institutions in projects, trust is very hard to come by," he says.

Aniszczyk doesn't

> ...think you could do open governance without assets being neutrally owned. At the end of the day, someone owns the domain, the rights to the trademark, some of the copyright, potentially. There are many great organizations out there that are super lightweight. There are things like the Apache Software Foundation, Software in the Public Interest, and the Software Freedom Conservancy.

The question of foundations can be a controversial one, especially with regard to the largest and most commercial ones. That list certainly includes the Linux Foundation, of which Aniszczyk is an executive. Some feel such foundations have grown too large and extract too much money from the ecosystem of participating projects and companies. And, while many of the most active open source projects are housed in foundations, others are not.

It's also worth observing that, in the case of open source projects, participants do have the option of forking a project if they find the stewardship of a company or foundation lacking in some way. There are arguably successful examples, perhaps most notably MariaDB's forking of MySQL after that database project's owner, Sun, was acquired by Oracle. However, as noted earlier, it can lead to a splintering of developer and other communities.

As with many aspects of open source communities and projects, the "right" approach to governance is very situational. Foundations—whether created for a specific project or with broader scope—are often seen as a more neutral collaboration point than projects solely under the control of a single company. However, they're not a prerequisite for successful projects. It just often takes more work to attract and retain outside contributors and raises the bar for demonstrating that processes for communicating, making decisions, and accepting contributions aren't biased in favor of the main project sponsor.

In addition to where the project will live, there's the question of *how* it will be governed. Some foundations, such as the Apache Software Foundation, have a fairly standard structure for projects. (At least ostensibly. The on-the-ground realities aren't always so neat and clean.) Others, like the Cloud Native Computing Foundation, take a more flexible approach based on the considerations of individual projects. Still others, like the OpenStack Foundation, were explicitly started to meet the needs of a specific project and its related subprojects.

At a detailed level, there are many additional decisions. Where will the code be hosted? How will communications take place? How will a selected governance model be implemented at a detailed level? Who makes the ultimate decisions, and who gets to commit code? How will you enable people to move from user to contributor? Is everything lumped together, or will you create Special Interest Groups (SIGs)? Will you have a dedicated community manager? What's your timeline?

And, of course, what's the project's name and what does the logo look like? (Topics that always seem to consume an outsized portion of time.)

Finally, iterate, iterate, iterate.

Who Is in the Community?

The simplest (but also simplistic) way to think about the developer community is through the lens of code contributions. The leader, maintainer, committer, and contributor taxonomy is fairly typical.

Leaders

Someone or someones need the authority to make final decisions about features, releases, and other activities. This may be a "benevolent dictator for life," a technical oversight committee, or some other voting group that has the explicit authority to make technical decisions.

Maintainers

Most projects delegate some of the decisions to people who are responsible for maintaining specific parts of the project, and in large projects, these maintainers may also delegate to people who are responsible for subcomponents of their portion. For example, Greg Kroah-Hartman is the current maintainer for the Linux kernel stable branch as well as for a variety of subsystems.

In a large project, maintainers can be more editors than coders. For example, Kroah-Hartman says that most of his work involves code review of the latest development kernel. He also talks about working with developers to help them learn how to be part of the Linux kernel development community, engagement that's often not all that technical in nature.[9]

Committers

In many projects, maintainers and committers are the same thing. However, especially in large projects, there's often a broader group of developers who are considered reliable and responsible enough to be allowed to directly submit code into the project's version control system without having to go through a maintainer gatekeeper.

---

[9]https://thenewstack.io/greg-kroah-hartman-commander-chief-linux-stable-branch/

Such contributions are still subject to review by maintainers or project leaders and may be reverted if there is a problem or processes weren't followed. For example, many projects require that code pass an automated test suite before it can be added to the project and code that doesn't will be rejected.

Contributors

Healthy projects also typically have a much broader pool of people who contribute in smaller ways. They may make a small bug fix or spot an error in the documentation. Their contributions are usually subject to a review from an experienced committer or maintainer, but the breadth of this group is often one of the hallmarks of broad support for an open source software project.

Providing a gentle on-ramp for new contributors and providing mentoring and other means to get them incrementally more involved in the project as they desire is one of the most important duties of community management.

Peters and Ruff offer guidelines for contributors in "Participating in Open Source Communities."[10]

They suggest that if you are a first-time contributor to a project, you might consider finding a mentor or an experienced project member who can review your work and provide you with some feedback as you prepare your first couple of contributions.

After submitting a contribution using the process described in the documentation, you will need to be available to respond to feedback. Common feedback would include questions about how something works or why you chose a particular approach along with suggestions for improvements or requests for changes. This feedback can be tough sometimes, so it helps to assume that the feedback is in the spirit of making your contribution better and avoid getting defensive. You may need to go through several rounds of resubmission and additional feedback before your code is accepted, and in some cases it may be rejected. There are many valid reasons why something might not be accepted, so don't take it personally if your code is rejected; and if possible, try to learn more about why your contribution was not accepted to help increase the chances of getting your next contribution included.

Keep in mind that if your contribution was accepted, you may be expected to maintain it over the long term. This is especially true for large contributions, new

---

[10]www.linuxfoundation.org/participating-open-source-communities/. Creative Commons Attribution-ShareAlike 4.0 International License.

features, or stand-alone code, like a driver for a specific piece of hardware. For small contributions and bug fixes, it is unlikely that there will be any long-term maintenance expected.

Why You Should Think About More Than Coders

Communities aren't just about coding though—or even about contributing tangible things that are an inherent part of the project like documentation, a website, or logos.

In *Producing Open Source Software: How to Run a Successful Free Software Project* (O'Reilly Media, 2005), Karl Fogel notes that not even all maintainers need to be coders at all. He writes:

> *There may be people who are very invested, and who contribute a lot, but through means other than coding. Plenty of people provide legal help, or organize events, or manage the bug tracker, or write documentation, or do any number of other things that are highly valued in the project. They often may have a level of influence in the community (and familiarity with the community's dynamics) that exceeds that of many committers.*[11]

Fogel argues that

> *The most important criterion is not technical skill or even deep familiarity with the code, but rather that a person show good judgement. Judgement includes knowing what not to take on. Someone might post only small patches, fixing fairly simple problems in the code, but if their patches apply cleanly, do not contain bugs, and are mostly in accord with the project's log message and coding conventions, and there are enough patches to show a clear pattern, then an existing committer should propose them for commit access.*

But as Diane Mueller, a director of community development at Red Hat, told me, it can be hard to get away from a code-centric mindset. "You only really talked to people when they were those people that were giving you code. We tried to flip this all on its head" with OpenShift Commons, she says.

---

[11]https://producingoss.com/

She adds that

> *In addition to all these people who were adding services, or providing infra-structure, or working with us on this, there was that whole other commu-nity out there, the customers, the people who were actually deploying OpenShift Origin [now OKD] or deploying OpenShift Container Platform. How do we get their feedback back to the contributors, the engineers, the service providers on this topic? What we did was try and create a new model, a new ecosystem that incorporated all of those different parties, and different perspectives ... A lot of it was about creating this peer-to-peer net-work model, wherein Red Hat got out of the way so the conversations could be common between Amadeus and a Clydesdale Bank or someone else.*

Users Get Involved

The direct involvement of software users in the open source development process isn't new. As we've seen, users wrote the first operating systems.

AMQP (Advanced Message Queueing Protocol) is another great study point. John O'Hara of JPMorgan Chase conceived of it in 2003 as a cooperative open effort. The company designed it over the next couple of years. In 2005, JPMorgan Chase approached other firms to form a working group that included Cisco Systems, IONA Technologies, iMatix, Red Hat, and Transaction Workflow Innovation Standards Team (TWIST). Implementations of AMQP became widely used in financial services and elsewhere where high-performance middleware messaging was needed.

However, the broad involvement by many types of end users in setting the direction of open source projects and working cooperatively on software that's relevant to entire industries has increased by such a degree as to be a difference in kind. Groups like Automotive Grade Linux, the Academy Software Foundation, and the Fintech Open Source Foundation all include broad representation from their respective industries as well as from more traditional technology vendors.

As with open source development carried out cooperatively by otherwise competing vendors, open source also lowers legal and other barriers to cooperation among software users.

Users Become Contributors

Users also can *become* contributors. Fogel observes that

> *Each interaction with a user is an opportunity to get a new participant. When a user takes the time to post to one of the project's mailing lists, or to file a bug report, she has already tagged herself as having more potential for involvement than most users (from whom the project will never hear at all). Follow up on that potential: if she described a bug, thank her for the report and ask her if she wants to try fixing it. If she wrote to say that an important question was missing from the FAQ, or that the program's documentation was deficient in some way, then freely acknowledge the problem (assuming it really exists) and ask if she's interested in writing the missing material herself. Naturally, much of the time the user will demur. But it doesn't cost much to ask, and every time you do, it reminds the other listeners in that forum that getting involved in the project is something anyone can do.*

How to Encourage New Contributors

In writing this section, I received a lot of great advice from my colleagues in Red Hat's Open Source Program Office who think about issues of community and open source contribution a lot. That's because one of the most challenging jobs of a community manager is growing the breadth of participation in their project.

This conversion of users into contributors is one important aspect of community management. Mind you. There's no rule that users always start contributing code or anything else. But many successful open source software projects have an on-ramp that makes it easy for casual or occasional contributors to begin participating on their own terms—while recognizing that others will be in a position to fully participate in a project at a high level from day one.

Projects tend to start as an in-group, whether employees of a single company or colleagues of another sort. This group may desire more outside participation in principle. But that generalized wish may not extend to making an explicit effort to be welcoming to outsiders, relinquishing control, or abandoning processes that cordon off decision making from newcomers.

Holding Onto Control: An Anti-pattern

These behaviors are natural, but they're also anti-patterns. Dave Neary writes that

> *Companies are used to controlling the products they work on. Attempting to transfer this control to a project when you want to grow a developer community will result in a lukewarm response from people who don't want to be second class citizens. Similarly, engaging with a community project where you will have no control over decisions is challenging. Exchange control for influence.*[12]

Neary also argues that the hesitancy to give up control can be part of a broader lack of understanding of the role of community in which the community is viewed through the lens of a resource that does stuff for you for free. Companies just expect other people to do work for them as directed. Neary writes of

> *...the technical director who does not understand why community projects do not accept features his team has spent months developing, or the management team that expects substantial contributions from outside the company to arrive overnight when they release software they've developed.*

Tidelift's Chris Grams has described this as the Tom Sawyer model of community engagement. He writes that

> *I've talked to people at companies who are considering "open sourcing" their product because they think there is an army of people out there who will jump at the chance to build their products for them. Many of these people go on to learn tough but valuable lessons in building community. It's not that simple. You can avoid the Tom Sawyer trap through some exercises in humility. A couple of questions for you: Why does it have to be your community and why do you have to build it? Do people have to come participate in your community, or might you consider joining their community?*[13]

As a general principle, think about the friction points that might inhibit someone—especially someone from outside your organization—from contributing to the project. I've already touched on some of these. Certain licenses or contributor license

---

[12]www.slashdata.co/blog/2011/01/open-source-community-building-a-guide-to-getting-it-right

[13]https://chrisgrams.com/2009/09/09/tom-sawyer-whitewashing-fences-and-building-communities-online/

agreements may be sensible from a legal, intellectual property, or business model perspective. Nonetheless, be aware that the choices you make there can affect how likely someone is to want to work on the project.

Tools also play a role.

Reducing the Friction of Tools

Amye Scavarda Perrin, formerly of the Gluster storage project, talks about how infrastructure was historically hard to open up to outsiders without a track record but that

> *...infrastructure tools like Ansible, Chef, and Puppet have become widely adopted and changed this. It's now possible to open source project infrastructure as code, with the same levels of access as any other contributor. This makes the process visible to contributors, allowing a pathway for contribution that might not be strict project code. You're no longer tied to the problem of only a limited amount of high-level contributors who have access.*[14]

More generally, both virtual machine- and container-based technologies simplify setting up replicable development environments quickly.

Conversely, obscure and difficult-to-use version control systems, oddball programming languages, complex procedures, hard-to-run test suites, and a litany of other frictions make it easy for a potential new contributor to quickly decide that "it's just not worth it" and move on. Very few organizations erect these roadblocks on purpose. Maybe their own engineers have gotten so used to convoluted legacy processes and tooling that it doesn't hurt so much any longer. But the more familiar you can make working with the code base (or otherwise contributing to the project), the more contributors you'll gain.

Mentoring

Formal mentoring programs can also help to get contributors up to speed. Examples include the Kubernetes Mentoring Initiatives and OpenStack Mentoring. The details vary. For example, OpenStack offers two different levels of mentoring in addition to a

---

[14]https://community.redhat.com/blog/2017/04/encouraging-new-contributors/

mentoring program that's longer term, but more lightweight, and is aimed at bringing together mentors and mentees who may not be co-located.

Neary observes that mentoring programs aren't always effective because of communication issues, excessive time commitments, and lack of follow-through.[15] He nonetheless argues that "Mentoring programs are needed to ensure that your project is long-term sustainable."

He likens mentoring to management and suggests going for quick wins while developing an ongoing relationship between mentors and "apprentices." He cautions that

> Just as not everyone is suited to being a manager, not everyone is suited to being a mentor. The skills needed to be a good mentor are also those of a good manager—keeping track of someone else's activity while making them feel responsible for what they're working on, communicating well and frequently, and reading between the lines to diagnose problems before it's too late to do anything about them.

However, he adds that "Mentoring is also an opportunity for developers who would like to gain management experience to do so as a mentor in a free software project."

The Importance of Culture

More broadly though, communities need to think about their culture. I was going to write here that communities need a healthy culture in order to attract new contributors. But that's (unfortunately) not quite right. Some projects are connected to sufficiently important commercial products that they can successfully attract developers in spite of themselves. Nonetheless, there's been enough repudiation of bad behaviors and lack of diversity in various open source projects that we can hopefully take cultures that value attributes like empathy, respect, and inclusiveness as aspirational even if they aren't always the norm.

Jono Bacon refers to the art of community as "building belonging." He writes that

> A sense of belonging is what keeps people in communities. This belonging is the goal of community building. The hallmark of a strong community is when its members feel that they belong. Belonging is the measure of a strong social economy. This economy's currency is not the money that you find in

---

[15]https://blogs.gnome.org/bolsh/2011/05/31/effective-mentoring-programs/

your wallet or down the back of your couch, but is social capital. For an economy and community to be successful, the participants need to believe in it. If no one believes in the community that brings them together, it fails.[16]

Structures and processes matter when welcoming contributors and maintaining communities more generally. However, at least as important are the intrinsic attitudes, norms, and culture of the community.

Steps to Maintain a Community

Part of maintaining a community is encouraging new contributions. Contributors leave projects all the time, and they don't necessarily leave because someone did something wrong. They may just move onto new things, need a break, or otherwise want to try something different. This means that the community needs to be constantly refreshed with new blood. It's therefore important that new contributors have a good experience and that community members be able to progress according to their interests.

Quick Responses

Josh Berkus thinks of making a contribution as akin to starting a timer.[17] He writes that

The longer maintainers take to respond to their submission, the lower the chance that person will ever contribute to the project again. While no one has done a specific study on this that I know of, my experience is that it drops by half in a couple of days and it gets very close to zero in only a few weeks. If you're running a young project and looking to attract lots of new contributors, there may be no higher priority than dealing with first-time contributions quickly. Minutes to hours is the target here.

It's not just the initial response that matters though. It's certainly a good thing to quickly acknowledge a contribution. But it's not enough if the contribution never gets added to the project for reasons that aren't ever made clear. This gets back to the importance of infrastructure that Perrin discussed earlier. Automated tooling and continuous integration/continuous delivery (CI/CD) systems can reduce the time to

---

[16]www.jonobacon.com/2011/05/31/the-art-of-community-building-belonging/
[17]https://community.redhat.com/blog/2017/04/contributors-speed-matters/

integrate and test new software. It doesn't eliminate the need for someone to work with a new contributor when, as is often the case, their submittal needs some additional work. But it does reduce a lot of the latency associated with manual processes.

Documentation: An Easy On-Ramp

Berkus adds that documentation is another good area to automate the integration of new content given that "it's one area where most open source projects need a lot more contributions and where acceptance of imperfect submissions carries relatively low risk."

The design of the software itself also plays into how people can engage with a project. For example, writing in 2013, Simon Phipps discussed some learnings from the LibreOffice project[18]:

> *The code base was hard to build, so the project set up automated Tinderbox continuous-integration build servers, allowing any developer to work on the code without needing to create their own complex build environment in multiple operating system environments. The code has been substantially cleaned up with translation of comments from German to English for more accessibility around the world (most developers have English as at least a second language). The clean-up also involved a great deal of refactoring of old approaches into more modern ones and the elimination of unused code left over from defunct platforms—this is 20-year-old code, after all.*

Modular Beats Monoliths

Greg DeKoenigsberg and Michael DeHaan talk about how modularity and "option value" have helped make the Ansible project successful, quoting from a 2005 paper by Carliss Baldwin and Kim Clark of Harvard Business School entitled "The Architecture of Participation: Does Code Architecture Mitigate Free Riding in the Open Source Development Model?"

---

[18]www.infoworld.com/article/2613624/open-source-software/what-you-can-learn-from-the-monster-libreoffice-project.html

Modularity is important because it

...provides a simple framework of platform and modules. The platform supports the modules and provides well-defined rules for module development; modules may then be developed or modified independently according to those rules, thus allowing contributors to add value in corners of the project, with minimum investment.

For its part, high option value means users can choose some modules but not others, or even to rewrite particular modules.

Combining the two makes it easier to identify ways of contributing immediately and to see the value of that contribution quickly. DeKoenigsberg and DeHaan add

In browsing through Ansible's libraries, one can find over 230 different modules, the vast majority of which were co-developed and co-maintained by multiple community developers over time. The Ansible "batteries included" philosophy helps to ensure that as new modules are developed, they are tested and integrated in Ansible's core, so that the maximum number of users get the maximum option value for the minimum collective effort.

Communicate, Communicate, Communicate

Effective communications are important for any team and not just an open source community. However, many open source communities bring to the fore considerations that haven't historically been as important for teams working together in a single location.

The Limits of Being Together

In a traditional in-office work setting, a lot of communication takes place fairly organically and informally. Impromptu meetings, bumping into coworkers in the hallway, eating lunch together, and making decisions by the water cooler. Communications could be thought of as embedded into the physical nature of the workplace. Indeed, we see this idea of collaboration through physical proximity as a stated benefit of the much-maligned open office plans that were so in vogue, at least prior to the COVID-19 pandemic.

Not that co-location was ever necessarily a panacea. Recalling one of her teams in which everyone sat next to each other, Red Hat chief Agile architect Jen Krieger observed to me that

> ...we didn't necessarily want to be in everybody's face all the time. If you are an engineer, it's really sometimes hard to be in a situation where you're constantly pulled out of what you're trying to think about. We would actually pick a day every week where everybody would be working from home, so that folks could focus on just getting their work done.

Best Practices for Distributed Teams

Many companies and teams experienced widespread remote work for the first time in 2020. And they've often found themselves adopting practices and behaviors that were already in wide use in many open source communities.

Even the best traditional practices break down with widely distributed communities. What may be less obvious is that they start to break down when communities are distributed to even a small degree. What happens is that you talk about software development or something else entirely with the local team over pizzas and beers and you make some collective decision. Then the two or three guys or gals in London or Hawaii only find out after the fact, perhaps completely by accident. "That's right. We made that decision over lunch last week. Sorry. We'll try and remember to tell you next time."

Brockmeier notes that water cooler decisions are the reason that the Apache Software Foundation has an "if it didn't happen on the mailing list, it didn't happen" rule. He says that "Any major decision that wasn't discussed on a mailing list could very well be reversed. 'Major decision' is very much up for interpretation, but I've seen a number of things backed out and put up for discussion because they violated this rule."

A very asymmetrically distributed team can be the most challenging. Krieger tells a story about how she was the sole distributed team member of a team trying Scrum for the first time:

> Everybody else was in our Miami office and they were all, on a daily basis, participating in live and active vocal conversation ... A lot of times, what would happen is they would have team meetings and they would forget to call me, because the phone exchange didn't allow direct call in, if they didn't call me, I just didn't go to the meetings.

She adds that water cooler conversations are going to happen in any case but

> *...when you are making decisions, the first thing I always like to tell people is, "Who you actually bring to the decision making room is actually a pretty important topic." If you are going to randomly make decisions in the hallway without all the people who need to be in that decision, it's probably not going to be a very good way for you to actually get consensus or drive change to your organization.*

This is good advice for both distributed and local teams.

More than one person has told me that, while many aspects of the pandemic have made coping with work harder, they appreciate that everyone is on their own video screen during a call. (I know a couple of teams that already had a rule whereby if any individual was calling in from their own phone or computer, everyone was expected to do so.) I've also found that, while the people I work with have long had pretty good discipline about using a shared collaborative agenda and meeting minute documents, the practice has now become essentially universal.

It's About People

Finally, Krieger advises that you think about team and community dynamics rather than purely mechanical processes around information exchange and decision making. For example, she says that

> *It's important for teams to understand, especially if you're committed to doing something together as a team, that you have a social responsibility to the folks that you're actually interacting with. It's not just, get on your team meeting and immediately start talking about work but it's asking somebody about their day, or finding out what they did over the weekend, or trying to make some sort of social connection so that it's easier for you to have casual conversation.*

This becomes all the more important with fully remote teams as many were forced to be during the pandemic. At an MIT Sloan CIO Digital Learning event in September 2020, Aarti Shah, senior vice president and chief information and digital officer, Eli Lilly and Company, emphasized the importance of virtual check-ins and ensuring people are taking time off. At the same event, Barry Libenson, global CIO, Experian, added, "We have had more virtual happy hours in the past six months than in the prior six years."

It's Also About Tools

There are a wide range of tools to make remote collaboration easier.

We call IRC, Google Chat, and Slack messaging tools, but you can almost think of them as an ambient distributed conversation that allows people to participate mostly when they have the time and feel like it. Code repositories like GitHub provide visibility into the software being developed. Shared documents and wikis can be used for agendas and to document decisions. Zoom and other video conferencing systems are good for lightweight real-time interactions. Companies can facilitate the rollout of tools and provide guidelines for using them appropriately and consistently. However, OASIS' Guy Martin suggests an approach that is "culture first, process second, tools last." Good tools are important, but they won't help if the culture and behaviors don't support collaboration.

It's also the case that the proliferation of different collaboration tools can be a very real challenge. Potential community members may have very strong preferences for an open source tool like IRC. Alternatively, they may see IRC and mailing lists as too old-school and just want to use Slack. To some degree, communities need to meet potential participants where they are or at least where they're willing to go. But this can lead to a degree of fragmentation.

The Limits of Virtual

Many have also experienced the limits of virtual activities as both day-to-day work and events went online in 2020. Even the current generation of collaboration tools lack the richness and serendipity of in-person communications.

In setting up OpenShift Commons originally, Diane Mueller said that, while she did a lot of things to try to make the virtual world work, she also realized that get-togethers shouldn't just be virtual. As a result, OpenShift Commons has regular "Gatherings," day-long meetings of a few hundred members from both developer and user communities spread around the world. (Of course, they're all virtual as I'm writing this.)

Krieger adds that another team she was working on was

> ...having a little bit of trouble actually working well together ... We brought everybody together so that they could meet each other, have food together. People bond while eating. It's just a thing. It's a universal thing, whether it be beer in the Czech Republic or Italian food in Little Italy in New York City, people bond over eating and drinking. It's just a thing that we do as humans.

In writing about "the importance of face-to-face," Jono Bacon adds that

...while there are often attempts in companies to provide functional meth-ods of building relationships (such as those cheesy team-building exercises most of us have suffered through), relationships usually form in more organic ways. Getting to know someone is often a mixture of chatting in the hallway, having breakfast together, sharing ideas at the end of a presenta-tion, having a couple of drinks together in a bar, and other ways of getting to know each other. The venue and proximity are not the only important pieces though. Relationships also typically form when there is a sense that personal barriers have been dropped a little. When people feel comfortable sharing experiences, expressing concerns, riffing on ideas, and confiding in each other, genuine relationships and alliances form.[19]

The pandemic has reinforced Bacon's observations. Many virtual events have done a good job of broadcasting content—often to far more people than would have been able to travel to an in-person event for reason of time, money, visas, or other reasons. Other aspects of virtual events have been harder, especially at scale, although the various event platforms continue to experiment with ways to conduct in-session polling, post-session interactive discussions, and other ways of increasing engagement. However, there's been near-universal agreement that replicating the so-called "hallway track" at conferences where people meet serendipitously, develop friendships, and compare restaurant notes has been...challenging.

There will always be frictions to communicating within a project and community. Differences in language time zones, and cultural norms have costs. These all take effort to overcome, and, in some cases, the frictions may just be too great. This then comes back to some of the other project characteristics that can make contributing easier. Modularity and bounding the scope of code are also useful for helping individuals and small groups to work in parallel. Communication still matters, but it's more tolerant of limited real-time, high-bandwidth interactions.

---

[19]https://opensource.com/life/15/10/the-importance-of-face-to-face

Bacon writes that

> *Peter Bloch, a consultant on learning, makes an important foundational observation about communication in a social economy: "community is fundamentally an interdependent human system given form by the conversation it holds with itself." When I first heard that quote, I realized that the mechanism behind communication in a community is stories. Stories are a medium in which we keep the river flowing ... when the characters in the stories are people in a community, the stories are self-referencing and give the community a sense of reporting. Communities really feel like communities when there is a news wire, be it formalized or through the grapevine.*

Determine If You're Successful

"Without data, you're just a person with an opinion." Those are the words of W. Edwards Deming, the champion of statistical process control who would come to be credited as one of the inspirations for what became known as the Japanese postwar economic miracle of 1950–1960. Ironically, Japanese manufacturers like Toyota were far more receptive to Deming's ideas than General Motors and Ford were in his own country.

Community management is certainly an art. It's about mentoring. It's about having difficult conversations with people who are hurting the community. It's about negotiation and compromise. It's about interacting with other communities. It's about making connections. In the words of Diane Mueller, it's about "nurturing conversations."

However, it's also about metrics and data.

Some have much in common with software development projects more broadly. Others are more specific to the management of the community itself.

I think of deciding what to measure and how as adhering to five principles.

Measuring Something Changes It

First, you should recognize that behaviors aren't independent of the measurements you choose to highlight.

In 2008, Daniel Ariely published *Predictably Irrational*, one of a number of books written around that time that introduced behavioral psychology and behavioral economics to the general public. One memorable quote from that book is the following: "Human beings adjust behavior based on the metrics they're held against. Anything you measure will impel a person to optimize his score on that metric. What you measure is what you'll get. Period."

This shouldn't be surprising. It's a finding that's been repeatedly confirmed by research. It should also be familiar to just about anyone with business experience. It's certainly not news to anyone in sales management, for example. Base sales rep bonuses solely on revenue, and they'll try to discount whatever it takes to maximize revenue even if doing so puts margin in the toilet. Conversely, want the sales force to push a new product line—which will probably take extra effort—but skip the spiffs? Probably not happening.

And lest you think I'm unfairly picking on sales, this behavior is pervasive, all the way up to the CEO, as Ariely describes in a 2010 Harvard Business Review article. "CEOs care about stock value because that's how we measure them. If we want to change what they care about, we should change what we measure," writes Ariely.

Developers and other community members are not immune.

What Actually Matters?

Second, you need to choose relevant metrics. There's a lot of folk wisdom floating around about what's relevant and important that's not necessarily true. Dave Neary offers an example from baseball. He notes that

> In the late '90s, the key measurements that were used to measure batter skill were RBI (Runs Batted In) and batting average (how often a player got on base with a hit, divided by the number of at-bats). The Oakland A's were the first major league team to recruit based on a different measurement of player performance, on-base percentage. This measures how often they get to first base, regardless of how it happens.[20]

Indeed, the whole revolution of sabermetrics in baseball and elsewhere, popularized in Michael Lewis' *Moneyball: The Art of Winning an Unfair Game* (W. W. Norton, 2004), often gets talked about in terms of bringing data into a field that historically was more about gut feel and personal experience. But it was also about taking a game that had actually always been fairly numbers-obsessed and coming up with new metrics based on mostly existing data to better measure player value. (The data revolution going on in sports today is more about collecting much more data than was previously available using video and other means and applying new techniques like deep learning to that data.)

---

[20]https://community.redhat.com/blog/2014/07/when-metrics-go-wrong/

Quantity May Not Lead to Quality

As a corollary, collecting lots of tangential but easy-to-capture data isn't better than just selecting a few measurements you've determined are genuinely useful. It's tempting in a world where online behavior can be tracked with great granularity and displayed in colorful dashboards to be distracted by sheer data volume even when it doesn't deliver any great insight into community health and trajectory.

This may seem like an obvious point. Why would I choose to measure something that isn't relevant? However, in practice, metrics often get chosen because they're easy to measure, not because they're particularly useful. They tend to be more about inputs than outputs. The number of developers. The number of forum posts. The number of commits. Collectively, measures like this often get called vanity metrics. They're ubiquitous, but most people involved with community management don't think much of them.

Number of downloads may be the worst of the bunch for open source projects. It's true that, at some level, they're an indication of interest. That's something. But it's sufficiently distant from actively using the project, much less engaging with the project deeply, that it's hard to view downloads as a very useful number.

Is there any harm in these vanity metrics? Maybe? Yes, to the degree that you start thinking that they're something to base action on. Probably more seriously, they can come to be seen by stakeholders like company management or industry observers as meaningful indicators of whether a project is winning or not.

What Does the Number Mean?

Understand what measurements really mean and how they relate to each other. Neary makes this point to caution against myopia. He tells the story of how

> ...in one project I worked on, some people were concerned about a recent spike in the number of bug reports coming in because it seemed like the project must have serious quality issues to resolve; however, when we looked at the numbers, it turned out that many of the bugs were coming in because a large company had recently started using the project. The increase in bug reports was actually a proxy for a big influx of new users, which was a good thing.

In practice, you often *have* to measure through proxies. This isn't an inherent problem, but the further remove you get from what you want to measure and what you're actually measuring, the harder it is to connect the dots. It's fine to track progress in closing bugs, writing code, and adding new features. However, those don't necessarily correlate with how happy users are or whether the project is doing a good job of working toward its long-term objectives.

Horses for Courses

Finally, different measurements serve different purposes. Some measurements may be nonobvious but useful for tracking the success of a project and community relative to internal goals. Others may be better suited for a press release or other external consumption. For example, as a community manager, you may really care about the number of meetups, mentoring sessions, and virtual briefings your community has held over the past three months. But it's the number of contributions and contributors that are more likely to grab the headlines. You probably care about those too. But maybe not as much depending upon your current priorities.

Still other measurements may relate to the goals of sponsoring organizations. The measurements most relevant for projects tied to commercial products are likely to be different from pure community efforts.

Because communities differ and goals differ, it's not possible to just compile a metrics checklist, but here are some ideas to think about. As Red Hat's James Falkner notes, "Each community has its own mission, goals, and central thoughts around which people collaborate, and the measurements you take must take those into account, without wasting yours or anyone else's time." The following are some common threads and themes with respect to measuring community and project health.

Understand Softer Aspects of Community

Conducting surveys and other studies can be time consuming, especially if they're rigorous enough to yield better than anecdotal data. It also requires rigor to construct studies so that they can be used to track changes over time. It's also a lot easier to measure quantitative contributor activity than it is to suss out if the community members are happier about their participation today than they were a year ago. However, given the importance of culture to the health of a community, measuring it in a systematic way can be a worthwhile exercise.

Breadth of community, including how many participants are unaffiliated with commercial entities, is important for many projects. The greater the breadth, the greater the potential leverage of the open source development process. It can also be instructive to see how companies and individuals are contributing. We saw earlier how Ansible contributions benefit from the modularity of the software. Projects can be explicitly designed to better accommodate casual contributors. (A particular challenge of tracking open source contributions is that many participants use a personal email address—or multiple ones—so identifying even relevant company contributions can be difficult.)

Are new contributors able to have an impact, or are they ignored? How long does it take for code contributions to get committed? How long does it take for a reported bug to be fixed or otherwise responded to? If someone asked a question in a forum, did anyone answer them? In other words, are you letting contributors contribute?

Advancement within the project is also an important metric. Mikeal Rogers of the Node.js community tells how

> *The shift that we made was to create a support system and an education system to take a user and turn them into a contributor, first at a very low level and educate them to bring them into the committer pool and eventually into the maintainer pool. The end result of this is that we have a wide range of skillsets. Rather than trying to attract phenomenal developers, we're creating new phenomenal developers.*

Whatever metrics you choose, don't forget why you made them metrics in the first place. I find a great question to ask is "What am I going to do with this number?" If the answer is to just put it in a monthly status report, that's not a great answer. Metrics should be measurements that tell you either that you're on the right path or that you need to take specific actions to course correct.

For this reason, Stormy Peters argues for keeping it simple. She writes that

> *It's much better to have one or two key metrics than to worry about all the possible metrics. You can capture all the possible metrics, but as a project, you should focus on moving one. It's also better to have a simple metric that correlates directly to something in the real world than a metric that is a complicated formula or ratio between multiple things. As project members make decisions, you want them to be able to intuitively feel whether or not it will affect the project's key metric in the right direction.[21]*

---

[21]https://medium.com/open-source-communities/3-important-things-to-consider-when-measuring-your-success-50e21ad82858

Back to the Bazaar

With healthy and well-governed communities, open source software can be an extremely effective software development model. We see examples everywhere in the software landscape today. The degree to which open source can reduce the friction of companies and individuals to collaborate took a long time to fully appreciate. Open source software may have often begun life as a lower-cost alternative to proprietary products. But today, whole categories of software default to open source in whole or in part.

That said, we can also look around and observe that, important as open source is, it's not the entire software universe. It's reasonable to ask why and where the open source development model hasn't displaced the alternatives.

Part of the reason relates to the business models that companies can successfully build in conjunction with open source software and open source development practices. I'll dive deeper on that topic later in this book. However, for now, suffice it to say that many companies built themselves around proprietary software development processes. Others use open source software to greater or lesser degrees but use it together with proprietary code and services. This doesn't mean an open source development model couldn't be effective in these cases, but rather that it's not a fit with how they want to run their businesses.

But what of the open source development process itself? It comes back to the hubbub of the bazaar, which no software program developed in an open community can escape entirely. A few statements about the nature of that bazaar broadly hold true.

It's a Bit of a Free-for-All

Open source tends to be about lack of restrictions, lack of forced approaches, and lack of guard rails. Some projects aren't quite that freewheeling, but upstream projects are often still likely to include features that are early-stage, experimental, or sometimes just broken. Commercial products mitigate this confusing picture to a certain degree by, paradoxically, constraining options and opinions.

Of course, the old proprietary world had plenty of differing opinions to choose from as well—and once you bought into one, you couldn't easily change your mind. Nonetheless, we can generalize that the open source landscape can be chaotic to navigate in the absence of a guide.

Open Source Is Duplicative

How many stalls filled with similar bangles and beads do you really need anyway? Shouldn't someone just herd them all into one organized marketplace?

Sounds like open source. Whether it's the many graphical user interfaces on desktop Linux systems, the almost overwhelming number of overlapping projects in the cloud-native computing space, or the wide range of Linux distributions, the apparent inefficiency can seem staggering. At best, it's Darwinian with a smaller number of successful projects gaining community and momentum over time—as Kubernetes has done in the container orchestration space.

This is one of the ways in which innovation happens, but it's a messy process.

Community Makes It Work

Ultimately, effective use of the open source development model requires that a community be able to coalesce and be willing and able to contribute to a project at the level needed to make it successful.

If we look across the open source software landscape at many of the successful projects, we can start to discern certain patterns. Linux, Kubernetes, the Apache web server—they're all infrastructure software projects that have broad horizontal applicability.

What you don't see much of is payroll, financial accounting, or software that's very specific to a particular profession or industry. There probably aren't a lot of people who want to casually contribute to dental records management in their spare time or who have either the inclination or the knowledge to update tax rules in an application every year.

Even when there are open source versions for these types of applications, the open source code tends to be primarily written by one company and exist in the market alongside proprietary "Pro" offerings with more features or hosted services.

Furthermore, popularity doesn't equate to funding. Even beyond some critical infrastructure components, which we've discussed, there are many popular projects in programming languages, media creation apps, and elsewhere that lack significant enterprise-level funding. Funding matters because the popular image of open source software being developed mostly by hobbyists on nights and weekends doesn't apply to just about any major open source project. And large communities also need support through sponsorships and other funding just to keep the lights on for basic community maintenance.

Open source communities can be an extremely powerful model to develop software. Creating and growing a community has to be deliberate work that's matched with the nature of and goals for the project. And it may still not work if another project gains the mindshare or if the project just isn't suited to community-based development. You can't put out a sign that says "Work on my stuff for free" and expect it to just happen as if by magic. You have to understand the open source development model and approach it deliberately.

Why the Development Model Matters

The open source development model wasn't originally the featured headline of open source. But user freedoms are amplified when there are effective communities developing the software. Especially as projects grow, that requires appropriate governance structures, community management, and having a meal or drinks together now and then.

Open Source's Connection to the Past

Open source took its present form in part because of some of the specific ways in which the computer industry and its surrounding environment developed. But open source also has roots in how companies have long collaborated—and innovation has taken place. Know-how and intellectual property have long been informally shared, even absent official sanctioned processes, throughout much of history. Researchers have also studied how communication takes place and how people are motivated since long before there was such a thing as open source software. Open source both benefits from such research and provides fodder for deeper study of these topics going forward.

The Machine That Drives Open Source

As we learned in the last chapter, clearly there's something new, different, and powerful in the open source development model and the way that it can be used by successful businesses. That makes understanding how and why open source works a matter of more than academic interest even if it's often academics who formally study how open source software development works as a process.

Furthermore, there's a suspicion—more than a suspicion really—that open source has insights to offer that go beyond software development. How best to innovate? How do people communicate and self-organize? What intrinsically motivates individuals to take on certain tasks? What should we be measuring in organizations?

These are all reasons to peer into open source software projects and communities, ponder possible insights, and consider what they may tell us about other aspects of interaction and organization within companies, between companies, and among

117

© Gordon Haff 2021
G. Haff, *How Open Source Ate Software*, https://doi.org/10.1007/978-1-4842-6800-1_5

individuals in both their professional and personal spheres. Open source is, after all, a product of a highly interconnected world. It's reasonable to assume that the forces ushering in open source also have had effects elsewhere.

Innovation

Innovation has been the subject of academic study for a long time. After all, technology has been dramatically changing how humans lived ever since there have been humans. Even the Industrial Revolution was just a dramatic acceleration of an established trend.

Innovation Through Collective Invention

One early paper that specifically focused on collective invention came from Robert C. Allen of the University of British Columbia in 1983.[1]

Allen was studying the 19th-century iron and steel industry and seeking to better understand the manner in which inventions took place. It was a milieu with little or no government funding and minimal academic research; even the firms themselves didn't pursue research and development in any formal way. With the exception of a few well-known inventors like Bessemer, the process seems to have been very diffuse.

In the course of his research, Allen concluded that a great deal of information about furnace designs was widely shared. He based this, in part, on the designs that companies made publicly available.

But it also stemmed from the nature of the inventions themselves. Most changes were incremental and experimental in a field that generally lacked theories about how to build a better blast furnace from first principles.

Allen speculated that output and profits could be greater if the "existing regime of trade secrets was replaced by a new regime of free information exchange." He also thought that firms might release information because "so many people would know the relevant information that it would have been costly to keep it secret." Secrecy can introduce frictions and transaction costs.

---

[1]Allen, R. C. (1983). "Collective Invention." *Journal of Economic Behavior and Organization.*

In conclusion, he writes:

An essential feature of collective invention was the release of technical information to actual and potential competitors. It was this behavior which allowed cumulative advance. All of the factors that account for this behaviour apply to the other institutions as well. Hence, one would expect to observe the wilful dissemination of technical knowledge under a variety of circumstances. And, indeed, even a casual acquaintance with recent engineering literature indicates that such behaviour is rampant today. To the degree that economists have considered this behaviour at all, it has been regarded as an undesired "leakage" that reduces the incentives to invent. That firms desire such behaviour and that it increases the rate of invention by allowing cumulative advance are possibilities not yet explored. They should be.

The Economics of Open

Eric von Hippel of MIT's Sloan School of Management has made something of a career out of studying innovation going back to the 1970s. "Spurred on by [Allen's] work and the evident success of open source software, quite a few of us then began trying to understand the economic benefits of open vs. proprietary information,"[2] von Hippel writes. For example, in 1987, he noted that

..."informal" know-how trading is the extensive exchange of proprietary know-how by informal networks of process engineers in rival (and non-rival) firms. I have observed such know-how trading networks to be very active in the US steel minimill industry and elsewhere, and they appear to represent a novel form of cooperative R&D.[3]

von Hippel and ETH Zurich's Georg von Krogh argue that "society has a vital interest in encouraging and rewarding innovation."[4] They write about how "open source software development is an exemplar of a compound model of innovation that contains elements of both the private investment and the collective action models."

---

[2]`https://evhippel.mit.edu/papers/section-3/`

[3]von Hippel, Eric. "Cooperation Between Rivals: Informal Know-how Trading." *Research Policy* 16, no. 6 (December 1987).

[4]von Hippel, Eric, and Georg von Krogh. "Open Source Software and the 'Private-Collective' Innovation Model: Issues for Organization Science." *Organization Science* 14, no. 2 (March 2003).

The private investment model is how products were traditionally brought to market and commercial software written. Innovation is supported by private investment with the profits going to the entity making the investments. With this model, any "spillover" of proprietary knowledge has historically been considered to reduce profits, hence the existence of trade secrets, patents, and other ways to reduce the ability of others to make money off innovations that you spent money creating.

By contrast, the collective action model applies to public goods, which have two characteristics. First, if one user consumes them, every other user has access to them. Second, the act of consuming the good doesn't mean there's less of it for everyone else. In economist speak, a public good is defined by its non-excludability and non-rivalry.

The collective action model operates in science and elsewhere. If a researcher publishes a paper proposing a novel use for a drug, that knowledge is now available to everyone, and one person making use of that knowledge doesn't mean that there's now less knowledge for everyone else.

They then add that

> *In the case of open source software development projects, we see an interest-ing compound of the private investment and collective action models of innovation. We term this compound the "private-collective" innovation model. In this model, participants in open source software projects use their own resources to privately invest in creating novel software code. In prin-ciple, these innovators could then claim proprietary rights over their code, but instead they choose to freely reveal it as a public good. Clearly, the net result of this behavior appears to offer society the best of both worlds—new knowledge is created by private funding and then offered freely to all.*

The Advantages of Collaborative Innovation

von Hippel and von Krogh wrote those words in 2003, still relatively early days for commercial open source software and even earlier days for open source driving large amounts of innovation as opposed to being primarily a less expensive alternative to proprietary software. However, they already recognized that something different was going on with the relationship of open source software to innovation that wasn't captured by traditional economic models.

In 2017, von Hippel expanded on his innovation work in *Free Innovation* (MIT Press). This book specifically focuses on innovation created by individuals in the absence of commercial transactions. However, many of the same principles apply to organizations participating in open source projects.

For example, he writes that

...a collaborative innovation project offers two major advantages over innovation projects carried out by individual free innovators. The first major benefit from a participant's perspective has to do with output value obtained: Each individual participant incurs the design cost of doing a fraction of the project work but, if intending to use it, obtains the value of the entire design, including additions and improvements generated by others... A second major advantage of collaborative projects over single innovator projects is that collaborative projects greatly expand the range of innovation opportunities that are viable for free innovators. This is because overall project costs are no longer limited to a level of design costs that are viable for a single individual.

He adds that

...protective measures would shrink the pool of potential contributors, and so shrink the overall scale of the project. The network properties of the collaborative innovation model (the fact that the value to everyone increases as the total number of contributors increases) mean that this reduction in the contributor pool would reduce the value of the project to the contributors who remain as well as to free riders.

This reinforces the idea that it's usually better to focus on taking full advantage of the open source development model rather than worrying about those who would use your software without giving back.

How Knowledge Gets Shared

Other research has focused on the role of networks and ties in innovation, including the sharing of knowledge.

For example, in 2008, Annapoornima Subramanian and Pek-Hooi Soh of the National University of Singapore did an analysis of open source projects through the lens of knowledge integration theory. They looked at the efficiency of integration, the extent to which projects accessed and utilized the specialized knowledge held by individual members. They considered flexibility of integration, the extent to which a project can access additional knowledge and reconfigure existing knowledge.

This research drew conclusions similar to other studies that emphasize the importance of communication in open source projects. The authors write that "In an open knowledge sharing environment such as OSS [open source software], effectiveness of the project greatly depends on the extent to which the project can integrate and build upon knowledge that is available in the public domain." They conclude that this phenomenon, also known as open innovation, is essential for technologies such as software, where the knowledge required for building the innovation is widely available.[5]

Collaboration and Communication

Inherent in cooperative ventures is the need to collaborate and communicate. Open source software projects—as well as other open projects like Wikipedia—have been a rich data trove for researchers in this area because so much communicating takes place on public mailing lists, code repositories, and chat systems like IRC. Open source projects are also interesting, if complicated as a result, because they can be a mix of people contributing on their own time and people contributing as part of their day job or even a blend of the two.

All this makes open source software development a useful study point for distributed teams generally. What's the effect of geographic distribution? Does being spread across many different time zones matter? What self-organizing structures appear? How does organization of a project team affect the resulting software?

The Limits of Communication

Take Conway's law. It's an adage named after computer programmer Melvin Conway, who argued in a 1968 *Datamation* article that "any organization that designs a system (defined more broadly here than just information systems) will inevitably produce a design whose structure is a copy of the organization's communication structure."[6] A common shorthand restatement is that "If you have four groups working on a compiler, you'll get a four-pass compiler."

---

[5]"Knowledge Integration and Effectiveness of Open Source Development Projects." *IIMB Management Review*, June 2008.

[6]www.melconway.com/Home/Committees_Paper.html

Conway's observation was mostly empirical. However, it rings true for many practitioners. An early 2000s example comes from an Amazon offsite meeting at which managers suggested that employees should be communicating with each other better—a perennial complaint that's pretty much par for the course at just about any large company. To their surprise, founder and CEO Jeff Bezos stood up and announced, "No, communication is terrible!"[7] Bezos' idea was that communication works better within small "two-pizza teams" (teams no bigger than two pizzas can feed) and that communication between different teams can be minimized by requiring that interactions between software written by each team only take place through well-documented public interfaces.

This is one of the ideas behind microservices, or service-oriented architectures more broadly. So long as you stick to the contract—that is, the documented interface—any team can theoretically make whatever changes they want to their code, including rewriting it in a new language or changing algorithms, so long as they don't make changes to the public application programming interface (API). In practice, you almost certainly don't want every team to be doing their own thing for a variety of reasons, but in principle they could.

In one study of the relationship between software and teams writing the software,[8] researchers found that as teams increase in size, forecasts regarding how long it would take to develop some piece of software tend to get more optimistic. (This bias shone through whether the forecast came from the team itself or someone outside the team.) Furthermore, they found that even though large teams thought they would be faster than smaller ones, they could actually be slower. This echoes Fred Brooks' observation in *The Mythical Man-Month* (Addison-Wesley Professional, 1975), an account of the design of the IBM System/360 family of computers, that "adding manpower to a late software project makes it later."

The problem, as organizational psychologist and expert on team dynamics J. Richard Hackman has pointed out in *The Psychology of Leadership: New Perspectives and Research* (Psychology Press, 2004), is that the number of links between people increases by about the square of the number of people. And it's the number of links that corresponds to communication difficulty and overhead.[9]

---

[7]http://blog.idonethis.com/two-pizza-team/

[8]www.opim.wharton.upenn.edu/~kmilkman/2012_OBHDPb.pdf

[9]To be precise, it's n(n-1)/2. Ten people have 45 links. One hundred people have 4,950. And so forth.

How Communication Affects Software Structure

Other research from MIT and Harvard Business School[10] compared the structure of proprietary software relative to open source counterparts developed by more distributed and loosely coupled teams. They concluded that the product developed by the loosely coupled organization was significantly more modular—that is, design changes in one component don't affect other components—than the product from the tightly coupled organization.

This is in keeping with the observations of community managers and others that it's easier to create communities around open source software that's modular. When software is monolithic and the team is distributed, the organizational structure is effectively fighting against the structure of the software.

There has also been research into social group size, which is potentially interesting for understanding how large open source communities—or at least their subgroups—can grow while still being effective. One frequently quoted number here is Dunbar's[11] number—popularized in Malcolm Gladwell's *The Tipping Point: How Little Things Can Make a Big Difference* (Little, Brown, 2000)—which is based on the idea that "there is a cognitive limit to the number of individuals with whom any one person can maintain stable relationships, that this limit is a direct function of relative neocortex size, and that this in turn limits group size."

That number is 150 people and is widely interpreted as the maximum size for cohesive social groups. However, as noted by Christopher Allen, that's misleading—or at least incomplete.[12] Dunbar's number applies to groups that have a strong incentive to stay together, which isn't always the case in open source communities. Lacking strong incentives, the number may be smaller. Allen cites some numbers from online gaming communities that suggest 50–60 active participants in a group may be a more realistic upper number.

---

[10]www.hbs.edu/faculty/Publication%20Files/08-039_1861e507-1dc1-4602-85b8-90d71559d85b.pdf

[11]www.cambridge.org/core/journals/behavioral-and-brain-sciences/article/coevolution-of-neocortical-size-group-size-and-language-in-humans/4290FF4D7362511136B9A15A96E74FEF

[12]www.lifewithalacrity.com/2004/03/the_dunbar_numb.html

Modularity Is Generally Better

Concepts like modularity and a desire to constrain the amount of communication that needs to take place come up time and time again in open source project data.

In 2008, Richard N. Langlois and Giampaolo Garzarelli argued that "open-source collaboration ultimately relies on the institutions of modularity."[13] They observed that, around the same time that Brooks was coining the "mythical man-month" phrase, David Parnas (1972) and other researchers were looking at software systems in a different light. Solving the problem of interdependency, these researchers argued, is not a matter of maximizing communication among the parts but rather of minimizing the need to communicate, just as Bezos told his managers.

Systems taking this approach are built from parts that do not need to communicate extensively with one another. In fact, they are forbidden from doing so by design. They're also, at least in principle, reusable. Parnas argued that "system details that are likely to change independently should be the secrets of separate modules; the only assumptions that should appear in the interfaces between modules are those that are considered unlikely to change."

Langlois and Garzarelli concluded that modularity is generally superior to monoliths (or integrality as they call it) across most dimensions in both software design and organizational structure. It's only in the setup costs that modularity costs more. This is consistent with what practitioners today observe with microservices and other modular software design patterns. There's an initial cost to carefully mapping out the service boundaries and determining how components will communicate with each other. The effort may not be justified for a small project and team. But such modular design patterns tend to win out as projects and teams grow.

How Contributors Interact in Open Source

Other research has looked at the interaction patterns in specific projects.

An analysis of Apache Software Foundation projects found "that a small group of contributors is responsible for the majority of commits."[14] This is a common pattern

---

[13]Langlois, Richard N., and Giampaolo Garzarelli (2008). "Of Hackers and Hairdressers: Modularity and the Organizational Economics of Open-source Collaboration, Industry and Innovation," *Industry and Innovation*, Volume 15, 2008—Issue 2: Online Communities and Open Innovation.

[14]Chełkowski, Tadeusz, Peter Gloor, and Dariusz Jemielniak. Inequalities in Open Source Software Development: Analysis of Contributor's Commits in Apache Software Foundation Projects.

in many open source projects and reinforces the importance of supporting casual contributors so that they have the potential to grow into major ones.

Jorge Colazo of Trinity University found that "... more successful teams in terms of both quality and productivity, seem to rely more on 'linchpin developers' that become more active as the team's TD [temporal distribution] grows and serve as 'bridges' between time zones"[15] in his study of 230 open source software projects. This sounds a lot like the role of the maintainers who have key responsibilities in large projects.

A 2012 study from Microsoft Research on the Eclipse IDE and the Firefox web browser code bases found that, while the developers of large modules could be geographically distributed, there was a tendency for smaller modules to be developed by contributors at a single site.[16]

The relative importance of location may vary by project though. Studying collaboration on the Linux kernel mailing list and interviewing developers, Dawn Foster concluded that "Location doesn't matter."[17] Among the things developers told her was that "The Linux community doesn't care where you're located, ever. You can be on the moon as long as you have a good Internet connection." Also "Similar time zones can be helpful because I can get a reply immediately. But it is not super important."

What was important? Relationships, including the ability to get together face-to-face. One developer told her, "At conferences you can really sit down with a beer, hash things out, and come to a consensus. The Linux Kernel Summit is massively useful for that kind of thing."

Foster's quantitative analysis bears out the interview results. Looking at the USB Linux kernel mailing list specifically, she found that social networks (previous interactions) and working for the same organization affected the level of interactions, but time zone did not.

I'd inject the caveat here that the Linux kernel is not a particularly representative open source project in some ways and almost certainly makes heavier use of inherently asynchronous communications mechanisms such as mailing lists relative to newer projects. The consensus among my professional peers is that direct collaboration

---

[15]Colazo, J. (2014). "Structural Changes Associated with the Temporal Dispersion of Teams: Evidence from Open Source Software Projects." 47th Hawaii International Conference on System Science.

[16]Christian Bird and Nachiappan Nagappan, "Who? Where? What? Examining Distributed Development in Two Large Open."

[17]www.slideshare.net/geekygirldawn/collaboration-in-linux-kernel-mailing-lists-81009604

becomes more difficult beyond about six time zones because of the difficulty of finding overlapping times for real-time conversations within normal working days. Nonetheless, especially in more modular projects (which many parts of the Linux kernel are), time zones are likely to be at least *less* important than other factors.

Participation

How do you encourage participation in open source projects, and what are the motivations for developers and others to do so?

How Participants Get Started

In 2014, researchers from the University of Helsinki and Stanford took a look at onboarding in open source projects.[18] They began by observing that

> *The general problem of introducing new people into an existing organization is especially pronounced in distributed settings with virtual teams— small, often temporary groups of knowledge workers, separated by geographical, temporal, and cultural distances that add to the communication challenges involved in getting them to work effectively.*

As we've seen in other work, geographic separation isn't necessarily a big issue in well-established projects among participants who already know each other. However, gaining initial trust can require different techniques than retaining participants and encouraging their ongoing involvement.

This study focused specifically on this very early stage of integrating newcomers or "climbing the learning curve in virtual teams" as the authors put it. This is important because, as we've seen, people come and go all the time in healthy communities, so efficiently bringing new members into the fold needs to happen continuously unless a community is to wither. Their study point was somewhat artificial—a short-lived collaboration project between Facebook and a number of universities to get students involved with open source. Nonetheless, it's interesting to see data that backs up the more anecdotal experience of communities like Kubernetes with respect to mentoring.

---

[18]Fagerholm, Fabian, Alejandro Sanchez Guinea, and Jürgen Münch. "Onboarding in Open Source Projects," University of Helsinki, Jay Borenstein, Stanford University, and Facebook. *IEEE Software*, November/December 2014.

Onboarding and Mentoring

In this case, the onboarding process consisted of two things: a co-located hackathon and mentoring. The mentoring subsequently took place through the usual open source project communication channels such as email and IRC chat. Although the study focused on the mentoring, the hackathon is also notable; virtual collaboration tends to work better when "in real life" get-togethers are also part of the mix. Mentors were tasked with recommending and detailing tasks, explaining the software architecture, and assisting in technical development details.

The students joined the project of their choice using the usual processes already in place for the project. Mentors would guide them to small tasks of interest suitable for a newcomer, eventually letting them take on tasks of greater complexity when they felt up to it.

The researchers then measured the activity of the mentored students as well as that of a random group of other equivalently inexperienced project participants. Activity was defined as the total number of commits, pull requests (requests to merge new or changed code into a project), and interactions by each developer as a proxy for how involved they were with the project.

The results showed that mentoring can have a significant positive impact. By the end of 16 weeks, the mentored developers had about twice the level of activity of the unmentored ones. It's worth observing that it took about three weeks for there to be any real difference. This suggests that mentoring isn't a quick hit, one-off task. It's an ongoing process.

The study authors acknowledge that this means the productivity of the developers doing the mentoring is going to be reduced; the amount varied by project, but it ranged from about 20% to 35%. But they concluded that

> *While the performance drop can be significant, it can be justified by the fact that it's limited to the onboarding period, and by the potential impact on increased productivity and increased innovation that could be gained from new project members. In practice, this opportunity cost must be evaluated on a case-by-case basis. In many situations, the cost of mentoring is overshadowed by the potential benefits of gaining new members, even if they're temporary.*

Motivation

Why do people participate in open source communities? What do they get out of it? Are they focused on their own needs, or are they mostly thinking about others? Given that people are involved, the answer—as you might guess—is complicated and varied.

One need only consider the behaviors we anecdotally observe in open source communities to very quickly intuit that there's no single force at work here. After all, on big open source projects, many, if not the vast majority, of the main developers are doing so as part of their day job. That doesn't mean they don't care about open source beyond a paycheck. But it does suggest different reasons for participation than the developer working nights and weekends on their own passion project. We also see developers who are focused on solving some interesting technical problems, while others are explicitly trying to bring about a societal benefit.

But that doesn't mean we can't suss out some common patterns. Not only has there been academic research into open source contributions specifically, but there's a whole body of psychology literature dealing with motivation. As a result, motivation is the lens we'll use here to examine the question of why developers (and others) participate in open source.

Research into Open Source Motivations

In 2012, four researchers at ETH Zurich (G. V. Krogh, S. Haefliger, S. Spaeth, and M. W. Wallin) surveyed the prior 10 years of study into open source software contribution based on the top 200 articles as ranked by Google Scholar.[19] Among their results, they were able to group the reasons for contributing into three categories: extrinsic motivation, intrinsic motivation, and internalized extrinsic motivation—as well as finding some common subgroupings within those broader categories.

Extrinsic Motivation

I suppose we could say that this type of motivator is about "Show me the money!" and leave it at that. Extrinsic motivation isn't quite that simple, but payment in whatever form that took during a given era and place has historically been the go-to way to get

---

[19]Krogh, G. V., S. Haefliger, S. Spaeth, and M. W. Wallin (2012). Carrots and Rainbows: Motivation and Social Proactive in Open Source Software Development.

people to do something. Whether to accumulate riches or provide themselves with basic necessities such as food and shelter. The idea that you do work you otherwise wouldn't bother with in exchange for something of personal value is deep-rooted in most human societies.

However obvious the existence of extrinsic motivation may seem to the average person, it wasn't really a field of formal study until the 1940s when behaviorist Clark Hull, later working with Kenneth Spence, came up with the idea of drive reduction theory. This theory focused on reducing primary drives like hunger and thirst. If you're hungry, you eat. If you're thirsty, you drink. Drive reduction theory fell out of fashion, in part because it didn't focus on things—like money—that could be used to reduce drives but only in a secondary way. However, we see echoes of drive reduction theory in familiar concepts like Maslow's hierarchy of needs. (See Figure 5-1.)

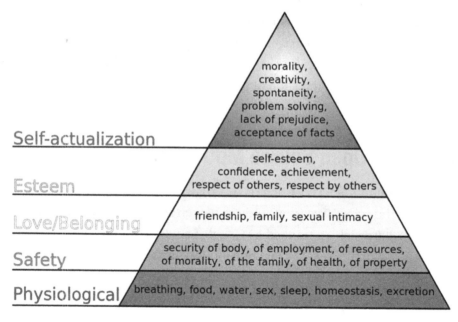

Figure 5-1. Maslow's hierarchy of needs. Source: J. Finkelstein, Wikimedia. Licensed under the GNU Free Documentation License

Coming back to what makes contributors work on open source, money can, of course, be a big carrot. Even going back 20 years or so, many major open source projects had a significant number of contributors who were paid by their companies to work on open source.

Career advancement goes hand in hand with pay. But is open source software any different from proprietary software development in this regard? It may be. Multiple researchers have found empirical evidence to support the argument that there are career advantages to developing code that's in the open and therefore available for others to look at and work with.

As a sidenote, the idea of a public code repository like GitHub as resume has become a common theme. That said, it's sometimes inappropriately used as a hiring filter to gatekeep those lacking the time, resources, or interest to program as a hobby.

Intrinsic Motivation

Research beginning in the 1970s started to focus on intrinsic motivations, which do not require an apparent reward other than the activity itself. Self-determination theory, developed by Edward Deci and Richard Ryan, would later evolve from studies comparing intrinsic and extrinsic motives and from a growing understanding of the important role intrinsic motivations can play in behavior.

With respect to open source software, it's perhaps the ideological or altruistic motivations that first come to mind. After all, in the case of free software at least, there was always an ideological and political element from the beginning even if there were also practical benefits for a user to have access to source code.

There's evidence from surveys that developers can be somewhat motivated by these factors. However, the research results are mixed. Some developers say on surveys that they're participating, in part, for ideological or altruistic reasons. But the effect is most pronounced among developers doing open source as a hobby. And while altruism certainly can influence professional developers, this mostly seems to be the case among developers who are also satisfied with their pay and other aspects of their career.

A variant of altruism is kinship amity. It's related to the concept of gift economies but is specific to family (kin) groups which don't expect a calculated quid pro quo. (In other words, family members do things for each other, but they don't typically keep a running tally, at least a systematic one, of who hasn't been pulling their weight recently.) It's different from altruism in that it is restricted to the group to which one belongs, such as an open source community. Here again the research is mixed. Studies have generally found a positive relationship between identified kinship amity and various measurements of effort, such as number of hours worked per week—but the correlation is often fairly weak.

Finally, there's just fun. This should come as no surprise to anyone who hangs around open source developers. Most of them like working on open source projects. One large study from 2007 (Luthiger and Jungwirth) determined that fun accounted for 28% of the effort (hours) dedicated to projects. However, again, it's easier to feel motivated by fun and altruism when it's either a hobby or you're otherwise satisfied professionally.

Internalized Extrinsic Motivation

Today's psychology literature also includes the idea of internalized extrinsic motivations. These are extrinsic motivations such as gaining skills to enhance career opportunities— but they've been internalized so that the motivation comes from within rather than coming as a direct result of a carrot being dangled by someone else. It's the difference between learning a new programming language because you know keeping current on new tech pays off over time vs. receiving a salary increase as a direct payoff for earning a certification.

Gaining a good peer reputation, among community insiders and potential employers, for work in open source is one good example of how this type of motivation can play out in open source development. A variety of surveys have supported the idea that peer reputation helps drive participation.

Learning also frequently gets mentioned as a big benefit of participating in open source projects. Learning may be intrinsically satisfying, but it can also be an important ingredient of career advancement. It can be hard to tease apart the intrinsic from the extrinsic here though. Is it learning for learning's sake? Or is it learning specific skills needed on the job or to mark a checkbox on a career development plan?

A final motivator in this category is what researchers call "own-use value" but is more recognizably described as something like "scratch your own itch." Develop something that you want for yourself and create something for others in the process. That something is ultimately an external reward to yourself, but no one is forcing you to do it.

What Lessons Can We Learn?

Motivations for many things are multifaceted, and contributing to open source software is no exception. However, here are three takeaways that you may find useful.

Don't expect non-extrinsic motivators to carry too much of the load. Many do contribute to open source projects for idealistic or altruistic reasons. But those are usually not the sole motivators and may not even be the most important ones. Especially in the case of projects that have commercial backing, pay and other professional working benefits also matter a great deal.

Amplify non-extrinsic motivators such as learning and peer recognition. While not replacements for more direct benefits such as money or career advancement, the opportunity to be recognized by peers and to work in new technology areas is a motivator. Organizations should consider peer recognition programs and explicitly encourage learning in order to make the best use of these motivational factors.

Motivators can be counterproductive when over-rotated. Precisely because motivations are multifaceted, don't place too big a bet on any single one. We already discussed the limitations of ideology and altruism. However, also consider something like "scratch your own itch." If that's the only reason someone contributes, they'll tend to wander in and out of a project as their own specific needs merit. That may be a perfectly fine outcome, but it's not a path to developing a long-term maintainer.

Measurement

I touched on the principles of metrics earlier, but it's worthwhile to close out the topic of research with a deeper dive into appropriate measurements for both the maturity of a project's software development process and its broader overall health.

Why Measure?

But why do we take measurements anyway? Is it to comfort us that everything is humming along without a glitch? Is it to warn us that something is amiss? Is it to provide evidence in the event of some unanticipated future meltdown?

Measurement can do all those things, but, fundamentally, it's the means by which we inform intelligent decisions and actions. Writing in 1973, Peter Drucker (who once appeared on a *BusinessWeek* magazine cover as "The Man Who Invented Management") argued that measurement is the basic element in the work of a manager. And, furthermore, few factors are as important to the success of an organization as yardsticks based on measurements.

Measurements Affect Behaviors

At the same time, it's important not to think of measurement as a dispassionate mechanistic system that sits outside the people and process being measured. As Robert Austin writes in *Measuring and Managing Performance in Organizations* (Dorset House, 1996):

> *Organizational subsystems are composed of people, most of whom maintain among their goals the desire to look good in the eyes of those responsible for evaluating and allocating rewards to the subordinate subsystems. The desire to be viewed favorably provides an incentive for people being measured to tailor, supplement, repackage, and censor information that flows upward.*

If you're responsible for a measurement that makes you look bad, others shouldn't be surprised if it goes missing or you reinterpret it in a more favorable light.

Much of the more formal work intended to formalize and standardize metrics—much of it based on traditional measures of software development activity—has tended to sidestep such cautions.

For example, IEEE Standard 1061 proposes direct metrics as a way to quantify attributes so that they can be compared to a target value. The idea is that direct measures, such as defects found during testing, are independent measures that aren't affected by other variables.

The Limits of Direct Measures

However, matters are rarely that simple. Writing for the 10th Annual Software Metrics Symposium in 2004, Cem Kaner and Walter Bond noted that

> *As soon as we include humans in the context of anything that we measure— and most software is designed by, constructed by, tested by, managed by, and/or used by humans—a wide array of system-affecting variables come with them. We ignore those variables at our peril. But if we take those variables into account, the values of our seemingly simple, "direct" measurements turn out to be values of a challenging, multidimensional function.*[20]

---

[20]Kamer and Bond, "Software Engineering Metrics: What Do They Measure and How Do We Know?"

Part of the problem is that there are, in fact, relatively few measurements that are both direct and useful. Quality of code is probably an unambiguously good thing. But that's mostly because we're effectively defining quality as an amorphous good as opposed to something that we can directly measure. Instead, we measure attributes like test coverage or bugs found. But what if we're doing a great job of finding minor surface problems that don't have much of an impact while missing deep-rooted flaws that could be showstoppers? Even under the best of circumstances, the proxy or surrogate measures that we're forced to use are ambiguous and indirect measures of the attribute we actually care about.

Furthermore, software quality does not exist in a vacuum. Software, as used in the physical world, is instantiated in hardware and as part of broader complex systems from which unanticipated properties and behaviors can emerge. Software correctness is therefore tied to larger systems engineering issues, as described in a safety context by the Systems-Theoretic Accident Model and Processes (STAMP) developed by MIT's Nancy Leveson. STAMP integrates into engineering analysis causal factors such as not only software but also hardware, human decision making, human factors, social and organizational design, and safety culture, which are becoming ever more problematic in our increasingly complex systems.

Measurements at Cross-Purposes

Another common problem arises from whether a given measurement fulfills a motivational or an informational purpose.

Motivational measurements are explicitly intended to affect the people being measured. If you don't do well enough on the certification exam, you won't pass, and you won't be able to apply for the better-paying job that requires the certification. Measurements of this type may also provide some guidance as to which skills need further development or where your aptitude may be highest. They can also help evaluate the effectiveness of training and hiring programs in the aggregate. However, for the most part, the primary purpose of motivational measurement is to use carrots (and sticks) to change behavior.

By contrast, Austin describes informational measurements as being "valued primarily for the logistical, status, and research information they convey, which provides insights and allows better short-term management and long-term improvement of organizational processes." As a result, you ideally want people to behave as if these measurement systems weren't even in place.

The software development version of the Heisenberg Uncertainty Principle means that this is a hard constraint to keep in place. You measure something and you tend to change it. In practice, it's hard to view processes that the numbers say are broken without reflecting on the role that individual human failures may have played. (And the individual humans know this.) Attempting to force compatibility between motivational and informational metrics can cause "dysfunction," to use Austin's word. But it's a common need of measurement systems that we should take into account as much as possible.

Understanding Community Health

An open source project is much more than just a software development project. It's a community too. And monitoring the health of that community through metrics is at least as important as making sure that quality software is getting written and deployed.

The idea that there's value in systematically understanding how people feel about an organization they belong to or an activity they participate in isn't new. The first employee surveys, then commonly known as employee attitude surveys, appear to have first surfaced in industrial companies in the 1920s. Over the next couple of decades or so, workplace motivation became a topic of academic study.

Morris S. Viteles was an influential researcher and writer in the field of industrial and organizational psychology and wrote the first comprehensive textbook about the field in 1932. Writing in *Motivation and Morale in Industry* in 1954 (W. W. Norton), he noted that

> *An interest in checking on morale conditions and finding ways to improve employee morale and relations within the company finds expression in reasons given for undertaking attitude surveys. Many companies expressed a desire to learn about the minor troublesome situations so that measures could be taken to prevent their growing into major ones. In general, statements made by the companies show clearly an expectation that the attitude survey would provide management with a measure of its own success or failure in personnel matters and, at the same time, locate unsatisfactory feelings and sources of irritation requiring remedial action.*

Shining More Light on Culture

Understanding how people fit into a software development project has been historically underappreciated and the metrics used fairly generic. However, the increased emphasis on culture as part of modern software development approaches such as DevOps (as well as being key to digital transformation initiatives) has helped to shine a light on organizational measurements that can also be relevant to open source projects.

For example, a 2014 report from market researchers Gartner[21] included organizational effectiveness among its categories for "Data-Driven DevOps" metrics. Some of the specific measures, such as retention, are fairly conventional and would apply to most company roles. However, Gartner also calls out mentoring, sharing, collaboration, and morale. These aren't metrics that most companies have focused on tracking historically. But they have clear relevance to open source projects and communities.

A relatively new effort to define metrics for community health came out of the CHAOSS (Community Health Analytics OSS) Metrics Committee, a Linux Foundation project, in 2017.[22] Researchers from academia and practitioners from industry got together in CHAOSS to define a neutral, implementation-agnostic set of reference metrics to be used to describe communities in a common way.

The organization plans initially focused on four open source project metrics: project diversity and inclusion, project growth-maturity-decline, project risk, and value. These "complex metrics" are constructed from multiple "activity metrics." Activity metrics include the usual dashboard numbers like new contributors and open issues but also factors that are less commonly tracked, for example, whether the path to leadership in the project has been published and how many rewards, shout-outs, recognitions, and mentions there are in pull requests or change logs.

Twelve Areas to Assess

Drawing from the CHAOSS work and first-hand experience, Red Hat has identified 12 areas that are important to the health of an open source project.[23] Some of these were covered in the course of discussing the open source development model. Others I will flesh out here.

---

[21]"Data-Driven DevOps: Use Metrics to Help Guide Your Journey." *Gartner*, May 2014.

[22]https://wiki.linuxfoundation.org/chaoss/metrics

[23]www.redhat.com/cms/managed-files/rh-measuring-open-source-health-brief-f25266pr-202009-en.pdf

Project life cycle. An open source project's life cycle affects many other considerations about a project's health. Important metrics for community and project health tend to shift over time. A given project may go through a growth spurt when a lot of attention should be devoted to how effectively new contributors are being onboarded and mentored. Later in life, the same project may shift more focus to how well it's doing moving existing contributors into leadership roles as current maintainers inevitably move on.

Target audience. Who is going to use and contribute to the project? Is that target audience likely to engage with competing or complementary projects? How do you plan to reach that audience, and how will you determine if you are succeeding?

Governance. What are the rules and customs under which the project operates? Are the rules fair? Is a single person or another entity really in absolute control when all is said and done?

Project leaders. In healthy projects, leaders are visible and easily identifiable. Leaders often coordinate project work and establish a project's vision, and usually have extensive knowledge of the project history. However, as we saw earlier, leadership is not all about coding, and that may not even be a leader's primary contribution. What is the leader's focus?

Release manager and process. In healthy projects, members have formally documented release processes and identified release managers to supervise those processes. It may be useful for both users and contributors to aim for a reasonably predictable cadence though that cadence will vary from project to project. Some projects may prioritize more occasional releases that prioritize the stability of a release. Others may have faster turns that emphasize new and experimental features.

Infrastructure. The most successful projects are those that have the tools they need to do their work—and keep those tools in good working order. This has often been something of a weak spot for many projects which took care of it on the cheap and on the side. As a result, this is an area that certain foundations have focused on providing for members in recent years.

Goals and road map. Healthy open source projects have publicly shared goals, clear processes for reaching those goals, and clear deadlines for tracking progress toward those goals. While flexibility is always needed, road maps should reflect the current state of the project and where it wants to be in six months, one year, or two years based on user and contributor priorities. One release may focus on reducing bugs and improving overall stability. Another release may be more focused on implementing some key new feature.

Onboarding processes. In addition to what's already been discussed, onboarding can even play into certain development priorities. For example, a project that is hard to install and get running for reasons of scanty or outdated documentation, poorly chosen defaults, or the lack of an easy-to-use installer is going to deter contributors from getting on board; it won't make potential users too happy either.

Internal communication. Issues affecting community health often emerge first on internal channels—such as mailing lists or chat platforms—where contributors and users interact. Questions to ask include the following: Does the project have sufficient communication channels? Can people find and use these channels effectively? (And are they the communication channels the participants *want* to use?) Are channels regularly moderated? Is channel communication governed by a code of conduct?

Outreach. Outreach is the process of actively promoting a project and making others aware of it. This can include meetups, blogs, hackathons, and other mechanisms. Outreach also plays into diversity and inclusion in that a strategy that makes reaching a broad set of participants an explicit goal looks different from one focused on "the usual suspects." Diversity also refers to the breadth of participation. Is everything coming from one or two companies? Are different types of organizations and different types of users represented?

Awareness. Of course, the desired outcome of outreach is awareness. And specifically awareness by your target audience. And it's really not just awareness. Can people in the target audience explain the project's uses, features, and advantages over alternatives? (And even articulate the use cases where your project *may not be* the best option.)

Ecosystem. Finally, what else does the project touch? This includes other projects. For example, in the cloud-native space, many of the projects interact with each other in either co-dependent or looser ways. Ecosystem can also be about attitudes. If your project is part of a broader ecosystem like security tools or cloud-native infrastructure, what do other players think about you? This can be as much about how they view you as a community member as about how they view your technology.

A Broader View of Health

To expand on ecosystem, projects don't exist in a vacuum. The health of their ecosystem—upstream, downstream, and related projects—matters too. What's the *aggregate* project tree heath, which is to say the combined health metrics of all linked dependencies? An individual project may be healthy, but if it's heavily dependent on other projects that aren't, it should correct the issues in the dependencies or switch away from them. Doing so may be fairly straightforward in the case of a library for which there are a variety of reasonable substitutes. It will be much more difficult for a project that's effectively a satellite orbiting a much larger project that's failing. (Conversely, a large successful project like Kubernetes can energize a wide range of smaller efforts that complement or expand the functionality of the mothership in various ways.)

Finally, any approach to measurement and metrics ultimately depends on the context of a given project. For example, mature projects might appear inactive if no new features are being developed even though the community remains responsive to bug reports and security issues. But that may just mean the project has attained its goal and the community sees no need to add features for the sake of adding features.

The nature of different projects also tends to make certain tasks easy and some hard. A project started within one company and then released as open source will often have to work hard to attract external contributions at all. This makes tracking the diversity of contributions—and putting the processes and code in place to simplify those contributions—paramount. In other cases, a degree of diversity comes naturally because of the way the project was formed, and collaboration among parties with sometimes divergent interests becomes a more interesting metric.

If all this sounds complicated, it is. And neither researchers nor expert practitioners have been able to reduce measurement of software development practices and community health to a template or a science. However, they have identified at least some approaches and ideas to increment on and some bad practices to avoid. As Kaner and Bond write in the conclusion of their 2004 paper:

> *There are too many simplistic metrics that don't capture the essence of whatever it is that they are supposed to measure. There are too many uses of simplistic measures that don't even recognize what attributes are supposedly being measured. Starting from a detailed analysis of the task or attribute under study might lead to more complex, and more qualitative, metrics, but we believe that it will also leads to more meaningful and therefore more useful data.*

Reflecting and Informing

On the one hand, much of what we know about open source software development is relatively new. Most research specifically into open source development and community practices is only about a decade or so old. Furthermore, what research exists from the early days of open source is arguably of limited relevance today when open source is so pervasive and often commercialized.

However, past research into fields as diverse as invention and innovation, collaboration, motivation, and measurement has produced findings that are often relevant to open source projects and communities. At the same time, precisely because open source software development happens in the open, it provides a rich data trove for new research into these topics as well.

Open source software is a test bed for how people (and organizations) work together, why people work together, and the types of measurements that we should be thinking about. Much of this is an art. But there's also science. This is why formal research is at least worth a look.

CHAPTER 6

Business Models and Accelerated Development

When many people first hear about businesses that make their living selling open source software, their first question is usually something like "How can you sell something that's available for free?" That complicated answer is addressed in this chapter.

Even restricting the discussion to "free as in beer" doesn't simplify it much. The business world is full of examples of free and paid services or products supporting and subsidizing each other in various ways. While common, it can be a hard formula to get right, and business models based on such approaches can rapidly shift with technology and consumer habits.

It's also probably misleading, or at least simplistic, to refer to an "open source business model" as if open source software existed outside of normal commercial relationships in which money is traded for a product or service of value.

This brings us to the other overarching theme that I'll cover. Open source software and the forces that have helped to shape it don't exist in a bubble. They're part of broader trends in software development, business interactions, and organizational culture generally.

How Can You Sell Something That You Give Away?

Free is a multifaceted word. Its meaning is less muddled in some languages. Latin and some languages deriving from it use different words for the concept of freedom (*liber* in Latin) and zero price (*gratis* in Latin). "Free" in modern English appears to have come from the Old English/Anglo-Saxon side of its language tree where *freagon* came

© Gordon Haff 2021
G. Haff, *How Open Source Ate Software*, https://doi.org/10.1007/978-1-4842-6800-1_6

to embody both meanings. (English also has language roots in Latin by way of Norman French; both Latin roots put in an appearance in words like liberty and gratuity.)

As we've seen, "free software" in the sense that we've been discussing here has always been about free as in freedom rather than free as in beer. As Stallman writes in the first footnote to the GNU Manifesto:

> *The wording here was careless. The intention was that nobody would have to pay for permission to use the GNU system. But the words don't make this clear, and people often interpret them as saying that copies of GNU should always be distributed at little or no charge. That was never the intent; later on, the manifesto mentions the possibility of companies providing the service of distribution for a profit. Subsequently I have learned to distinguish carefully between "free" in the sense of freedom and "free" in the sense of price. Free software is software that users have the freedom to distribute and change. Some users may obtain copies at no charge, while others pay to obtain copies—and if the funds help support improving the software, so much the better. The important thing is that everyone who has a copy has the freedom to cooperate with others in using it.*

Freedom doesn't pay the bills though.

The GNU Manifesto offers up some possibilities that apply mostly to individuals. For example, "People with new ideas could distribute programs as freeware, asking for donations from satisfied users, or selling hand-holding services." Stallman also makes some more questionable suggestions such as "Suppose everyone who buys a computer has to pay x percent of the price as a software tax. The government gives this to an agency like the NSF [National Science Foundation] to spend on software development."

None of these really look like scalable business models. And there are good reasons to be skeptical or even critical of "business models" that seem closer to patronage or dependence on the kindness of others than an exchange of something of value for cash.

The Linux Foundation's Chris Aniszczyk argues that

> *...it even enables what I call an open source developer-focused gig economy where people are expecting donations but they're not making enough money. I've actually done a lot of research and there are very few developers out there being sustained by donations. I think it's a poor model. Instead,*

we should be teaching them how to find jobs or build businesses around the cool stuff they've done so they can actually sustain themselves with a great business or with salary with benefits and all that goodness.

So how does one go about building a business around open source?

Is There an "Open Source Business Model"?

In *Free: The Future of a Radical Price* (Hyperion, 2009), former *Wired* magazine editor-in-chief Chris Anderson refers to "free" as the "most misunderstood word" and describes many of the ways in which giving things away gratis can be profitable. In all, he describes 50 business models that fall into three broad categories.

Categories of Business Models

There are direct subsidies. For example, Apple gives away many types of Apple Store Genius Bar tech support as part of the package you get when you buy an Apple phone or computer.

There are three-party or two-sided markets in which one customer class subsidizes another. Ad-supported media, including companies like Facebook, fall broadly into this category in that they're giving away a service to consumers while charging businesses for access to that audience (and thereby allowing consumers to effectively sell their attention in exchange for that free service).

Finally, there's freemium. A certain class of service or product is free, but you need to pay to upgrade. Freemium is a common approach for selling many types of software. In-app purchases on iPhone and Android smartphones are classic examples of this approach. You can download the basic app for free, but you need to pay money to remove ads or get more features.

There are various problems with all of these models.

Subsidies only work so long as no one can unbundle your product. When Craigslist gutted the classified newspaper advertising business, newspapers no longer could use classified ads to subsidize the foreign news bureaus or investigative journalism teams that gave them prestige and brought them readers. But weren't viable as stand-alone businesses given their high cost.

Advertising generally, especially in its often obtrusive, targeted digital forms, makes many experiences less pleasant and is increasingly hard to untangle from partisan news and non-news.

For our purposes here, however, let's focus on approaches that don't include advertising and which have an open source project as an essential component of the mix.

Getting the Balance Right

We start with a commercial product that adds capabilities and value to an open source project in some manner.

Many of us are familiar with freemium in the context of software. Beyond the app store model mentioned in the preceding text, we often see software and software services offered in multiple pricing tiers at increasingly higher prices and increasingly greater capabilities on one or more dimensions.

For example, higher tiers of an online collaboration product might support more users and provide more storage space. Other products may focus on features that large businesses often need, such as Microsoft Active Directory integration, but which individual users generally don't care about.

A general challenge with freemium is getting the balance of free and paid right. Make free too good and your conversion rate to paid might not be high enough to be profitable—even among people who would have been willing to pay if they had to in order to use the product at all. I use a variety of proprietary programs and software services that are useful enough to me that I'd probably be willing to pay for them if I had to. However, the free tier meets my needs well enough; I may not even value the incremental features of the paid version at all.

On the other hand, cripple the free version too much and it becomes uninteresting in its own right. If this happens, you don't get many people to try your software.

Take the example of a not-so-hypothetical online storage provider trying to grow its customer base. They could offer a free trial. That has pros and cons but probably isn't a good fit in this case. (Users will upload things, and some of them will lose their only copies of those things when the trial ends. They'll be mad. Probably not a great plan.)

Instead, they decide that users will be able to freely sign up to be given some storage that they'll be able to keep using forever at no charge. But if they want more storage, they'll have to pay some tiered monthly fee depending upon how much they want. But how much should you give them?

You could be a cheapskate and give them 10 megabytes. Seriously? You can store one MP3 song with that amount. No one's going to bother to use that; you might as well not bother with a free tier at all. OK. How about 10 terabytes—a million times as much? That's more storage than all but a tiny sliver of individuals need. You'll get lots of sign-ups (assuming the service is otherwise useful) but few paying customers who require more space.

Finding the right balance is hard especially given that the needs and price sensitivity of your user base are likely anything but homogeneous.

Building the Funnel with Free

The nice thing about a freemium model done properly though is that it's a good way to acquire users with the product itself. They're not *paying* customers yet, but they're well into your sales funnel (in marketing speak). To be precise, they're probably in an evaluation phase, which is often listed as the third phase of the funnel after awareness and interest.

They're using your product. They still have to like it. And they still have to decide to buy it. But getting a potential customer to evaluate your product is a big step. Freemium models for software, especially relatively simple-to-use software, make getting from initial awareness to evaluation a relatively quick and low-friction process if the experience for new users is otherwise solid.

What Does This Mean for Open Source?

Many business models that incorporate open source software can be thought of as variants on freemium. The community project is the free part. The product is everything else.

However, be careful with this simplistic framing.

If the "everything else" is just basic support, that doesn't add a lot of value and hasn't proven to be a very successful approach in general. Better is surrounding the project with all the other capabilities that make it a commercial product. At a minimum, if you're providing support, customers will typically expect you to bring expertise and capabilities to your support that couldn't be brought by a more generic support organization. In an open source context, this means that, even if you're not the original creator of the project, you're an active participant in the upstream community.

Consulting for companies that want to use a project is another common path. But, with consulting, the real question should be whether it's a good *consulting business* that happens to involve an open source project or projects for which you presumably have some particular expertise.

Open Core vs. Open Source

Another approach that's been around for a while but has attracted some criticism in recent years is open core.

With open core, a company gives away a free product that is open source but then sells additional proprietary software that complements it in some way. This often takes the form of something like a "community" edition that's free and an "enterprise" edition that requires either a license or a subscription fee. A typical distinction is that the enterprise edition will include features that tend to be important for large organizations running software in production but aren't as big a deal for individuals or casual use. Andrew Lampitt is credited with coining the open core term.

The MySQL database—acquired by Oracle when it bought Sun—is a typical case. MySQL Enterprise Edition

> *...includes the most comprehensive set of advanced features, management tools and technical support to achieve the highest levels of MySQL scalability, security, reliability, and uptime. It reduces the risk, cost, and complexity in developing, deploying, and managing business-critical MySQL applications.*

Thus, even though you can use the base MySQL project for free, many of the features that you probably want as an enterprise user are behind the paywall.

In part because the upsell features are often not clearly partitioned off from the core project, many open core products require their contributors to sign a contributor license agreement (CLA), which assigns rights to the commercial owner of the product. (It may or may not assign copyright, but, in any case, it usually gives the owner the right to use the contributions under a proprietary license if they want to.)

Pure open source projects may use CLAs as well, but in that case, they serve a somewhat different purpose. For example, the Eclipse Contributor Agreement gives as its rationale the following: "It's basically about documenting the provenance of all of the intellectual property coming into Eclipse. We want to have a clear record that you have agreed to the terms under which the Eclipse community has agreed to accept contributions." In this case, some recommend the use of a Developer Certificate of Origin rather than a CLA.

Many vendors are attracted to open core because it's a business model that makes use of open source but often skirts directly embracing open source development practices and obligations that may come with them. What's being sold is the proprietary add-ons. The vendor's hope is that they've gotten the free and paid balance right. That the free is good enough to attract users and even outside contributors. But that most customers who would have been willing and able to pay anyway will pony up for the premium version.

As a former president of the OSI, Simon Phipps, writes:

> *Open core is a game on rather than a valid expression of software freedom, because it does not [provide] software freedom for the software user ... to use the package effectively in production, a business probably won't find the functions of the core package sufficient, even in the (usual) case of the core package being highly capable. They will find the core package largely ineffective without certain "extras," and these are only available in the "enterprise version" of the package, which is not open source. To use these features, you are forced to be a customer only of the sponsoring company. There's no alternative, no way to do it yourself if the value delivered doesn't justify the expense involved, or if you are time-rich and cash-poor. Worse, using the package locks you in to the supplier.*

Are You Taking Advantage of Open Source Development?

That's the perspective from the users of the software. But what about from the vendor's perspective? Is this just an argument that open core is not a sufficiently ideologically pure approach to building a business based on open source?

For some, it's the "open" that rankles. As we saw when we discussed licenses, open core isn't open source as the term's been historically used, but vendors who use the term seem to be trying to draft off the increased interest that companies and governments have, sometimes with legislative mandates, in purchasing open source products.

From a customer's perspective, if you need the enterprise features, you need the proprietary product. The fact that there's an open source version lacking features you need isn't all that relevant. It's no different from a freemium approach to traditional proprietary software or software-as-a-service. You can't try out what you don't have access to. The power of freemium to get potential users in the door can be significant.

It's just that open core isn't uniquely different from proprietary approaches to selling software just because open source is part of the mix.

But take both the Ideologically and the customer flexibility that open source software brings off the table. Open core only partially benefits from the open source development model.

The power of open source as a development approach isn't that anyone can see your code. It's that individuals and companies can collaborate and work together cooperatively to make better software. However, open core almost can't help sending off a vibe that the vendor owns the open source project and its community given that proprietary extensions depend on the open source core. It can be hard to attract outside contributors in this situation—which can be a community management challenge under the best of circumstances. The result is often an open source project that is open source in name only.

Open core can still be a sensible approach in some situations. But adopting this approach can also be a way to avoid making some of the trade-offs that may be involved with tapping into open source community development.

Enterprise Software with an Open Source Development Model

At Red Hat, we describe ourselves as an enterprise software company with an open source development model. I think that captures things nicely because it both describes the objective and (one of) the many means needed to achieve that objective. How did open source get here?

The Rise of the Independent Software Vendor

It's difficult to identify the first company to sell software that wasn't also hawking hardware (which is to say, the first Independent Software Vendor (ISV)). However, Cincom Systems—founded in 1968—is a good candidate. It sold what appears to be the first commercial database management system not to be developed by a system maker like IBM. Fun fact: Not only is Cincom still extant as a private company in 2021 but one of its founders, Thomas Nies, is the CEO.

Over time, pure-play or mostly pure-play software companies packaging up bits and selling them became the dominant way in which customers acquired most of their software. As we've seen, ISVs like Microsoft selling closed-source proprietary software even became major suppliers of the operating systems and other platform software that historically were supplied by vendors as part of a bundle with their hardware.

When open source software came onto the scene, it didn't bring with it the same requirement to purchase an up-front license. However, many users still wanted the other benefits associated with having a relationship with a commercial entity.

Open Source Support Arrives

Probably the first company to systematically provide support for open source software in a formal way was Cygnus Solutions. It was founded by John Gilmore, Michael Tiemann, and David Henkel-Wallace in 1989 under the name Cygnus Support. Its tagline was: Making free software affordable.[1]

Cygnus Solutions maintained a number of the key GNU software products, including the GNU Debugger. It was also a major contributor to the GCC project, the GNU C compiler.

As Tiemann described the company in 1999's *Open Sources: Voices from the Open Source Revolution* (O'Reilly Media):

> *We wrote our first contract in February of 1990, and by the end of April, we had already written over $150,000 worth of contracts. In May, we sent letters to 50 prospects we had identified as possibly interested in our support, and in June, to another 100. Suddenly, the business was real. By the end of the first year, we had written $725,000 worth of support and development contracts, and everywhere we looked, there was more opportunity.*

In the same book, Tiemann also touched on something else that would come to be important to successful open source businesses when he wrote:

> *Unless and until a competitor can match the 100+ engineers we have on staff today, most of whom are primary authors or maintainers of the software we support, they cannot displace us from our position as the "true GNU" source (we supply over 80% of all changes made to GCC, GDB, and related utilities).*

---

[1]www.oreilly.com/openbook/opensources/book/tiemans.html

Shortly after Tiemann wrote those words, Red Hat—which had just gone public in August 1999—acquired Cygnus. Red Hat dates back to 1993 when Bob Young, incorporated as the ACC Corporation, started a mail-order catalog business that sold Linux and Unix software accessories out of his home. The following year, Marc Ewing started distributing his own curated version of Linux, and he chose Red Hat as the name. (He picked that unusual name because he was known for wearing his grandfather's red Cornell lacrosse hat when he worked at his job helping fellow students in the computer lab at Carnegie Mellon.)

Young found himself selling a lot of copies of Ewing's product. In 1995, they joined together to become Red Hat Software, which sold boxed copies of Red Hat Linux, an early Linux distribution.

Linux Distributions Appear

Distributions, or "distros" as they're often called, first appeared in 1992, but more active projects arrived the next year. That's when Patrick Volkerding released Slackware based on the earlier but not well-maintained SLS. 1993 saw Ian Murdock's founding of Debian and its release near the end of the year.

Distributions brought together the core operating system components, including the kernel, and combined them with the other pieces, such as the utilities, programming tools, and web servers needed to create a working environment suitable for running applications. Distributions were a recognition that an operating system kernel and even the kernel plus a core set of utilities (such as those that make up GNU in the case of Linux) aren't that useful by themselves.

Over the next decade, the number of distributions exploded although only a handful were ever sold commercially.

Support was one of the first things to get added to commercial Linux distributions. Initially, this meant pretty much what it did with traditional retail boxed software. You called a helpdesk if you were having trouble installing something, the software didn't work as promised, or you wanted to report a bug. However, support in isolation doesn't begin to describe the many aspects of a commercial software product. As Steven Weber writes, it's all about "building profitable economic models around the open source process."

Subscriptions: Beyond Support

What does a product subscription look like in the context of open source software? After all, it's open source, so it's not like you lose access to the code if you let your subscription lapse as would be the case with Adobe Creative Cloud, for example.

It developed over time. It came about through experimenting, innovating, and perfecting a community-based model. It came through experiencing how to best participate in communities; adding features and functionality desired by customers; and then testing, hardening, compiling, and distributing stable, workable versions to customers. We covered many of the ways in which commercial products extend projects when we looked at the open source development model.

One of the things that Michael Tiemann wrote back in 1999 that's still very relevant today is that part of a business model for open source software is establishing in-house expertise in the design, optimization, and maintenance of the products being sold. This may be an obvious point in the case of proprietary software that is written by a single company. However, with open source software, it's difficult to provide effective support in the absence of active participation in the communities developing the software. That participation is what leads to having the expertise to solve difficult support problems.

And it goes beyond support. Users of software often want to influence product direction or the development of new features. With open source software, users can do so directly. However, working with the communities in which the software is developed isn't necessarily easy or obvious to a company that isn't familiar with how to do so. As we've seen, there's not really a template. Communities have different governance models, customs, and processes. Or just quirks. Even those organizations that do want to participate directly in setting the direction of the software they use can benefit from a guide.

Focusing on Core Competencies

Furthermore, many organizations don't want to (or shouldn't) spend money and attention on developing all the software that they use. When I was an industry analyst in the early 2000s, I would talk with the banks and other financial institutions who were among the earliest adopters of Linux after the Internet infrastructure providers. Large banks had technologists with titles like "director of kernel engineering." But here's the thing. Banks are not actually in the business of writing and supporting operating systems. They need operating systems. But they also need bank branches. Yet they're not in the construction business.

Over time, banks and other end users did increasingly participate in community-based open source development. They created standards of mutual interest like AMQP. Today, there are many software foundations in which end users increasingly participate. However, especially for platforms that are primarily infrastructure, most enterprises prefer to let companies that specialize in computer hardware and general-purpose software do much of the heavy lifting while they focus on the technology and other capabilities that differentiate them from their competitors.

Ultimately, subscribers can choose the degree to which they participate in and influence technology and industry innovation. They can either use the open source product as they would any other product. Or they can actively take a role in setting the development direction to a degree that is rare with proprietary products.

Open source software subscriptions do indeed provide fixes, updates, assistance, and certifications in a way that doesn't look that different from other commercial software products. And that may be enough for many customers. However, the ability to participate in the open source development model creates opportunities that don't exist with proprietary software.

Aligning Incentives with Subscriptions

Furthermore, subscriptions create different incentives for vendors than up-front licenses do. The usual way that proprietary software licenses work is that there's an up-front license fee and upgrade fees for major new versions, as well as ongoing maintenance charges. In the case of complex software, there may be a significant consulting component as well. As a result, there's a strong incentive for vendors to encourage upgrades. In practice, this means that—while the company selling the software has contractual obligations to fix bugs and patch security holes—they would actually prefer that customers upgrade to new versions when they become available. There's thus an active disincentive to add new features to existing software.

With a subscription model, on the other hand, so long as a customer continues to subscribe, it doesn't matter so much to the vendor whether a customer upgrades to a new version or not. There's still some incentive to get customers to upgrade over time. It takes effort to add new features to older versions, and, at some point, it can just become too hard to continue providing support of an older version. But there's no financial impetus creating an artificial urgency to force upgrades.

Subscriptions do sometimes get a bad rap, especially in proprietary consumer software and services. But that's mostly because, with most subscriptions of this type,

154

you only retain access to the software so long as you pay the subscription fee. For someone only running some piece of software occasionally and casually, that can be a bad deal compared to just using a five-year-old software package that's no longer supported but works fine for the task at hand.

Open source subscriptions are different because you retain full control over and access to software even if you let a subscription lapse. That's fundamental to free and open source software. It's yours to do with as you please. That's at the heart of a business model that makes profitable companies built around open source possible.

The Cloud Wrinkle

This business model discussion has, so far, mostly focused on selling open source software in the context of traditional software that you install and run on your own computers. Of course, that's often not the case today.

Simply running the same software on computers owned and operated, to a greater or lesser degree, by someone else doesn't change the fundamentals much. You're still acquiring and have primary responsibility for maintaining that software even if the hardware and power are someone else's responsibility.

However, once we start talking about consuming software in the form of a service from a third-party provider, *many* dynamics change, not least of which are associated software business models, especially those related to open source software.

This shift from on-prem software to software running as a service is one of the most profound shifts happening in the IT industry today. The next chapter will dive into this topic deeply. However, the rest of this one will look at some of the ways that businesses work together and develop software generally have shifted in parallel with the rise of open source software and corresponding changes to business models.

From Competition to Coopetition

Some of these other changes arguably take their cues directly from the open source development model. Others more likely result from some of the same influences that helped make the widespread adoption of open source software possible. These include the Internet and inexpensive computers.

One of the broad changes that has paralleled the rise of open source is an increasing trend toward greater coopetition—cooperative competition.

Coopetition Gets Coined

The coopetition term dates back to the early 20th century, but it started to see widespread use when Novell's Ray Noorda started to use the term to describe the company's business strategy in the 1990s. Novell was planning, at the time, to get into the Internet portal business, which required it to seek partnerships with some of the same search engine providers and other companies with which it would also be competing.

In 1996, Harvard Business School's Adam Brandenburger and Yale's Barry Nalebuff wrote a *New York Times* best-selling book (*Coopetition*, HarperCollins) on the subject, adopting Noorda's term and examining the concept through the lens of game theory. They described it as follows:

> *Some people see business entirely as competition. They think doing business is waging war and assume they can't win unless somebody else loses. Other people see business entirely as cooperative teams and partnerships. But business is both cooperation and competition. It's coopetition.*

The basic principles have been around forever. Marshall University's Robert Deal describes in *The Law of the Whale Hunt: Dispute Resolution, Property Law, and American Whalers, 1780–1880* (Cambridge University Press, 2016) how

> *Far from courts and law enforcement, competing crews of American whalers not known for their gentility and armed with harpoons tended to resolve disputes at sea over ownership of whales. Left to settle arguments on their own, whalemen created norms and customs to decide ownership of whales pursued by multiple crews.*[2]

Many situations aren't ruled solely by either ruthless competition or wholly altruistic cooperation.

Why Coopetition Has Grown

The theory behind coopetition isn't that well established with the result that there's debate over where coopetition is most effective and what the most effective strategies are. However, a 2012 paper by Paavo Ritala notes that "it has been suggested that it

---

[2]http://legalhistoryblog.blogspot.com/2016/04/deals-law-of-whale-hunt.html

occurs in knowledge-intensive sectors in which rival firms collaborate in creating interoperable solutions and standards, in R&D, and in sharing risks."[3]

That's a good description of the IT industry, but it's an increasingly good description of the *many* industries that are increasingly selling products and services that are enabled by software or simply are software. "Software is eating the world," as venture capitalist (and co-author of the first widely used web browser) Marc Andreessen famously put it in a 2011 *Wall Street Journal* piece. It seems at least plausible that coopetition's high profile of late is the result of complexity levels and customer demands that make it increasingly difficult to successfully avoid cooperation.

By way of contrast, I still remember one day in the early 1990s when I received an email from a sales rep. He was livid because he had learned that a networking card in a new computer system, for which I was product manager, was made by Digital Equipment, a major competitor. The rep's choice words included something along the lines of "I'm fighting with these guys every day and you go and stab me in the back."

I tell this story because it nicely illustrates the degree to which the computer systems market has changed. Today, the idea that having commercial relationships with a competitor to supply some part or service would be scandalous or even especially notable would generally seem odd. There are echoes of this sort of behavior in the scuffles between the likes of Apple, Google, and Amazon in smartphones, voice assistants, and app stores. But those are notable mostly because they're not really the norm.

Coopetition is at the heart of most larger open source projects in which the participants are mostly developers working on the software as part of their day jobs. Look through the top contributors to the Linux kernel, and you'll see multiple semiconductor companies, software companies with Linux distributions, computer system vendors, and cloud service providers.[4] Companies within each of these groups are often direct competitors. When the OpenStack Foundation was created, it was in large part to explicitly create a structure that could accommodate participation by competing corporate interests. Most open source foundations serve a similar role as part of their function as do standards organizatins and trade associations, such as 501(c)(6) organizations in the United States.

---

[3]https://onlinelibrary.wiley.com/doi/epdf/10.1111/j.1467-8551.2011.00741.x
[4]www.linuxfoundation.org/2017-linux-kernel-report-landing-page/

Open Source: Beneficiary and Catalyst

Open source software development has both benefited from and been a catalyst for coopetition. Seeing companies working cooperatively on an open source project, it's easy to dismiss the novelty of working together in this way. After all, companies have often cooperated in joint ventures and other types of partnerships forever.

What we observe with open source projects, however, is a sharply reduced level of overhead associated with cooperation. Companies do indeed work together in a variety of ways. But many of those ways involve contracts, nondisclosure agreements, and other legal niceties. While open source projects may have some of that—they may require contributor license agreements, for example—for the most part, starting to work on a project is as simple as submitting a pull request to let others know that you have pushed code to a repository and you'd like it to be merged with the existing code base.

Extensive involvement in a major project tends to be more formal and more structured of course. The details will depend on the project's governance model. Nonetheless, the overall process for working together in an open source project tends to be lighter weight, lower overhead, and faster than was historically the case for companies working together.

One specific change in this vein that we've seen is the way that software standards are now often developed.

Coopetition and Standards

Typically, we talk about two types of standards. One type is *de jure* standards, or standards according to the law. These are what you get when industry representatives, some of which are probably competitors, sit down as part of a standards organization or other trade organization to create a standard for something. The process can be very long and arduous—and also infamous for often producing long and technically rigorous, in an academic way, specifications that don't actually get used much in the real world.

The Open Systems Interconnection model (OSI model—not to be confused with the Open Source Initiative), dating to the late 1970s, is one example. While OSI's conceptual seven-layer model has been widely adopted as a way to talk about layers of the networking software stack, the great deal of software developed at considerable cost to directly implement OSI was never much used.

By contrast, TCP/IP, the Transmission Control Protocol (TCP) and the Internet Protocol (IP), came out of research and development conducted by the Defense

Advanced Research Projects Agency (DARPA) in the late 1960s. Today, they're among the core communication protocols used by the Internet. Although TCP/IP was subsequently ratified as a formal standard, it started out as a *de facto* standard by virtue of widespread use. Widely used proprietary products such as Microsoft Windows or x86 processors can also be viewed as *de facto* standards.

Open source has developed something of a bias toward a *de facto* standardization process that is effectively coopetition and standardization through code—or, if you prefer, "code first."

We've seen this play out repeatedly in the software containers space. While they were subsequently standardized under the Open Container Initiative, image runtime and image formats existed as implementations before they became a standard. The same is true of container orchestration with Kubernetes evolving to be the most common way of orchestrating and managing a cluster of containers. It's a standard based on the size of its community and its adoption rather than the action of a standards body.

This approach is very flexible because it allows companies to work together developing software and then iterate as needed. There's another advantage as well. One of the problems with specifications is that they rarely fully specify everything. As a result, software that's based on standards often has to make assumptions about unspecified details and behaviors. This can lead to interoperability problems. (The slow pace of formal standards adoption can also lead to vendors basing products on draft specs causing further issues, as was the case with the Fibre Channel standard in the storage networking space during the 1990s.)

By contrast, a standard achieved through a code-first approach is its own reference implementation. It's therefore a more effective approach to coopetition than developing a specification in committee only to have parties go off and develop their individual implementations—which can be subtly incompatible to the degree it becomes a real interoperability problem.

The Need for Speed

The ascendency of the open source development model as an approach for collaboration and innovation wasn't the only interesting IT trend taking place in the mid- to late 2000s. A number of things were coming together in a way that would lead to both new platforms and new development practices.

From Physical to Virtual

Server virtualization, used to split physical servers into multiple virtual ones, was going mainstream, and IT shops were becoming more comfortable with it. Virtualization on servers was initially focused on reducing the number of physical servers needed and thereby cutting costs, an important consideration during the tech downturn of the early 2000s. However, it came to have other uses as well. Ubiquitous virtualization meant that IT organizations were becoming more accepting of the idea that they didn't necessarily know exactly where their applications were physically running. In other words, another level of abstraction was becoming the norm as has happened many times in many places over the history of computing.

A vendor and software ecosystem was growing out alongside and on top of virtualization. One specific pain point this ecosystem addressed was in the area of "virtualization sprawl," a problem brought about by the fact that virtualization made it so easy to spin up new systems that the management burden could get out of hand. Concepts like automation, policy-based administration, standard operating environments, and self-service management were starting to replace system admin processes that had historically been handled by one-off scripts—assuming they weren't simply handled manually.

The Consumerization of IT

IT was also consumerizing and going more mobile. By the early 2000s, many professionals no longer used PCs tethered to a local area network that required a physical connection. Instead, they used laptops with a mobile connection to Wi-Fi networks. Then Apple introduced the iPhone in 2007. Soon smartphones were everywhere, usually purchased by employees even though they were often used for both personal and business purposes. They were no longer primarily business-issued work devices as they mostly were during the Blackberry era. Meanwhile, on the software side, users were getting accustomed to responsive, slick consumer web properties like Amazon and Netflix during this post-dot-com Phase 2 of the Web. Stodgy and hard-to-use enterprise software looked less attractive than ever.

Line of business users in companies also started noticing how slow their IT departments were to respond to requests. Enterprise IT departments rightly retorted that they operate under a lot of constraints—whether data security, detailed business requirements, or uptime—that a free social media site does not. Nonetheless, the consumer Web increasingly set an expectation, and, if IT couldn't or wouldn't meet it, users would go to online services—whether to quickly put computing resources on a credit card or to purchase access to a complete online application.

It wasn't necessarily that enterprise IT departments were doing a bad job relative to historical benchmarks. But they could see that the speed at which big Internet businesses such as Amazon and Netflix could enhance, update, and tune their customer-facing services was at a different level from what they could do. Yet a miniscule number of deployments caused any kind of outage. These companies were different from more traditional businesses in many ways. Nonetheless, they showed what was possible.

This brings us to DevOps.

The Rise of DevOps

I touched upon DevOps earlier in the context of security. DevOps increasingly goes by DevSecOps as a sort of reminder of how important security is throughout IT development and operations. But DevOps touches many different aspects of the software development, delivery, and operations process. At a high level, it can be thought of as applying open source principles and practices to automation, platform design, and culture. The goal is to make the overall process associated with software faster, more flexible, and incremental. Ideas like continuous improvement based on metrics and data that have transformed manufacturing in many industries are at the heart of the DevOps concept. Amazon and Netflix got to where they are in part by using DevOps.

The DevOps Origin Story

DevOps grew out of Agile software development methodologies, which were formally laid out in a 2001 manifesto[5] although they had roots going back much further. For example, there are antecedents to Agile and DevOps in the lean manufacturing and continuous improvement methods widely adopted by the automobile industry and elsewhere. The correspondence isn't perfect; lean approaches focus to a significant degree on reducing inventory, which doesn't cleanly map to software development. Nonetheless, it's not hard to find echoes of principles found in the Toyota Way (which underlies the Toyota Production System) like "respect for people," "the right process

---

[5]http://agilemanifesto.org/

will produce the right results," and "continuously solving root problems" in DevOps. Appreciating this lineage also helps to understand that, while appropriate tools and platforms are important, DevOps is at least equally about culture and process.

The DevOps term was coined by Belgian consultant Patrick Debois who had been frustrated about the walls of separation and lack of cohesion between application practices and infrastructure practices while on an assignment for the Belgian government. A presentation by John Allspaw and Paul Hammond at the O'Reilly Velocity 09 conference entitled "10 Deploys a Day: Dev and Ops Cooperation at Flickr" provided the spark for Debois to form his own conference called Devopsdays (as he capitalized it at the time) in Ghent, Belgium, in 2009 to discuss these types of issues. DevOpsDays expanded as a grassroots community effort to the point where dozens of these events were being held every year around the world.

According to Frederic Paul in an InfoQ video interview from April 2012, Debois admitted that naming the movement was not as intentional as it might seem: "I picked 'DevOpsDays' as Dev and Ops working together because 'Agile System Administration' was too long," he said. "There never was a grand plan for DevOps as a word."[6]

Another noteworthy DevOps moment was the publication of *The Phoenix Project: A Novel About IT, DevOps, and Helping Your Business Win*, written by Gene Kim, Kevin Behr, and George Spafford in 2013 (IT Revolution Press). This book is a sort of fable about an IT manager who has to salvage a critical project that has bogged down and gotten his predecessor fired. A board member mentor guides him through new ways of thinking about IT, application development, and security—introducing DevOps in the process. Although DevOps has both evolved and been written about more systematically since then (including *The DevOps Handbook: How to Create World-Class Agility, Reliability, and Security in Technology Organizations* by Gene Kim, Patrick Debois, Jez Humble, and John Willis (IT Revolution Press, 2016)), *The Phoenix Project* remains an influential text for the movement. Kim's *The Unicorn Project: A Novel about Developers, Digital Disruption, and Thriving in the Age of Data* (IT Revolution Press, 2019) is a recent retelling.

---

[6]https://blog.newrelic.com/2014/05/16/devops-name/. Debois actually advocates for capitalizing the term as Devops rather than DevOps.

DevOps: Extending Beyond Agile

DevOps extended Agile principles to encompass the entire application life cycle including production. Thus, operations and security skills needed to be added to the cross-functional teams that included designers, testers, and developers. Improving collaboration, communication, and the level of cross-functional skills is an important DevOps tenet.

Taken to an extreme, there might even no longer be devs and ops people, but DevOps skill sets. More commonly, this view of DevOps focuses on "two-pizza" cross-functional teams—small, multidisciplinary groups that own a service from its inception through its entire life cycle. This works in part because such services are autonomous, have bounded context, and can be developed independent of other services and groups, so long as they honor their API contract. It also assumes that these "generalist" teams have the necessary skills to operate the underlying platform.

Abstractions to Separate Concerns

However, especially in larger organizations, DevOps has evolved to mean something a bit different than closely communicating cross-functional teams, developers on pager duty, or traditional sysadmins writing code. Those patterns may still be followed to greater or lesser degrees, but there's a greater focus on clean separation of concerns. It's about enabling ops to provide an environment for developers and then get out of the way as much as possible.

This is what Adrian Cockcroft, Netflix's former cloud and DevOps guru—he's now at Amazon Web Services (AWS)—was getting at with the "No Ops" term when he wrote about it.[7] Netflix was and is a special case because of its unique needs as an extremely high-traffic video streaming site. But Cockcroft was hinting at something that's broadly applicable: In evolved DevOps, a lot of what ops does is put core services in place and get out of the way. There's value in creating infrastructure, processes, and tools in a way that means devs doesn't need to interact with ops as much—while being even more effective. (Netflix largely operates using Amazon cloud services, so they have relatively little infrastructure they operate themselves, in spite of their vast scale.)

---

[7]http://perfcap.blogspot.com/2012/03/ops-devops-and-noops-at-netflix.html

As discussed earlier, reducing the friction of interactions between devs and ops doesn't always mean making communication easier. It can also involve making communication unnecessary. You do not, in fact, want to communicate with a bank teller more efficiently. You want to use an ATM. You want self-service.

With this model of DevOps, key aspects of operations happen outside of and independent of the application development process.

Of course, communication between devs and ops (as well as other disciplines such as security) still matters. The most effective processes have continuous communication. This enables better collaboration, so that teams can identify failures before they happen; feedback, to continuously improve and cultivate growth; and transparency. But that communication shouldn't become a bottleneck.

Site Reliability Engineers

At this point, it's worth mentioning Site Reliability Engineering. The term came out of Google in about 2003 when a team led by Ben Treynor was tasked with making Google's sites run smoothly, efficiently, and more reliably. Like other companies with large-scale infrastructures, Google was finding that existing system management paradigms didn't provide either the reliability or the ability to deploy new features that they needed quickly enough.

The idea is that a site reliability engineer (SRE) will spend about half their time on ops-related tasks like manual interventions and clearing issues. However, because the goal is to make the underlying system as automated and self-healing as possible, an SRE also spends significant time writing software that reduces the need for manual interventions or adds new features. Conceptually, this is somewhat like how a traditional system admin would write a script after they had to do the same task a few times. But the SRE concept puts that practice on steroids and shifts the ops role into one with a much larger software development component.

Google's Seth Vargo and Liz Fong-Jones argue that SRE is a variant of DevOps or "DevOps is like an abstract class in programming, and SRE is one possible implementation of that class" as they put it. I think of it more as an evolved form of ops for a separation-of-concerns DevOps model given that SRE teams support the groups actually developing software services. That said, an SRE approach may indeed shift the location of the boundary between ops-centric roles and dev-centric roles. A concrete example might be one which embeds an application's operational domain knowledge for a cluster of containers as in the case of the Operators initially created by CoreOS.[8] But I'd argue that it's still effectively a specialized ops function.

Open Source and DevOps

Open source relates to DevOps across aspects that include platforms and tooling, process and automation, and culture.

Platforms and Tooling

A DevOps approach can be applied on just about any platform using any sort of tooling. DevOps can even be a good bridge between existing systems, existing applications, and existing development processes—and new ones. The best tools in the world also won't compensate for broken processes or toxic culture. Nonetheless, it's far easier to streamline DevOps workflows with the right platform and tools.

Open source tooling is the default in DevOps. A fairly early-on 2015 DevOps Thought Leadership Survey by market researcher IDC found that a whopping 82% of early DevOps adopters said open source was "a critical or significant enabler of their DevOps strategy." What's more, the further along the survey respondents were in implementing DevOps initiatives, the more important they thought open source and DevOps open source tools were.

At the platform level, a key trend pushing the use of new technologies is a shift from static platforms to dynamic, software-defined platforms that are programmable, which is to say controllable through APIs.

Containers and their associated technologies are another important element of modern distributed application platforms. Containers modernize IT environments and processes and provide a flexible foundation for implementing DevOps. At the organizational level, containers allow for appropriate ownership of the technology stack and processes, reducing hand-offs and the costly change coordination that comes with them. This lets application teams own container images, including all dependencies, while allowing operations teams to retain full ownership of the production platform.

---

[8]https://coreos.com/blog/introducing-operators.html

With a standardized container infrastructure in place, IT operations teams can focus on building out and managing clusters of containers that meet their security standards, automation needs, high availability requirements, and ultimately their cost profiles.

When thinking about the toolchain associated with DevOps, a good place to start is the automation of the continuous integration/continuous deployment (CI/CD) pipeline. The end goal is to make automation pervasive and consistent using a common language across both classic and cloud-native IT. For example, Ansible is an open source project and product that allows configurations to be expressed as "playbooks" in a data format that can be read by both humans and machines. This is an example of Infrastructure as Code (IaC). Documenting deployment patterns in this way makes them easy to audit with other programs and easy for non-developers to read and understand. Automation generally is a critical component of DevOps, as we saw earlier with relation to security automation, in part because it's one of the ingredients needed to ensure repeatability.

A wide range of other open source tools are common in DevOps environments including code repositories like Git, monitoring software like Prometheus, logging tools like Fluentd, and container content tools like Buildah.

Process

We also see the congruence of open source development processes and those of DevOps. While not every open source project puts in the up-front work to fully implement DevOps workflows, many do.

For example, Edward Fry relates the story of one community that found

> *...there are some huge benefits for part-time community teams. Planning goes from long, arduous design sessions to a quick prototyping and story-boarding process. Builds become automated, reliable, and resilient. Testing and bug detection are proactive instead of reactive, which turns into a happier clientele. Multiple full-time program managers are replaced with self-managing teams with a single part-time manager to oversee projects. Teams become smaller and more efficient, which equates to higher production rates and higher-quality project delivery. With results like these, it's hard to argue against DevOps.*[9]

---

[9]https://opensource.com/article/18/4/devops-compatible-part-time-community-teams

Whether or not they check all the DevOps boxes, significant open source projects almost can't help but to have at least some characteristics of a DevOps process.

For example, they need a common and consistent view into code. DevOps and open source projects are both well adapted to using a distributed approach whereby each developer works directly with their own local repository with changes shared between repositories as a separate step. In fact, Git, which is widely used in platforms for DevOps, was designed by Linus Torvalds based on the needs of the Linux kernel project. It's decentralized and aims to be fast, flexible, and robust.

And remember the earlier discussion about creating a good experience for new contributors by providing them with rapid feedback and incorporating their code when it's ready? Automation and CI/CD systems are a great way to automate testing, build software more quickly, and push out more frequent releases.

Iteration, Experimentation, and Failure

At a higher level, DevOps embraces fast iteration, which sounds a lot like the bazaar approach to software development. They don't align perfectly; software developed and operated using a DevOps approach can still be carefully architected. However, DevOps has a general ethos that encompasses attributes like incremental changes, modularity, and experimentation.

Let's talk about experimentation a bit more, because it has a flip side: failure.

Now that's a word with a negative vibe. Among engineering and construction projects, it conjures up the *Titanic* sinking, the Tacoma Narrows Bridge twisting in the wind, or the space shuttle *Challenger* exploding. These were all systematic failures of engineering design or management.

Most failures in the pure software realm don't lead to the same visceral imagery as in the preceding text, but they can have widespread financial and human costs all the same. Think of the failed Healthcare.gov launch in the United States, the Target data breach, or really any number of multimillion-dollar projects that basically didn't work in the end. In 2012, the US Air Force scrapped an enterprise resource planning (ERP) software project after racking up $1 billion in costs. That's hardly an isolated failure.

In cases like these, playing the blame game is customary. Even when most of those involved don't literally go down with the ship—as in the case of the *Titanic*—people get fired, careers get curtailed, and the Internet has a field day with both the individuals and the organizations.

But how do we square that with the frequent admonition to embrace failure in DevOps? If we should embrace failure, how can we punish it?

Not all failure is created equal. Understanding different types of failure and structuring the environment and processes to minimize the bad kinds is the key to success. The key is to "fail well," as Megan McArdle writes in *The Up Side of Down: Why Failing Well Is the Key to Success* (Penguin Books, 2015).

In that book, McArdle describes the Marshmallow Challenge, an experiment originally concocted by Peter Skillman, the former VP of design at Palm.[10] In this challenge, groups receive 20 sticks of spaghetti, one yard of tape, one yard of string, and one marshmallow. Their objective is to build a structure that gets the marshmallow off the ground, as high as possible.

Skillman conducted his experiment with all sorts of participants from business school students to engineers to kindergarteners. The business school students did worst. I'm a former business school student, and this does not surprise me. According to Skillman, they spent too much time arguing about who was going to be the CEO of Spaghetti, Inc. The engineers did well, but also did not come out on top. As someone who also has an engineering degree and has participated in similar exercises at reunions, I suspect that they spent too much time arguing over the optimal structural design approach using a front-loaded waterfall software development methodology writ small.

By contrast, the kindergartners didn't sit around talking about the problem. They just started building to determine what works and what doesn't. And they did the best.

Setting up a system and environment that allows and encourages such experiments enables successful failure in Agile software development. It doesn't mean that no one is accountable for failures. In fact, it makes accountability easier because "being accountable" needn't equate to "having caused some disaster." In this respect, it changes the nature of accountability.

We should consider four principles when we think about such a system: scope, approach, workflow, and incentives.

Scope

The right scope is about constraining the impact of failure and stopping the cascading of additional failures. This is central to encouraging experimentation because it minimizes the effect of a failure. (And, if you don't have failures, you're not experimenting.) In

---

[10]www.tomwujec.com/design-projects/marshmallow-challenge/

general, you want to decouple activities and decisions from each other. From a DevOps perspective, this means making deployments incremental, frequent, and routine events—in part by deploying small, autonomous, and bounded context services (such as microservices or similar patterns).

Approach

The right approach is about continuously experimenting, iterating, and improving. This gets back to the Toyota Production System's *kaizen* (continuous improvement) and other manufacturing antecedents. The most effective processes have continuous communication—think scrums and kanban—and allow for collaboration that can identify failures before they happen. At the same time, when failures do occur, the process allows for feedback to continuously improve and cultivate ongoing learning.

Workflow

The right workflow repeatedly automates for consistency and thereby reduces the number of failures attributable to inevitable casual mistakes like a mistyped command. This allows for a greater focus on design errors and other systematic causes of failure. In DevOps, much of this takes the form of a CI/CD workflow that uses monitoring, feedback loops, and automated test suites to catch failures as early in the process as possible.

Incentives

The right incentives align rewards and behavior with desirable outcomes. Incentives (such as advancement, money, recognition) need to reward trust, cooperation, and innovation. The key is that individuals have control over their own success. This is probably a good place to point out that failure is not always a positive outcome. Especially when failure is the result of repeatedly not following established processes and design rules, actions still have consequences.

Culture

I said there were four principles. But something else is more important still. A healthy culture is a prerequisite for both successful DevOps projects and successful open source projects and communities. In addition to being a source of innovative tooling, open source serves as a great model for the iterative development, open collaboration, and transparent communities that DevOps requires to succeed.

The right culture is, at least in part, about building organizations and systems that allow for failing well—and thereby make accountability within that framework a positive attribute rather than part of a blame game. This requires transparency. It also requires an understanding that even good decisions can have bad outcomes. A technology doesn't develop as expected. The market shifts. An architectural approach turns out not to scale. Stuff happens. Innovation is inherently risky. Cut your losses and move on, avoiding the sunk cost fallacy.

One of the key transformational elements is developing trust among developers, operations, IT management, and business owners through openness and accountability.

Ultimately, DevOps becomes most effective when its principles pervade an organization rather than being limited to developer and IT operations roles. This includes putting the incentives in place to encourage experimentation and (fast) failure, transparency in decision making, and reward systems that encourage trust and cooperation. The rich communication flows that characterize many distributed open source projects are likewise important to both DevOps initiatives and modern organizations more broadly.

Changing Culture

Shifting culture is always challenging and often needs to be an evolution. For example, Target CIO Mike McNamara noted in a 2017 interview that

> What you come up against is: "My area can't be agile because ..." It's a natural resistance to change—and in some mission-critical areas, the concerns are warranted. So in those areas, we started developing releases in an agile manner but still released in a controlled environment. As teams got more comfortable with the process and the tools that support continuous integration and continuous deployment, they just naturally started becoming more and more agile.[11]

It's tempting to say that getting the cultural aspects right is the main thing you have to nail in both open source projects and in DevOps. But that's too narrow, really. Culture is a broader story in IT and elsewhere. For all we talk about technology, that is in some

---

[11]https://enterprisersproject.com/article/2017/1/target-cio-explains-how-devops-took-root-inside-retail-giant

respects the easy part. It's the people who are hard. Or as George Westerman of the MIT Sloan School of Management, moderating a 2020 MIT Sloan CIO panel, put it, "The first law of digital innovation: Technology changes quickly. Organizations change much more slowly. Unfortunately organizational cultures change even more slowly." Yet, you have to do it because as Shamim Mohammad, the chief information and technology officer of CarMax, put it at the same event, "[culture is] the operating system that runs the company."

Writing in *The Open Organization Guide to IT Culture Change*, (Red Hat, 2017)[12] Red Hat CIO Mike Kelley observed how

This shift to open principles and practices creates an unprecedented challenge for IT leaders. As their teams become more inclusive and collaborative, leaders must shift their strategies and tactics to harness the energy this new style of work generates. They need to perfect their methods for drawing multiple parties into dialog and ensuring everyone feels heard. And they need to hone their abilities to connect the work their teams are doing to their organization's values, aims, and goals—to make sure everyone in the department understands that they're part of something bigger than themselves (and their individual egos).[13]

Pervasive Open Source

Business models associated with open source software products are important to get right. It takes viable business models that involve not just using but contributing back to projects to sustain healthy open source communities. While many individuals are motivated to contribute to open source projects on their own time, the vast amount of open source software powering today's world depends on corporations contributing as part of a profitable business plan.

Business models don't exist in isolation though. For software businesses, they have a critical and symbiotic relationship to development models and practices like DevOps that have grown up alongside open source. And all of this exists within the context of broader organizational culture.

---

[12]https://github.com/open-organization/open-org-it-culture/blob/master/open_org_it_culture_1_0.pdf

[13]https://opensource.com/open-organization/resources/culture-change

The Challenges Facing Open Source Today

This book comes from a place where open source software is a great success and transformational technology force. Indeed, it would be hard to credibly argue that open source ideas and practices *haven't* greatly influenced how software gets developed and how cooperative innovation happens more broadly.

But even the most positive storylines embed other narratives that don't make it into press releases. Some of these are just blemishes. Others are more fundamental questions about balancing the desires of users and communities, creating sustainable business models, and continuing to flourish in an IT landscape that has fundamentally changed since open source first came onto the scene. Some of this I've touched on already. Some deserves greater expansion. But the most fundamental questions concern the role of open source in a world where software is increasingly delivered as some form of service rather than locally installed on a user's server or desktop computer. So that's where I'll begin.

The IT Industry Has Changed

Open source remains an instrument for preserving user flexibility, portability, and sustainability.

When everything is proprietary, it's harder for software co-evolving with an ecosystem of projects to become a platform for other platforms. Look at the way Linux has evolved to be the foundation for new types of software and new types of open source platforms and technologies. Consider the development of the cloud-native space more broadly. This in turn has helped sustain the value of open source overall, which arguably comes most of all from its effectiveness as a software innovation accelerator.

© Gordon Haff 2021
G. Haff, *How Open Source Ate Software*, https://doi.org/10.1007/978-1-4842-6800-1_7

But can open source software continue to sustain itself moving forward?

We live in a world increasingly distant in time from the Unix wars, which played a significant role in the genesis of open source. Yet open source has continued to grow and thrive even though the importance of source code for supporting a fragmented collection of hardware platforms is mostly far behind us. Horizontal software stacks built on standardized hardware are the norm (albeit becoming more heterogeneous with new processor architectures and various types of accelerators). But the IT industry of 2021 is a much different one from that of 2000 or even, really, 2010.

The Rise of the Cloud

Google's then-CEO Eric Schmidt is often credited with coining the "cloud computing" term in 2006, although it probably first appeared in a Compaq Computer business plan a decade earlier. As is so often the case with technology, closely related concepts had been germinating for decades. For example, in a 1961 speech given to celebrate MIT's centennial, artificial intelligence pioneer John McCarthy introduced the idea of a computing utility.

As recounted by, among others, Nick Carr in his book *The Big Switch*: Rewiring the World, from Edison to Google (W. W. Norton & Company, 2008), the utility take on cloud computing metaphorically mirrored the evolution of power generation and distribution. Industrial Revolution factories in the late 19th century built largely customized, and decentralized, systems to run looms and other automated tools, powered by water or steam turbines.

These power generation and distribution systems, such as the machine works of Richard Hartmann in Figure 7-1, were a competitive differentiator; the more power you could locally produce, the more machines you could run, and the more goods you could manufacture for sale. The contrast to the electric grid and huge centralized power generation plants, such as the Hoover Dam shown in Figure 7-2, is stark.

Until recently, we'd been living in an era in which the pendulum had clearly swung in favor of similarly distributed computing. Computers increasingly migrated from the "glass house" of IT out to the workgroups, small offices, and desktops on the periphery. Even before Intel and Microsoft became early catalysts for this trend's growth, computers had been dispersing to some degree for much of the history of computing. The minicomputer and Unix revolutions were among the earlier waves headed in the same general direction.

You could think of these as analogs to the distributed power systems in the Industrial Revolution and part and parcel of the environment that gave rise to open source. Where infrastructure is a competitive differentiator, the parts and knowledge to construct that infrastructure are valuable.

Today, however, that pendulum is swinging back. Amazon Web Services (AWS), Microsoft Azure, and Google Cloud Platform have emerged as the dominant global providers of cloud infrastructure services—which is to say pay-per-use building blocks to write your own applications. Huawei is another major player, especially in China, and there are many regional providers. These, and many other, companies also offer consumers and businesses complete hosted applications. G Suite, Facebook, and Salesforce are among the most familiar examples.

The Amazon Web Services Story

By the time that CEO Jeff Bezos appeared on the cover of *Time Magazine* as 1999's Person of the Year, Amazon.com had already started to significantly expand beyond its roots as the "world's biggest bookstore." By then it was also selling not only CDs and movies but power tools, toys, and televisions. It was also still losing hundreds of millions of dollars per year—a loss that, however fashionable in the dot-com bubble era, was still a lot of money. That was partly because Amazon was reinvesting so much of its revenue into expanding its business. But it was also because then, as now, retail margins were razor-thin—especially for the sort of mass-market commodities that made up much of Amazon's business, constrained as they were by the prices charged by both other web retailers and brick-and-mortar stores.

As a result, Amazon has long eyed related and complementary businesses that didn't involve directly selling tangible "stuff" that they had to inventory and distribute on their own nickel. For example, by 1999, Amazon had started its "zShops" program (which became the "Amazon Marketplace" in 2006)—essentially a complete hosted ecommerce infrastructure for third-party merchants. Amazon's attraction to this sort of business was that, a la eBay, it was effectively collecting "tolls" on every transaction processed while being called on to do little more than provide access to the company's transactional infrastructure and the network effects that came from being a popular shopping hub. Yes, it's a pricey and complicated infrastructure to get set up in the first place (hence the aforementioned reinvesting in the business). But, at least over time, incremental scale could be added relatively inexpensively.

For our purposes here though, it was the late 2006 introduction of three pure utility infrastructure offerings—Elastic Compute Cloud (EC2), Simple Storage Service (S3), and Simple Queue Service (SQS)—that was most notable. These were the first mainstream infrastructure service offerings to truly deliver on McCarthy's utility computing vision; you paid for these services based only on what you used.

Since 2006, AWS has expanded its offerings to a vast number of services that span not only traditional infrastructure like storage and compute but middleware such as databases, data analysis tools, and other offerings. Users would have historically needed to install such software on their own computers and operate it themselves—a fact that will become important to our discussion about the relationship of open source to these cloud providers.

As a sidenote, a pervasive myth about the early AWS was that it was simply a way to use Amazon's excess compute capacity at times when the retail operation didn't need it. After all, retail demand varies enormously depending upon the time of day and the time of year. "Black Friday" (the day after Thanksgiving in the United States) through Christmas sees much of a year's total shopping for many types of items. However, Werner Vogels, Amazon's CTO, has repeatedly debunked this saying

> *The excess capacity story is a myth. It was never a matter of selling excess capacity, actually within 2 months after launch AWS would have already burned through the excess Amazon.com capacity. Amazon Web Services was always considered a business by itself, with the expectation that it could even grow as big as the Amazon.com retail operation.*

Figure 7-1. *Machine works of Richard Hartmann in Chemnitz, Germany. The factories of the Industrial Revolution were built around localized and customized power sources that, in turn, drove local mechanical systems deriving from those power sources. Source: Wikimedia, in the public domain*

Figure 7-2. *The Hoover Dam (formerly Boulder Dam). Electric power as a utility has historically depended on large centralized power sources. Source: Across the Colorado River, 1942, by Ansel Adams. In the public domain from the National Archives*

Is the Public Cloud the Only Future?

At the same time, it's also worth observing that the shift toward public cloud hasn't quite played out the way that the most enthusiastic (or self-interested) predicted.

For example, one-time chief technology officer of Sun Microsystems, Greg Papadopoulos, one suspects hyperbolically and with an eye toward something IBM founder Thomas J. Watson probably never said, suggested that "the world only needs five computers," which is to say there would be "more or less, five hyperscale, pan-global broadband computing services giants" each on the order of a Google. And the aforementioned Vogels long promoted the idea that going all in on public cloud was a question of when, not if. Most acknowledged that conservative enterprises would hang onto legacy hardware architectures, software, and practices for decades. But surely the economics of the big public clouds would place company-owned and company-operated datacenters increasingly on the wrong side of history.

Others, including myself, weren't so sure. As I wrote in CNET in 2009[1]:

> *And there are economically interesting aspects to this change. No longer do you need to roll in (and finance) pallets of computers to jump-start a company; you go to the Web site for Amazon Web Services. One implication is lower barriers to entry for many types of businesses.*

> *But that's not the sort of near-term economic shift that the electric grid brought about. Rather, it made both unnecessary and obsolete the home-grown systems of the enterprises of the day. And it did so relatively quickly.*

> *And that is what I don't see happening any time soon, on a substantial scale with cloud computing. So far, there is scant evidence that, once you reach the size of industrialized data center operations (call it a couple of data centers to take care of redundancy), the operational economics associated with an order of magnitude greater scale are compelling.*

Today, I argue that, important as public clouds and the many software-as-a-service (SaaS) applications are to individual consumers, developers, and companies, they're not the only future—at least for practically interesting time horizons. And that view has crystallized around hybrid cloud and edge computing in a way that also has implications for open source.

Distributing Computing to the (Many) Edges

Even the most enthusiastic proponents of public cloud computing always acknowledged that there would be physical devices out at the edge of the network. These could be user devices like phones. Or they could be something that interacted with the physical world whether passively like a sensor or actively like an actuator.

This is more or less the simple model we see playing out with many consumer Internet-of-Things (IoT) devices. A consumer's voice assistant communicates directly to Amazon's cloud. The browser on a Chromebook talks back and forth with a website somewhere.

---

[1]www.cnet.com/news/there-is-no-big-switch-for-cloud-computing/

In reality, things aren't really that simple if only because of the networking. If using Wi-Fi, that consumer likely has a router that's the source of their Wi-Fi network, and that router is in turn connected to a cable modem or local network provider gear. And if that consumer is using a phone connected to their cellular provider, well, there are lots of cell towers and other physical telco gear sitting between their handset and "the cloud."

Now, at this point, you might say, "But that's networking stuff! It's not computing." (At which point, you'd be in the good company of all the computer people historically who drew a picture of a cloud whenever networking was involved and firmly declared the details weren't relevant to whatever computer architecture they were trying to diagram.) However, at least some of the details do increasingly matter given the increased convergence between traditional computing concerns and equipment and those concerns associated with telecommunications. Furthermore, even if we set the networking domain off to the side, computing (and storage) also increasingly takes place at many intermediate locations between the device edge and a core datacenter (whether on-prem or in a public cloud) as illustrated in Figure 7-3.

But why?

Why Distribute

Centralized computing has a lot of advantages. The computers are in a controlled environment, benefit from economies of scale, and can be more easily managed. There's a reason the industry has generally moved away from server closets to datacenters.

But you can't always centralize everything. Consider some of the things you need to think about when you design the architecture for a distributed network of computers.

Bandwidth. Moving bits around costs money in networking gear among other things. You might not want to stream movies from a central server to each user individually. (This is the type of "fan-out" problem that Akamai originally solved and which has grown to the point where content delivery networks are ubiquitous.) Alternatively, you may be collecting a lot of data at the edge that doesn't need to be stored permanently or that can be aggregated in some manner before sending it home. This is the "fan-in" problem.

Latency. Moving bits also takes time. Process control loops or augmented reality applications may not be able to afford delays associated with communication back to a central server. Even under ideal factors, such communications are constrained by the speed of light and, in practice, can take much longer.

Resiliency. Furthermore, you can't depend on communication links always being available. Perhaps cell reception is bad. It may be possible to limit how many people or devices a failure affects. Or it may be possible to continue providing service, even if degraded, if there's a network failure.

Edge computing can also involve issues like data sovereignty; you may want to control the proliferation of information outside of a defined geographical area for security or regulatory reasons.

A lot of this isn't exactly new though. Why today?

This decentralization counter-trend is fueled by emerging use cases like IoT, AR/VR, robotics, machine learning, and telco network functions. These are best optimized by placing service provisioning closer to users for both technical and business reasons. Traditional enterprises are also starting to expand their use of distributed computing to support richer functions in their remote/branch offices, retail locations, and manufacturing plants.

That's a very quick overview of edge computing. How does it relate to the hybrid cloud idea?

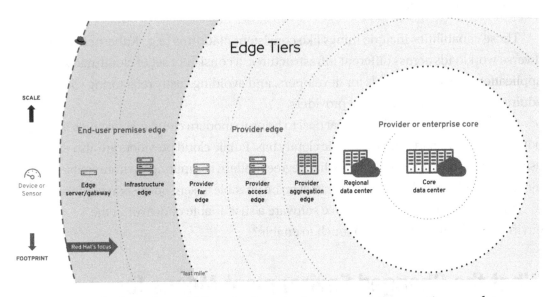

Figure 7-3. *The location of "the edge" varies by use case. Computing can be distributed across any of the multiple tiers shown in this diagram. Source: Red Hat*

The Hybrid Cloud

The idea behind a hybrid cloud is that it brings a unifying element to edge computing architectures as they extend across multiple tiers of computing, including public clouds and core datacenters. Of course, unification, like portability and "single pane of glass management," is something of an aspiration. Organizations may use features native to a single public cloud for good reasons. Or they may use a SaaS application that isn't meaningfully integrated with other aspects of their computing environment—nor does it need to be. However, unification still speaks to the idea that not every edge tier should be a silo and that using open source software can provide consistency, not just across those tiers at the very edge but multiple public clouds as well.

Stefanie Chiras, the GM of the Red Hat Enterprise Linux Business Unit, puts it this way:

> *Hybrid cloud is about a capability. It's not about an end state. It's not about having this percentage in public cloud, and this percentage in a private cloud, and this percentage on bare metal. It's about the ability and the capability to be able to move and adapt and adjust as you see fit, and based upon your needs.*

Those capabilities include things like consistent platforms (e.g., Kubernetes) running diverse workloads across different infrastructures, a consistent set of cloud-native application services and tools for developers, and avoiding costly refactoring when adding or changing public cloud providers.

Open source therefore has a great deal to bring to modern cloud architectures including both the on-prem parts and the public cloudy bits. Public cloud providers are also extensive users of open source. It's unclear to what degree modern computing environments, including public cloud providers, would even be possible absent open source software.

But is the creation of open source software a sustainable endeavor in the environment that it has done so much to enable?

What the Changed Environment Means for Open Source

The absence of a wholesale shift to public clouds notwithstanding, we must acknowledge that public cloud is a popular and powerful form of computing. It also recreates an approach that has similarities to the vertically integrated stacks that predated the horizontal computing era.

Not completely of course. The proprietary Unix era embraced many hardware and software industry standards and made more use of common hardware components than was the case in the mainframe and minicomputer era. Likewise, public clouds, while they may have many services specific to a single cloud (and incompatible with corresponding services on other clouds), nonetheless offer many familiar programming languages and frameworks, middleware like databases, operating systems, and applications.

Furthermore and critically, public clouds don't generally force users to use their native cloud-specific features; customers can largely maintain portability by running their own software on a cloud provider's base-level infrastructure. (SaaS applications tend to be much less portable, although data can usually be exported in some manner.)

Open source projects are ubiquitous throughout this new stack. Even Microsoft, now under CEO Satya Nadella, supports Linux workloads and has dropped the overt hostility to open source, which once characterized the company.

Some cloud giants have made significant contributions to open source projects. For example, Google created Kubernetes, now the leading open source project for orchestrating software containers, based on the infrastructure it had built for its internal use. Facebook has open sourced both software projects like React and hardware projects like the Open Compute Project.

But these dominant companies have also been criticized for making use of open source to create what are largely proprietary platforms to a significantly greater degree than they have reinvested through ongoing software development and other contributions to the commons. Insofar as large tech companies, both cloud providers and others such as Apple, take substantially more from the open source commons than they contribute back, this at least raises concerns about open source sustainability over the long run.

On the Device

Personal devices, like laptops, are not a primary focus of this book. While modern Linux distributions are a solid desktop experience, support for the proprietary applications, not least of which games, that many users want to run has always been hit-and-miss on Linux. And, while open source alternatives to popular productivity software like Microsoft Office and Adobe Photoshop exist, they're generally less polished and have never been the recipient of the vast resources applied by the likes of Microsoft and Adobe to their products.

In any case, today, while laptops and desktops still have their (important) uses, the focus of activity has shifted elsewhere. And that new focus looks more locked down than was the case with general-purpose PCs—even those running a proprietary operating system like Windows.

These new personal devices, along with other small connected devices like the thermostats and sensors in the general SmartHome category, have important differences from those of the personal computer era of distributed computing.

Your iPhone is a walled garden that only lets you browse the Web or install Apple-approved applications on an Apple-developed software stack. The nature of the process effectively makes open source, at least in the sense of an iterative open development process, impossible.

Android phones run a variant of Linux, but you still can't easily modify them in the same manner as a PC. SmartHome devices often run open source software as well but typically depend on centralized services and, in any case, are usually designed as black boxes that resist user tinkering.

Thus, we increasingly find ourselves in a computing landscape largely composed of monolithic public clouds at the core and mostly locked-down appliances or walled garden mobile devices on the perimeter.

At this point, let's consider how users play into this landscape. After all, any consideration of open source sustainability in this new landscape has to take into account user needs and desires.

What Users Want

User needs have also changed. In some respects, this applies more to individual consumers than to corporate buyers. But, as IT consumerizes, the boundaries between those groups blur and fade to the point where it can sometimes make sense to think about users broadly. It turns out that, while attributes like simplicity and ease of acquisition may take different forms for a teenager and an enterprise architect, their needs may not be as different as you would think.

The New Bundles

Bundling is a broad concept, and there's perhaps no more better historical example than newspapers.

Newspapers bundle together many things that are just loosely related like syndicated and local news, sports, and political reporting, along with advertising, classifieds, weather, comic strips, shopping coupons, and more. Many of the economic woes of the newspaper can be traced to the splitting of this bundle. Craigslist took over the classifieds—and made them mostly free. Online severed the connection between news and local ads. While ads run online as well, the economics are something along the lines of print dollars devalued to digital dimes.

As NYU professor Clay Shirky wrote in 2008:

> *For a long time, longer than anyone in the newspaper business has been alive in fact, print journalism has been intertwined with these economics. The expense of printing created an environment where Wal-Mart was willing to subsidize the Baghdad bureau. This wasn't because of any deep link between advertising and reporting, nor was it about any real desire on the part of Wal-Mart to have their marketing budget go to international correspondents. It was just an accident. Advertisers had little choice other than to have their money used that way, since they didn't really have any other vehicle for display ads.[2]*

Software, both historically and today, has also been a bundle in various respects. As IT industry analyst Stephen O'Grady observed in *The Software Paradox: The Rise and Fall of the Commercial Software Market* (O'Reilly Media, 2015), software used to be mostly something that you wrote in order to be able to sell hardware. It wasn't something considered valuable on its own. In many respects, we've increasingly returned to that way of thinking whether we're talking iOS on an iPhone or Linux on a web cam.

One of the core challenges around business models built directly on open source software is that open source breaks software business models that depend on bundling. If all you care about is the code in the upstream project, that's available to download for free. An open source subscription model doesn't require you to keep paying in order to retain access to an application as a proprietary subscription does. You'll lose access to professional support and other benefits of the subscription, but the software itself is gratis. In fact, open source is arguably the ultimate force for unbundling. Mix and match. Modify. Tinker. Move.

Online consumer services in particular have also just led to a mindset that you don't have to directly pay for many things. Your data is being mined and you're being targeted

---

[2]www.edge.org/conversation/clay_shirky-newspapers-and-thinking-the-unthinkable

by advertising, but your credit card isn't being billed monthly. Or you're buying something else from the company in question and the software you use is simply in support of that. There's a widely held expectation that, if it's digital, it should be free or at least a lot cheaper than any physical counterpart. This echoes *The Software Paradox* again.

Users Want Convenience

There's another aspect of bundles worth exploring.

Bundles, like other aspects of packaging, are prescriptive. They can be seen as a response to *The Paradox of Choice: Why More Is Less* (Brilliance Audio), a 2004 book by American psychologist Barry Schwartz, in which he argues that consumers don't seem to be benefiting psychologically from all their autonomy and freedom of choice. Whether or not one accepts Schwartz's disputed hypothesis, it's certainly the case that technology options sometimes seem to proliferate endlessly with less and less real benefit to choosing one tech over another—and certainly little benefit to having to wade through all the options.

When sellers create bundles, they also do so for a variety of reasons that often have to do with getting people to pay for stuff that they don't really want to pay for. The auto manufacturer who will only install leather seats if you also buy a sunroof and an upgraded trim package isn't doing so primarily because it wants to make life easier for the buyer. It's doing so because not everyone who *really* wants leather seats would normally be willing to also pay for those other options given the choice.

But the experience and convenience of a well-designed bundle that extends beyond the core product is at least a side effect in many cases.

Unbox a computer a couple of decades ago, and, if you were lucky, you might find a sheet of paper easily identifiable as a "Quick Start" guide. (This itself was an improvement over simply needing a field engineer to swing by.)

Today the unboxing experience of consumer goods like Apple's iPhone—as well as many more mundane and less expensive products—has become almost a cliché, but it's no less real for that. In the words of Grant Wenzlau, "Packaging is no longer simply about packaging the object—it is about the unboxing experience and art directing. This is where the process starts for designers today: you work backward from the Instagram image to the unboxing moment to the design that serves it."[3]

---

[3]www.thedieline.com/blog/2016/1/13/emerging-packaging-design-trends-of-2016-essentialism

O'Grady also writes about the power of convenience that bundled services can help deliver:

> One of the biggest challenges for vendors built around traditional procurement patterns is their tendency to undervalue convenience. Developers, in general, respond to very different incentives than do their executive purchasing counterparts. Where organizational buyers tend to be less price sensitive and more focused on issues relating to reliability and manageability, as one example, individual developers tend to be more concerned with cost and availability—convenience, in other words.[4]

The enterprise architect may not mind meeting with a sales rep and other members of the vendor team. In fact, they may appreciate the free lunch. The purchasing agent likely doesn't have an issue negotiating a price; that's their job after all, and maybe they'll even get rewarded for driving a tough bargain. The developer mostly wants to download (for free) and go.

O'Grady argues that, while Napster became popular in part because people could download music for free, it was also more convenient than driving to the mall and buying an album on a CD. Today, paid streaming accounts for the majority of music industry revenue with over 30 million subscribers in the United States. It turns out that many, perhaps most, consumers don't want to manage their own local digital music library, even though a great many songs can be found online for free given a modicum of effort.

Using open source software doesn't need to be about self-supporting a bag of parts downloaded off some repository on the Internet. Some communities, such as those around Linux distributions, do provide streamlined installation and curated groups of components aimed at different use cases. Commercial software subscriptions go further; they turn community projects into supported and curated products. Nonetheless, there's at least a tension between the idea of open source software as malleable, customizable, and free (in either meaning of the word) and a bundle that, by design, is prescriptive, abstracts away underlying complexity, and excludes or at least de-emphasizes technologies not deemed supportable and sufficiently mature for the target buyer.

---

[4]http://redmonk.com/sogrady/2012/12/19/convenience/

Maintaining a Positive Feedback Loop

So we mix up the open source development model, the changing nature of computing, shifts in user expectations, and, really, the overall dynamics of a world that's increasingly dependent on software for just about everything. What needs to change relative to open source's pretty spectacular trajectory, especially over the past ten years or so?

A good lens through which to examine this question comes from Jim Zemlin and the Linux Foundation in Figure 7-4. This particular diagram emphasizes a commercial feedback loop between projects, products, and profit—which is indeed important to the widespread success of open source software as a platform for IT industry innovation. However, something similar applies even if there is no product and project participants seek other types of value in addition to just money. Maintaining the links in this feedback loop depends on there being answers to some important questions.

Figure 7-4. *The positive feedback loop of projects (developers), products, and profits (or value more generally). Source: Linux Foundation*

Projects

We've already covered many of the aspects of projects and their associated communities that are important to get right. But, as Zemlin notes, there are always ways to improve.

"How do we create more secure code in upstream projects? How do we take the responsibility of this code being used in important systems that impact the privacy or the health of millions of individuals?" he asks. He adds that you may want to think explicitly about how your project fits into this feedback loop. "When I build my next project or a product, I should say, that project will be in line with, in a much more effective way, the products that I'm building."

Perhaps the biggest mindset shift over the past few years has been a broader recognition of the relationship of projects to value. As Zemlin puts it, "To get the value, it's not just consumed, it is to share back. There's not [just] some moral obligation, although I would argue that that's also important. There's an actual incredibly large business benefit to sharing as well." That said, it's hard to say free riding on the open source contributions of others is a solved concern for the open source model given how one-sided the participation of many organizations, including large IT vendors and cloud providers, can be.

Products and Solutions

Other questions relate to how products and other solutions work as part of an open source ecosystem. For example, there are many nuances involved in balancing competing requirements for stability and new technology across projects and commercial products. There is no single right answer here either. Tensions will always exist between upstream projects and downstream products—which in turn creates frictions that wouldn't exist in an idealized open source development model.

At the same time, commercial adoption and a community of support providers often need to move forward together and create a stable base upon which users and buyers are comfortable putting a project into production. Balancing the requirements for projects and products is hard. But finding a balance that works (whatever the compromises required) is necessary.

Successful products and other commercial solutions are often a necessary economic input into the open source feedback loop. Without that input—that is, customers paying for something they need—there may be no value created for those in a position to provide the inputs, such as developer salaries, which go into moving a project forward.

Profit and Broader Value

It's a feedback loop, and, as Zemlin argues, all three cogs are important. However, even if all aspects of open source as a development model and means for cooperation aren't solely about profit, that's an important point to probe if open source is going to continue to be a game changer.

Benefits such as societal good, better interoperability, and the creation of new companies are all well and good. But systematic success for open source depends on contributors to projects and their users realizing value—whether efficiency, speed of innovation, or reliability—which increases their opportunity to deliver profits. And for those contributors and users reinvesting patches, features, and resources into the project community, increasing the hiring of developers and others with expertise.

Value creation and reinvestment is central; the lack could impinge on the viability of open source as an ongoing development model. This isn't *necessarily* profit in the case of projects that are primarily hobbies for a community of developers. However, even in these cases, the need for developers to eat and maintain a sustainable lifestyle can't be dismissed.

Breaking the Value Chain

Let's now zoom in on the value capture aspect of the open source feedback loop. You've successfully gotten project and product dynamics worked out. What are some of the roadblocks you might face, and what might you be able to do about them?

Software Is Generally Devaluing

One high-level challenge is that the commercial value that can be extracted from software has just declined more broadly. This might seem odd given how software and other technologies are indisputably central to more and more business processes and customer services. It is the central apparent contradiction that O'Grady considers in the aforementioned *The Software Paradox*. He argues that

> *Software, once an enabler rather than a product, is headed back in that direction. There are and will continue to be large software licensing revenue streams available, but traditional high margin, paid upfront pricing will become less dominant by the year, gradually giving way to alternative models.*

In other words, software enables organizations to extract value from other things that they sell. Apple has been so successful, in part, because it sells a complete integrated product of which the macOS operating system is an incidental part. (The foundation of macOS (beginning with OS X) is Darwin, which is based in part on FreeBSD and the Open Software Foundation Mach kernel). Apple's services business has only been increasing as a percentage of its total revenue.

It's Always Been a Bigger Problem with Open Source

Open source models arguably exacerbate the issue. O'Grady has also written that

> *The numbers, on the surface, would indicate that the various economic models embraced by open source firms are not in fact favorable to the firms that embrace them. Closed source vendors are typically appalled at the conversion rates of users/customers at firms like JBoss (3%) and MySQL (around 1%, anecdotally, on higher volume) [both companies were subsequently acquired by Red Hat and Sun Microsystems respectively]—and those firms are more or less the most popular in their respective product categories. Even with the understanding that these are volume rather than margin plays, there are many within the financial community that remain skeptical of the long term prospects for open source (even as VC's pour money in in hopes of short term returns).*[5]

He wrote those words over 10 years ago, but Red Hat's success notwithstanding, there remains a dearth of companies that have been able to turn pure open source plays into significant revenues and profits. By just about any measure, Red Hat has been the most successful enterprise software company based on a pure open source development model; it was bought by IBM in 2019 for $34 billion and continues to operate under the Red Hat name.

Red Hat has done many things right in terms of both strategy and execution. Analyst Krish Subramanian attributes it "to 1) Being the first to understand OSS model and establish themselves well before the industry woke up to OSS 2) Picking the right OSS projects and *contributing code* to these projects. You can't win in OSS without code contribution."

However, in general, building a significant business around selling open source software is clearly not straightforward, or a lot more companies would have done so. It's also worth observing that even Red Hat, which had about $3 billion in annual revenues as of 2018, was still quite small compared to either traditional proprietary software vendors or the new cloud vendors who depend upon open source.

---

[5]http://redmonk.com/sogrady/2006/07/31/billion-dollar-open-source-businesses/

The industry has also developed a better appreciation for some approaches to business using open source that just don't work. Developer tools have always been a tough business, even with expensive proprietary products. Selling open source subscriptions for client devices is also hard; lack of good business models isn't the only reason that we've never seen "The Year of the Linux Desktop," but it hasn't helped. We see similar dynamics with the Internet-of-Things. The web cams, temperature sensors, and smoke alarms may be running open source software, but essentially no one is willing to pay for that directly in the consumer market especially.

Centers of Gravity Shift

Where has open source software development had the greatest impact? The easy response is the operating system—notably Linux. You wouldn't necessarily be wrong. Linux brought a Unix-like operating system to mass-market hardware and unified the non-Microsoft Windows computing world to a degree that might well have never happened otherwise. (And, if not Linux, the unifier would likely have been another open source Unix variant like BSD.) Linux is big in mobile, by way of Android, and it is relentlessly filling other niches that were once reserved for proprietary operating systems.

A more complete response would take a broader view that included software such as the Apache web server, innovations in software-defined storage and networking, container platforms, and more. However, whether we take the narrow view or the broader one, the focus of open source development has mostly been on infrastructure software, the software plumbing of datacenters that's largely independent of an organization's industry or specific application requirements.

It's then a short step to argue that at least some of this base plumbing is well understood and mature. It may not exactly be a commodity; for example, security incidents highlight the need for ongoing operating system support and updates. But it's hard to argue with a general assertion that software value is shifting to applications that businesses use to create differentiated product and service offerings. Furthermore, computing infrastructure is precisely what cloud providers offer. It's not necessary to install and operate it yourself.

This is all true. However, open source software development already has a long history of moving into new areas. In part, it's about moving up the stack from the operating system layer to software that builds on and expands on the operating system, such as container orchestration. Or into expanding middleware for both traditional enterprise applications and new areas such as IoT or edge computing more broadly.

Today, we also see the value of projects and products that comes from integration and curation. Thus, while a container project like Kubernetes could reasonably be classified as just infrastructure, complete container platforms like OpenShift pull together an integrated and curated set of cloud-native projects in order to provide a better experience for operations, developers, and security teams.

What of Software and Services?

The most pressing concerns around building a sustainable business are shifting from a focus on the competition that comes from the free community project to the competition that can come from public cloud providers.

The reason for this shift stems from two major factors.

The first is that many companies and individuals increasingly want to consume services rather than install and run software locally. Doing so is often more convenient. Of course, many do still run software on their own computers whether for technical, regulatory, or control reasons. Nonetheless, the shift from running software to consuming services is the overall trend.

The second is the recognition that public cloud providers are a new class of competitors for software vendors. And they embody this shift toward services. As a result, vendors looking to sell software based on an open source project fear that cloud providers will take their project and turn it into a service that competes directly with either their on-prem product or their own managed software service.

Is This a Problem?

The large public cloud providers are formidable competitors. That's not in dispute. Furthermore, public clouds, AWS in particular, have stood up services that compete with what were, at least initially, fully open source software projects. This includes Elasticsearch, whose permissively licensed code base AWS forked in order to offer a competing search service.

To some, this strikes at the heart of open source. In 2019 in the aftermath of AWS' Elasticsearch announcement, Sharone Revah Zitzman wrote that "I've been trying to gather my thoughts since the AWS Open Distro for Elasticsearch was announced this week, and explain why I think this is such a devastating move for the open source world as whole." She adds that "This is Amazon seeing someone's shiny toy, and just wanting it for themselves. MINE MINE MINE. This is called a fork."

Matt Asay, the head of open source strategy and marketing at AWS, perhaps unsurprisingly, has a different perspective. While hardly a disinterested observer, he said to me in 2020 that open source and cloud feed off each other:

> *I'm starting to think that there's no way of talking about one without the other and that they are inextricably bound up together and depend on each other for their success. The larger question is around whether cloud accelerates open source and whether open source accelerates cloud and I think it's the symbiotic relationship.*

O'Grady makes the point that open source vendors need to focus on their own cloud services. "It's not hard to see commercial open source company fortunes rising in tandem with their cloud businesses, not licensing gymnastics."

There's certainly a tension between major open source projects and the cloud vendors offering managed services based on those projects. Some of this is a natural consequence of the big public clouds being 800-pound gorillas in the computing landscape generally. It's also true that, early on, most of the public clouds gave back far less than they took and generally acted in ways that were guided by what they could do rather than what they should have done with respect to their use of open source. It's not really productive to debate whether public clouds and other large companies do their fair share for open source overall. Any answer would only be a snapshot in time anyway as, just over the last 12 months, major providers have taken various actions arguably deserving of either praise or approbation. However, overall, the relationship between the major public clouds and open source software seems to be on at least a mildly positive trajectory.

Food for Thought

The tension between, and interdependencies between, open source and public clouds is nothing new. I wrote a research note titled "The Cloud vs. Open Source" in 2008. But the two trends I've highlighted—the overall shift toward services and the increased importance of public cloud providers—have brought urgency to debates concerning open source profitability and hence sustainability in an increasingly cloud world. Furthermore, as venture capital has flowed into open source at an increasing rate, one suspects that capital is seeking outsized growth and revenue increases that exceed what's been historically possible for even successful open source–based businesses. As a result, VCs are seeking to find ways to stack the deck in their favor with licensing or other changes.

Many are skeptical that licenses attempting to forestall cloud provider competition will have the intended effect. O'Grady asks:

> *What are the implications [of such approaches] long-term? Typically it's not good. You're going to have, probably in most cases, problems with adoption, problems with usage, and problems with essentially getting to the ubiquity that you want and in fact need for a lot of open source commercial models.*

I get increasingly pulled into conversations with young companies trying to figure out what they should do to productize and profit from an open source project in a cloud computing world. Every case is different, and ultimately each company will need to figure out their own business plan and routes to market. But here are some questions I ask and advice I give.

Why do you want to have an open source project? To some, open source is something of a brand. It's hard to say they're completely wrong given that many IT decision makers associate attributes like higher-quality software, better security, and access to the latest innovations with enterprise open source.[6] Presumably, a lot of the ruckus over licenses that purport to be open source but don't conform to the Open Source Definition stems from this view. Companies want to be seen as having "open source" projects but don't really have much interest in actively participating in open source communities or compromising on the level of control that would be needed.

Competition means you're doing something right. Easy for me to say of course. But, as Asay puts it, "The biggest problem for any startup isn't collecting cash. The far bigger problem is getting noticed, attracting users." Or as Chef co-founder Adam Jacob argues:

> *When you think about somebody building and taking your software and trying to build another product to compete with you on it, what they're actually doing is building the top of your funnel. They're making the funnel*

---

[6]"The State of Enterprise Open Source: A Red Hat Report." 2020 research conducted by Illuminas.

at the top bigger. And since that impact is so outsized, the number of opportunities they create for you is bigger than the amount you lose at the bottom in competition every now and again.

Obscurity probably sinks way more companies than competition sinks successful companies with a first mover advantage.

Open source is a development model. If you've made it this far, you probably have that phrase memorized by now. If an organization views open source solely as a brand or even as a try-before-you-buy funnel, they're missing the great opportunity to participate in the open source development process. To be sure, many projects are mostly aligned with a single company even if those projects are, in fact, run in an open and transparent way. But, if a company does genuinely want to engage with a broader community, they should plan to do so from the start rather than hope it's something that may just happen someday.

From products to ecosystems. Finally, I counsel that they shouldn't be thinking solely in terms of a product based on an open source project in some manner. Rather, they need to be thinking about the ecosystems within which their business exists and how to use open source to participate.

Ecosystems Matter

Vertical integration was a common model for 20th-century industrial companies. As *The Economist* notes:

> *Some of the best known examples of vertical integration have been in the oil industry. In the 1970s and 1980s, many companies that were primarily engaged in exploration and the extraction of crude petroleum decided to acquire downstream refineries and distribution networks. Companies such as Shell and BP came to control every step involved in bringing a drop of oil from its North Sea or Alaskan origins to a vehicle's fuel tank.*[7]

In its heyday, Eastman Kodak owned its own chemical company to meet its needs for the vast quantities of ingredients needed to manufacture and process film.

We've already seen how commonplace this model was in the computer industry with mainframes; minicomputers; and, to an only somewhat lesser degree, Unix systems.

---

[7]www.economist.com/node/13396061

It could be an effective way to control access to inputs. It could also increase the market power of a dominant supplier. Indeed, regulators and lawmakers have at times restricted certain forms of vertical integrations as well as other types of tying together products and services. For example, manufacturers have often tried to make using hardware like a printer contingent on buying a profitable stream of printer supplies like ink from them, rather than going to a discount third party.

Today though we see the rise of coopetition. We see markets demanding interoperability and standards. We see more specialization and disaggregation.

Furthermore, ecosystems are only expanding. Management consultants McKinsey refers to "competing in a world of sectors without borders."[8] They go on to write that

We've all experienced businesses that once seemed disconnected fitting together seamlessly and unleashing surprising synergies: look no farther than the phone in your pocket, your music and video in the cloud, the smart watch on your wrist, and the TV in your living room.

In another report, McKinsey talks of a "radical reframing of what IT is and how CIOs manage it—not as an internal collection of information technologies (IT) but as a broad network of ecosystem technologies (ET)."[9] Their "four-layered IT" model based on this perspective is illustrated in Figure 7-5.

---

[8]www.mckinsey.com/business-functions/mckinsey-analytics/our-insights/
competing-in-a-world-of-sectors-without-borders
[9]www.mckinsey.com/business-functions/digital-mckinsey/our-insights/
adopting-an-ecosystem-view-of-business-technology

Overview of four-layered IT

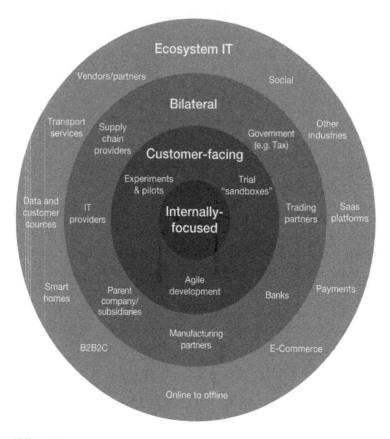

McKinsey&Company

Figure 7-5. *McKinsey argues that to fully benefit from new business technology, CIOs need to adapt to emerging technology ecosystems. Source: "Adopting an ecosystem view of business technology," February 2017*

Together, these suggest an environment that naturally aligns with organizations working together on technologies and other projects for mutually beneficial reasons. Open source software isn't the only way to do so. But much of today's technology is software. Standards are increasingly developed first through code. Open source development can almost be thought of as a communication platform for disparate companies working together to achieve business objectives.

It's Not Just About the Code

I've laid out some of the challenges that open source faces in today's world. IT organizations can increasingly use global cloud providers rather than operate their own infrastructure. That same infrastructure is being commoditized in many cases, and community code, downloaded for free, is good enough for many purposes. This in turn can choke off the reinvestment that the open source development model needs to work.

Furthermore, the viability of software as a stand-alone business seems to be declining. Users increasingly don't want to explicitly pay out of pocket for software. They expect it as part of a bundle whether that means hardware or paying implicitly through advertising and other forms of monetization, which makes their attention something of a product to be sold.

And users want convenience. Open source was born from an era where using software meant installing it on a computer someplace. Today, they're more likely to consume a service, the operational details of which are hidden away and largely irrelevant. Software abstracted in this manner can be less valuable for a company looking to profit from it and reinvest some of those proceeds in its ongoing development.

At the same time, it's not all doom and gloom. Open source is a good fit with developing ecosystems and businesses that need to work together on technology.

However, there's a bigger point, which is the topic of this book's final chapter. Open source principles have indeed led to an extremely effective software development model that can form the basis for equally effective enterprise software products—products that bring not just code, but also expertise, support, and other capabilities to solve business problems, to customers. That model has also started to influence the way that software is developed more broadly.

It also goes beyond software. Many principles, or at least analogs to them, can influence approaches to data, to education, to organizations. There's more inertia in many of these areas than in software. But there are also enormous opportunities.

CHAPTER 8

Open Source Opportunities and Challenges

The prior chapters of this book focused on "open" primarily as it relates to software code and the software development model.

As we have seen, opening up code solved practical problems facing a computer industry with a fractured hardware and software landscape. Later, the open source development *process* became an increasingly important component of open source. In this case, the practical problems involved improving cooperation, innovation, and interoperability.

However, many of the same principles and practices—or at least echoes of them—can apply to other areas. And, indeed, we see that happening. This chapter explores openness as it extends beyond source code.

In some cases, it involves the sharing of and collaboration around different types of digital artifacts, whether raw data or other forms of information. Interactive communication and development of knowledge is also part of the education and research process. Open source principles can be applied to hardware. Finally, there are the big questions of structure and the way organizations work. Do open source communities have anything to teach us?

© Gordon Haff 2021
G. Haff, *How Open Source Ate Software*, https://doi.org/10.1007/978-1-4842-6800-1_8

Opening Data

Determining what it means for data to be open, why we might want (or not want) data to be public, how datasets interact, and the practical difficulties of moving data has a lot of different angles. But considering value, transparency, ownership, and privacy hits most of the high points.

Value from Data

Data and computer programs have a close relationship. A program often takes in one set of data—for example, a grid of temperature, humidity, and atmospheric measurements over a region of ocean—and transforms it into another set of data, perhaps a storm track or intensity prediction. Absent data—and, in this case, data that's very recent—the most powerful supercomputer and sophisticated weather model is worthless.

Data has long had value of course, but it was in the mid- to late 2000s that a widespread appreciation of that fact began to sink in.

In 2006, Clive Humby, a UK mathematician and architect of Tesco's Clubcard, coined the since widely quoted statement "Data is the new oil." Less quoted is his follow-up, which emphasized that raw data has to be processed and analyzed to be useful. "It's valuable, but if unrefined it cannot really be used. It has to be changed into gas, plastic, chemicals, etc. to create a valuable entity that drives profitable activity; so must data be broken down, analyzed for it to have value," he said.

However, in 2008, *Wired* magazine's Chris Anderson made something of a counterpoint in an article titled "The End of Theory: The Data Deluge Makes the Scientific Method Obsolete." His thesis was that we have historically relied on models in large part because we had no other choice. However, "with enough data, the numbers speak for themselves."[1]

It was a provocative argument at the time, and it remains a likely deliberate overstatement even today. However, the intervening decade has seen dramatic increases in machine learning performance across a large number of areas. For example, in certain types of tests, computers can actually outperform humans at image recognition today.

While the techniques to use data effectively continue to be refined, many of the most impressive "AI" achievements draw heavily from work that Geoff Hinton did back in the 1980s on a generalized back-propagation algorithm for training multilayer

---

[1] `www.wired.com/science/discoveries/magazine/16-07/pb_theory`

neural networks. These advances have come about partly through increases in compute power, especially in the use of graphics and specialized processors like Google's Tensor Processing Units (TPU). They also depend on huge datasets used to train and validate the machine learning models.

It's not as simple as saying "it's all about the data," but there's clearly been a shift in value toward data. As a result, companies like Google and Facebook are far more amenable to participating in open sourcing code than they are at opening their data (and the specific ways they work with that data such as search algorithms).

An Open Map

One example of open source principles and practices being applied to data is OpenStreetMap.

Steve Coast founded the project in 2004; it was initially focused on mapping the United Kingdom, where Ordnance Survey mapping data wasn't freely available. (By contrast, in the United States, map services and data downloaded from The National Map maintained by the US Geological Survey (USGS) are free and in the public domain.) In April 2006, the OpenStreetMap Foundation was established to encourage the growth, development, and distribution of free geospatial data and provide geospatial data for anybody to use and share. OpenStreetMap is a particularly good example of open data because the data generated by the OpenStreetMap project is considered its primary output rather than map tiles or other services that can be created from the data.

According to the project, "OpenStreetMap emphasizes local knowledge. Contributors use aerial imagery, GPS devices, and low-tech field maps to verify that OSM is accurate and up to date." It also allows for automated imports of data from sources that use appropriate licenses.

The resulting data is under the Open Database License. It is free to use for any purpose so long as OpenStreetMap and its contributors are credited. While there's generally been less discussion around open data licenses than has historically been the case with software licenses, that's slowly changing. For example, in 2017, the Linux Foundation introduced two Community Data License Agreements (CDLA): a sharing license that encourages contributions of data back to the data community and a permissive license that puts no additional sharing requirements on recipients or contributors of open data. Both encourage and facilitate the productive use of data.

Comparing the quality of OpenStreetMap with commercial services such as Google Maps is difficult because quality tends to be a function of both the location and which features are important to you. For example, OpenStreetMap lacks the real-time information about road and traffic conditions needed to do the most effective routing. On the other hand, commercial services often draw data from sources that don't emphasize features such as hiking trails.

In general, though, both the quantity and quality of data in OpenStreetMap have improved dramatically over the past decade or so, and it's a valuable open data resource for many purposes.

Transparency Through Data

Data can be valuable in the monetary sense. It enables services that are useful and for which consumers and organizations are willing to pay. As machine learning seems poised to be an integral part of more and more technology from automobiles to conversational assistants like Amazon's Echo, data seems certain to only become more valuable—leading to increased tensions between opening data and profiting from it.

However, another aspect of data openness is the increased availability of data from public institutions and others so that citizens can gain insight into government actions and the environment they live in.

There are nuances to open data in this context.

Not all data collected by a government is or should be publicly available. The specifics will differ by country and culture—for example, salary information is more public in some countries than in others—but individuals and institutions will always (properly) have their secrets.

Furthermore, when data is opened, it needs to be done in a way that it's actually useful. Red Hat's Melanie Chernoff writes that

> *What we, as policy advocates, want to encourage is that the data that governments do and should publish is done so in a way to ensure equal public access by all citizens. In other words, you shouldn't have to buy a particular vendor's product in order to be able to open, use, or repurpose the data. You, as a taxpayer, have already paid for the collection of the data. You shouldn't have to pay an additional fee to open it.*[2]

---

[2]https://opensource.com/government/10/12/what-%22open-data%22-means-%E2%80%93-and-what-it-doesn%E2%80%99t

It's often easy to find fault with governmental and corporate lack of transparency generally. However, the overall trajectory of making public data available is mostly positive.

For example, in May of 2013, then–US president Obama signed an executive order that made open and machine-readable data the new default for government information. Over a quarter of a million datasets are currently available.[3]

Many municipalities also make various types of data available about crime, traffic infractions, health code violations, zoning, and more.

How is this data used?

A common technique is to "mash up" data with maps. Humans are visual creatures, so presenting temperatures, crime statistics, or population densities on a map often makes quickly discerning patterns and spatial relationships easier than presenting the same facts as a boring table.

Some uses are mostly tactical and practical. USGS water level data is used by whitewater paddlers and others to plan their trips. The National Weather Service, or specifically the forecasts based on it, helps you decide whether to pack an umbrella in the morning.

However, other types of data can give insight into the "health" of cities or actions taken by public employees. One example from New York City revealed that police officers were routinely ticketing cars in locations where it was, in fact, legal to park under an amended law.[4] Other examples include heat maps of where different types of crime occur. Individuals and companies can also build on public data to create applications that make it easier to use mass transit effectively or to more easily find out whether a restaurant has been cited for health concerns.

A common theme is that combining a multiplicity of datasets can often yield nonobvious insights.

Ownership of Data

The flip side to transparency and one that is much on the minds of regulators and others as of 2018 is the ownership of data and privacy issues associated with it.

---

[3] https://www.data.gov/

[4] http://iquantny.tumblr.com/post/144197004989/
the-nypd-was-systematically-ticketing-legally

Eben Moglen of the Software Freedom Law Center once referred to Google and its ilk as a "private surveillance system that [the government] can subpoena at will." He went on to describe this as a "uniquely serious problem." It's hard to dispute that such services create an unprecedented centralization of data—both for data explicitly placed into their cloud and that generated with each search or purchase. This is anathema to those who saw open source and inexpensive computers as a great victory for the decentralization of computing and information.

The monetization of essentially private behaviors like browsing the Web for advertising and marketing purposes is part of the impetus behind regulations such as the European Union's GDPR. The widespread availability and archiving of so much data have also exposed some of the fault lines between overall US and European attitudes toward free press, free speech, and privacy.

At a higher level, societies as a whole have also not really come to grips with what it means for so much data about individuals to be so widely available and combinable. It's easy to focus on the usual suspects. Facebook. Equifax. Google. They're profiting from mining our online behaviors and selling the results to advertisers and marketers. They make convenient bogeymen. (And governments are scrutinizing them ever more closely.)

But there are broader questions. As we've seen, sharing data can be a positive. Speaking at the 2018 MIT Sloan CIO Symposium in May, Elisabeth Reynolds, the executive director of the Work of the Future Task Force, observed that "the regulatory framework is often opposed to sharing data for the greater good."

For example, data about vehicle traffic, electricity usage, or personal health metrics could potentially be aggregated and studied to reduce congestion, optimize power generation, or better understand the effectiveness of medical treatments.

Maintaining Privacy

However, the more fine-grained and comprehensive the dataset, the harder it is to truly anonymize.

The problem is only compounded as you start mixing together data from different sources. Gaining insights from multiple data streams, including public datasets, is one of the promises of both IoT and AI. Yet, the same unexpected discoveries made possible by swirling enough data together also make it hard to truly mask identities.

Furthermore, there's personal data that's public for sound policy reasons, often to do with transparency. The sale of your house and your deed are public documents in the United States. But there's a difference of degree that's sufficient to become a difference of kind when all those public records are a mouse click away and ready to be combined with countless other datasets that are also online rather than filed away deep in some dusty county clerk's office.

Openness of data is mostly a good thing. But it can be hard to strike the appropriate balance. Or even to agree what the appropriate balance should be.

One conceptually simple approach to working with sensitive data is to directly anonymize the data. For example, medical images might be shared to compare the effectiveness of different diagnostic techniques; removing the patient's name and other specific identifying information could work in such a case. (Often such data is actually pseudonymized, with a trusted party replacing personally identifiable information fields with one or more artificial identifiers, or pseudonyms.)

It's also common to generalize fields. The patient's age, or age range, in our example may be relevant. Their specific birthday probably isn't. So a field with a birthday of 1/1/90 may simply become a field of age 30 or 30–35. But surely a given birthday isn't an identifier! Not by itself, but one of the big challenges with anonymization is that it's not always clear what can be used to identify someone and what can't–especially once you start correlating with other data sources, including public ones. Even if a birthday isn't a unique identifier, it's one more piece of information for someone trying to narrow down the possibilities.

Even combining data so that only the aggregated data is seen isn't a panacea.

Imagine this scenario. A company runs an employee satisfaction survey that includes questions about the manager each person reports to. The aggregated results for the entire company are shared with all; managers also see what those reporting up to them answered in aggregate. There's not much anonymity if a manager has only one person- or even just a few–reporting to them. (A common approach for this sort of situation is to only show results that are aggregated across some minimum number of people.)

At a much larger scale, organizations like the US Census have long had to deal with the challenges of publishing large numbers of tables that cut up data in many different ways. Over time, there's been a great deal of research into the topic; this has led to the creation of various guidelines for working with data in this manner.

Particularly challenging today is that, rather than being published in static tables, datasets are now often available in electronic form for ad hoc queries. This makes it much easier to narrow down results to one or a small number of identifiable individuals or companies by running multiple queries. Even in the absence of a single field that uniquely identifies someone, the totality of data like zip code, age, salary, home ownership, and so forth can, at a minimum, narrow down the possibilities.

One of the problems with traditional anonymization methods is that it's often not well understood how well they're actually protecting privacy. Techniques like those described, which collectively fall under the umbrella of statistical disclosure control, are often based on intuition and empirical observation.

However, in a 2006 article, Cynthia Dwork, Frank McSherry, Kobbi Nissim, and Adam D. Smith provided a mathematical definition for the privacy loss associated with any data release drawn from a statistical database. This relatively new approach brings more rigor to the process of preserving privacy in statistical databases. It's called "differential privacy" (specifically ε-differential privacy). A differential privacy algorithm injects random data into a dataset in a mathematically rigorous way to protect individual privacy.

Because the data is "fuzzed," to the extent that any given response could instead have plausibly been any other valid response, the results may not be quite as accurate as the raw data, depending upon the technique used. But other research has shown that it's possible to produce very accurate statistics from a database while still ensuring high levels of privacy.

Differential privacy remains an area of active research. However, the technique is already in use. For example, the Census Bureau used differential privacy to protect the results of the 2020 census.

Opening Information

The first phase of the Web, including the dot-com bubble, majored in static websites and ecommerce. There was an increasing amount of information online, but the typical web user wasn't creating much of it.

As the industry recovered from the burst dot-com bubble, that began to change.

The Read/Write Web

One aspect of this shift was "Web 2.0," a term coined by O'Reilly Media to describe a web that was increasingly characterized by connections, which is to say a form of data describing relationships. In Tim O'Reilly's words:

> Web 2.0 doesn't have a hard boundary, but rather, a gravitational core. You can visualize Web 2.0 as a set of principles and practices that tie together a veritable solar system of sites that demonstrate some or all of those principles, at a varying distance from that core.[5]

Another way to look at this phase comes from the inventor of the World Wide Web, Tim Berners-Lee, who used the term "read/write" Web to describe a Web in which everyone created as well as consumed.[6] This was around the time that blogging was really taking off and content created by users became an important part of the data and information underpinning the Web.

Besides the Web as a whole, the best example of a specific large-scale collaboratively created open information resource is probably Wikipedia.

Wikipedia

Launched in 2001 by Jimmy Wales and Larry Sanger, Wikipedia wasn't the first (or last) attempt to create a crowdsourced encyclopedia. In a 2011 article, Megan Garber, writing for Nieman Lab, counted six prior attempts. Subsequent attempts at different takes on the Wikipedia model, such as Google's Knol and Quora, were likewise largely unsuccessful. (What has worked to various degrees are smaller sites tackling a narrow topic such as a TV show.)

The reasons for Wikipedia's success have never been completely clear. In 2011, research by Berkman fellow and MIT Media Lab/Sloan School of Management researcher Benjamin Mako Hill[7] suggested it attracted contributors because it was a familiar product (an encyclopedia), focused on content rather than technology, offered low transaction costs to participation, and de-emphasized individual ownership of content.

---

[5]https://www.oreilly.com/pub/a/web2/archive/what-is-web-20.html?
[6]http://news.bbc.co.uk/2/hi/technology/4132752.stm
[7]www.niemanlab.org/2011/10/the-contribution-conundrum-why-did-wikipedia-succeed-while-other-encyclopedias-failed/

One also suspects that it stumbled into a governance model that struck at least a workable balance between autocratic control structures and a crowdsourced free for all. There's no shortage of complaints, even today, about various aspects of how Wikipedia is administered, and certainly quality can be uneven. However, it's hard to dispute the fact that Wikipedia mostly works and is a valuable resource.

Independent Contribution

Other sites are open and collaborative in the sense that they provide a platform for many users to contribute content, under a Creative Commons open source license or otherwise. YouTube is well known for videos. Flickr, now owned by SmugMug, is one example for photos although—in terms of sheer numbers—more social media-oriented properties like Instagram (owned by Facebook) are much larger.

The differences in the collaborative approach between Wikipedia and these other sites are probably rooted in the type of content. Collaboratively edited encyclopedia articles may suffer a bit from not having the coherence that a single author or editor can bring. But diverse perspectives that also guard against bias and self-promotion are usually a net win. On the other hand, collaboration on a posted photograph or video doesn't really make sense in most cases other than remixing or incorporating into new works.

Another large digital library is the Internet Archive, founded by Brewster Kahle in 1996, which has a stated mission of "universal access to all knowledge," including nearly three million public domain books. The Internet Archive allows the public to upload and download digital material, but much of its data is collected automatically by its web crawlers, which work to preserve copies of the public Web except where owners explicitly request otherwise. This service, which allows archives of the Web to be searched and accessed, is called the Wayback Machine, a play on the time machine in "Peabody's Improbable History," a recurring feature of the 1960s cartoon series *The Adventures of Rocky and Bullwinkle and Friends.*

Certainly, vast quantities of information remain behind paywalls and firewalls—or locked up on paper, microfilm, or microfiche—but the amount of information that is readily available with limited restrictions on its use would still be almost unfathomable just a few decades ago.

Opening Education

Probably the simplest (if incomplete) definitions of open education focus on reducing barriers to education, whether admission requirements, cost, or other factors.

Of course, teaching and learning took place long before there were formal educational institutions. Our distant ancestors didn't sign up for courses in wooly mammoth hunting in order to learn how to feed themselves.

Precursors

In the United States, an early example of what starts to look like an open education program comes from 4-H clubs. (4-H derives from the organization's original motto: head, heart, hands, and health.) It grew out of a desire to expose children to practical and "hands-on" learning that connected public school education to country life—and, in turn, expose their parents to the new agricultural approaches and technologies they tended to resist. According to the organization:

> *A. B. Graham started a youth program in Clark County, Ohio, in 1902, which is considered the birth of 4-H in the United States. The first club was called "The Tomato Club" or the "Corn Growing Club." T.A. Erickson of Douglas County, Minnesota, started local agricultural after-school clubs and fairs that same year. Jessie Field Shambaugh developed the clover pin with an H on each leaf in 1910, and by 1912 they were called 4-H clubs.*

4-H and related programs persist in many rural and semirural communities today as seen in the many country fairs that are a summer and autumn staple in parts of the United States.

MIT OpenCourseWare

Fast forward to the Internet age and hit pause at 2001. That was the year that the Massachusetts Institute of Technology first announced MIT OpenCourseWare, which is an obvious point at which to start our look at where open education stands today. It was formally launched about two years later.

The concept grew out of the MIT Council on Education Technology, which was charged by MIT provost Robert Brown in 1999 with determining how MIT should position itself in an environment where other schools were increasingly offering distance learning options to paying students.

MIT took a rather different approach. For one thing, the content was made available for free under an open license.

As Carey Goldberg of *The New York Times* reported, Steven Lerman, the faculty chairman, argued that "Selling content for profit, or trying in some ways to commercialize one of the core intellectual activities of the university seemed less attractive to people at a deep level than finding ways to disseminate it as broadly as possible."[8]

For another, the emphasis was on providing the raw ingredients for educators rather than an education in and of itself. In announcing the initiative, MIT president Charles Vest said that

> *We are not providing an MIT education on the Web. We are providing our core materials that are the infrastructure that undergirds an MIT education. Real education requires interaction, the interaction that is part of American teaching. We think that OpenCourseWare will make it possible for faculty here and elsewhere to concentrate even more on the actual process of teaching, on the interactions between faculty and students that are the real core of learning.*

Many other schools announced programs in the same vein over the next few years, and, in general, these commons of educational resources have grown over time.

We'll return to this idea of open educational resources (OER) shortly, but, first, no discussion of open education would be complete without mentioning massive open online courses (MOOCs).

MOOCs

As Vest noted, the commons populated by MIT OpenCourseWare and other resources of its type were intended to be the raw ingredients for learning rather than a course in a box. In addition to the reasons Vest gave, one suspects that the additional distance

---

[8]https://www.nytimes.com/2001/04/04/us/auditing-classes-at-mit-on-the-web-and-free.html

this approach placed between in-person MIT courses and MIT OpenCourseWare ones made the concept an easier sell to MIT's various internal constituencies. At a practical level, ubiquitous video and audio recording of lectures and other events also wasn't yet a thing.

However, this wasn't what a lot of potential students were looking for; they wanted a virtual version of a university course. As the 2000s progressed, many were becoming accustomed to watching instructional videos and lectures on YouTube. Various academics and others were also starting to see an opportunity to broaden the reach of elite university educations to populations that were underserved in their access to that level of education.

Precursors had been around for a while, but it was in 2012 that MOOCs exploded onto the scene including both venture capital–funded (Coursera and Udacity, both with Stanford professors attached) and nonprofit (edX, initially begun by MIT and Harvard). As *The New York Times*' Laura Pappano wrote at the time, "The shimmery hope is that free courses can bring the best education in the world to the most remote corners of the planet, help people in their careers, and expand intellectual and personal networks."

Courses were free and sign-ups were often massive—up to 150,000 or so massive—although the drop-out rate was correspondingly high, with numbers in excess of 95% common. Not really surprising given the lack of any real commitment required to hit the register button.

MOOCs are still around, but their record has been mixed.

From an open source perspective, they always seemed closer to free as in beer, rather than free as in speech. By design, most MOOCs follow a fairly traditional format for a university course with short talking-head and virtual whiteboard videos standing in for the lecture hall experience. Grades (remember extrinsic motivation) mostly come from various autograded tests and homework including multiple choice, numerical answers, and computer program output.

Courses often do encourage participation in discussion forums, and they often enlist past students as teaching assistants. However, many courses don't follow a rigid schedule. Furthermore, the practical realities of holding meaningful discussions among thousands of students at vastly different levels of educational background and English language ability make MOOCs much more of a broadcast medium than a participatory one, much less one where participants can choose what material is covered, learn from each other, or even guide the overall course direction.

(Experiences with formal learning and conferences during the pandemic in 2020 have followed a similar pattern. Broadcast works well, but personal interactions, especially at scale, are a major challenge.)

For the VC-funded Udacity and Coursera in particular, the difficulties of making money given free content also became troublesome. A number of MOOCs started out by offering a "verified certificate"—using the same sort of tools used for online proctoring of other types of certifications—for a fee. The problem was that a lot of employers didn't see a lot of value in a verified certificate relative to an unverified one, assuming they saw value in completing a MOOC at all. Over time, MOOCs have generally come to make all grades and certificates paid add-ons; some have even eliminated tests and other exercises from the free version. In 2013, Udacity would "pivot" (in Silicon Valley jargon) to simply charging for classes and focusing on vocational training.

This last point reflects what much of the audience for MOOCs ended up becoming anyway. For example, in 2013, after six months of high-profile experimentation, San Jose State University "paused" its work with Udacity because students in the program actually were doing worse than those in normal classes.[9] The student body of a typical MOOC tends to be populated heavily by early- to mid-career professionals, often with advanced degrees. On the one hand, MOOCs continue to be a great resource for those educated and self-motivated learners. But they've been a bitter disappointment for those who saw them as a viable alternative to the high prices and inefficiencies of traditional university education, which can act as barriers against those who lack money and family support.

Collaboration vs. Consumption

There are also those who argue that MOOCs were a bad model anyway.

In 2013, Rolin Moe wrote that

> *Had Udacity been able to provide a modicum of quality education to underrepresented populations, criticism would have remained to argue the pedagogy of such learning. With Udacity shifting away from underrepresented populations, the criticism is now about what is left in the wake of 2+ years of hyperbole and 0 years of results. And we cannot confuse what has shifted. It is not the narrative but only their business model; the narrative is still a system in crisis and searching for some low-cost, tech-savvy gizmo to*

---

[9]https://www.insidehighered.com/news/2013/07/18/citing-disappointing-student-outcomes-san-jose-state-pauses-work-udacity

do the job because we only need 10 schools and unions are the problem and our kids don't know enough STEM and plumbers make more money than college grads anyway.[10]

MOOCs essentially solved the problem of bringing a lecture to those who couldn't be physically present. But that's been a more or less solved problem since the advent of VHS tape. MOOCs make the lecture more consumable, but it's still basically just a lecture.

Martin Weller has written about how connectivism as a learning theory

as proposed by George Siemens and Stephen Downes in 2004–2005, could lay claim to being the first internet-native learning theory. Siemens defined connectivism as "the integration of principles explored by chaos, network, and complexity and self-organization theories. Learning is a process that occurs within nebulous environments of shifting core elements—not entirely under the control of the individual."

He went on to say that "What was significant about connectivism was that it represented an attempt to rethink how learning is best realized given the new realities of a digital, networked, open environment, as opposed to forcing technology into the service of existing practices." Yet, "while connectivism provided the basis for MOOCs, the approach they eventually adopted was far removed from this and fairly conservative."[11]

My Red Hat colleague Gina Likins argues that we should be thinking about education in terms of broader participation. For example, "people should be expected to fork the educational materials. What one classroom needs can't be expected to work in another. Students will come from different backgrounds with different experiences. The textbook is only the start."

Likins also points to other examples of open source community development that could apply to education. For example, many educational materials—textbooks in particular—follow a philosophy of not releasing before they're final. There are valid reasons for some of this. And, especially at the secondary school level, there are complex political considerations with some topics like history as well. But it's another way in which educational resources are developed with feedback from only a relatively small insular group, often with a limited set of perspectives.

---

[10]https://allmoocs.wordpress.com/2013/11/15/udacity-shifting-models-means-never-having-to-say-youre-sorry/

[11]http://blog.edtechie.net/pedagogy/25-years-of-edtech-2010-connectivism/

Academic research is also seeing open access movements. Some institutions have adopted open access policies to grant the public access to research materials. The Public Knowledge Project maintains an open source publishing platform called Open Journal Systems, which editorial teams can use to reference and publish (largely open access) academic journals outside the traditional publishing system.[12] It's also become more common to publicly circulate drafts and other preprint versions of research as a way of soliciting broader feedback.

Opening Hardware

Open source hardware has less of a cleanly established storyline than in the case of software.

Indeed, if you go back just a few years, you would probably conclude that outside of the "maker" world of hobbyists and tinkerers, open hardware had largely failed. There was quite a bit of standardization in computer system designs, but an open processor design like OpenSPARC from Sun had little impact.

This is starting to change though, especially in the guise of RISC-V.

RISC-V

RISC-V is a free and open instruction set architecture (ISA) that hardware designers can modify and experiment with. The unique aspect of RISC-V is that its design process and the specifications are truly open. The design reflects the community's decisions based on collective experience and research. Although the ISA is free, the processor implementation need not be: vendors can create commercial products without disclosing the underlying processor design. This is similar to the open source model for software in that derivative work and modifications are allowed. Additionally, for any new design to use the RISC-V name or trademark, it has to maintain compatibility with the ISA.

While some other architectures are open to greater or lesser degrees, RISC-V's active ecosystem sets it apart for now, highlighting again the importance of community and collaboration. (Ecosystems are vitally important in hardware as well as software. Ecosystem is one reason why ARM, a licensed family of architectures, while not open is challenging x86. Apple's M1 chip as well as its iPhone processor designs make heavy use of ARM.)

---

[12]https://opensource.com/resources/what-open-education CC-BY-SA

The RISC-V instruction set was developed by Professor Krste Asanović and graduate students Yunsup Lee and Andrew Waterman in May 2010, as part of the Parallel Computing Laboratory at the University of California, Berkeley. In 2015, the RISC-V Foundation (riscv.org), a nonprofit corporation controlled by its members, was founded to build an open, collaborative community of software and hardware innovators based on the instruction set. In November 2018, the RISC-V Foundation announced a joint collaboration with the Linux Foundation that provides operational, technical, and strategic support.

Possible application areas range from embedded microcontrollers to general-purpose and high-performance servers. The potential is great, and RISC-V cores are already being used in embedded systems and IoT devices. In the next couple of years, RISC-V will likely begin to move up into the server market.

Examples of RISC-V adoption range from announcements of support in the near future from Alibaba and the European Processor Initiative to finished products from Western Digital, NVIDIA, SiFive, and Espressif.

Ham Radio Kicks Off Maker Culture

However, it was among amateurs that the sharing of hardware designs took off first.

One early example of open source-ish sharing of hardware designs is amateur radio. The common term "ham radio," as amateur radio came to be known, was born of a slur. Professional wired telegraph operators used it in the 19th century to mock operators with poor Morse code sending skills ("ham-fisted"), and its use carried over to the amateurs experimenting with wireless telegraphy at about the beginning of the 20th century.

Factory-built gear wasn't readily available as ham radio was getting started, so amateurs began handcrafting vacuum tube-based transmitters and receivers. After World War II, surplus military gear also became widely available.

Amateur radio publications encouraged this sort of grassroots experimentation with hardware. In *Ham Radio's Technical Culture (Inside Technology)* (MIT Press, 2008), Kristen Haring recounts how, in 1950, *CQ Amateur Radio* magazine announced a "$1000 Cash Prize 'Home Brew' Contest" and called independently built equipment "the type of gear which has helped to make amateur radio our greatest reservoir of technical proficiency."

This hobbyist homebrew culture gave rise to the once widespread RadioShack chain. Started in 1921 by two brothers, Theodore and Milton Deutschmann, Radio Shack provided equipment for the then-nascent field of ham radio from a downtown Boston retail and mail-order operation. The "radio shack" term came from a small, wooden structure that housed a ship's radio equipment.

The company had ups and downs and ownership changes over the years before its owners largely shut it down in 2017. However, for a few decades after its acquisition by Tandy in 1963, RadioShack stores (as they were called by then) were popping up in shopping malls and city centers across the United States and elsewhere. And, in so doing, becoming a sort of home for electronics enthusiasts of all stripes, including early personal computer hobbyists. The TRS-80, introduced in 1977, was one of the first mass-produced PCs and initially outsold the Apple II by harnessing the power of RadioShack's retail channel and its thousands of locations.

To be sure, some of the nostalgia is selective. The company may have been the most convenient place for what I now call "makers" to pick up a needed resistor or capacitor. But its ubiquity also made it the default for less-knowledgeable consumers to pick up often subpar audio products and other consumer electronics in the days when the alternative was usually either a specialty retailer or a department store.

A Shift from Making

RadioShack was doomed in large part by some of the broad changes in electronics retailing dating to roughly the beginning of the 21st century. Ecommerce, big box stores, and the emergence of smartphones were all in that mix, and RadioShack never really adapted.

However, there were also technology shifts happening that affected the DIY tinkerers who viewed RadioShack so fondly even while the company was still successful in the 1990s.

Through about the 1980s or so, it was possible to design, build, and share plans for nontrivial electronics projects more or less from scratch. The Heath Company sold electronic test equipment like oscilloscopes, home audio gear, TVs, amateur radio equipment, and more in kit form under the Heathkit brand. A certain satisfaction and knowledge (if often frustration!) came from soldering and hand-assembling a complete working device from components, even if you were just working from cookbook instructions.

Byte, a mainstream computer magazine, carried a regular column by Steve Ciarcia called "Circuit Cellar" that introduced a variety of electronics projects that readers could build. As in the case of the code the computer magazines printed, there was usually no explicit license attached to these types of designs, but there was an implicit understanding that they were there to use, modify, and share.

The first thing to affect the traditional electronics DIYers was the personal computer. Many early PCs were something of a DIY project on their own. But it was more in the vein of connecting together assembled boards and other prebuilt parts such as disk drives and then figuring out why the thing wouldn't work. The process certainly involved problem solving and learning, but it was certainly different from creating from scratch.

But PCs, after you got one working, also drew many hobbyists from hardware to software. To many, software seemed to provide more opportunities to build "real" things. It was certainly easier to share your work with others who could benefit from it. Although open source software in a formal sense wasn't very widely known in the 1980s, "freeware," "shareware," and source code published for educational purposes widely circulated on bulletin board systems and on disks sold at the computer shows that targeted this new type of hobbyist.

It was also the case that electronics were simply getting harder to tinker with. Components were miniaturizing. They were getting faster and more complex. The devices that most people were in a position to design and build at home looked increasingly primitive compared to what you could buy off the shelf, often for less money.

The New Makers

Things remained in more or less this state until the mid-2000s.

The Arduino project started in 2003 as a program for students at the Interaction Design Institute Ivrea in Ivrea, Italy. Its goal was to provide a low-cost and easy way for novices and professionals to create devices that interact with their environment using sensors and actuators. The project's products are distributed as open source hardware and software, allowing anyone to manufacture Arduino boards and distribute the software.

In addition, being open source, Arduino was significant because it offered a good model for hobbyists and others to practically build interesting hardware projects in the modern era. Arduino board designs use a variety of microprocessors and controllers and are equipped with digital and analog input/output (I/O) pins that may be interfaced to various expansion boards and other circuits (Figure 8-1). Effectively, an Arduino embeds and abstracts away a lot of the complexities involved with interfacing with the physical world.

Figure 8-1. *Arduino microcontrollers can be used to build devices interact with the physical world through sensors and actuators. Source: Wikimedia. CC-BY-SA 2.0*

One person who recognized this was Limor Fried, who started Adafruit in her MIT dorm room during 2005 to sell electronics components and kits, including Arduinos. Now, it's a New York City company that she runs to make open source electronics kits and components for the growing tide of DIYers. For example, you can build a robot or a giant timer display.

In a 2011 interview with *Wired* magazine, Fried said that

> *One of the things about doing projects is that documenting them and sharing them with people used to be really difficult. Now we see so many people putting up videos, and it's so easy. I can make a five-minute video in an hour, with a preface and edits and nice audio and everything. And I think that makes a difference, because when people are exposed to this stuff and they actually get to see it, they get inspired.*

Another more recent hardware project is the Raspberry Pi, which is, in effect, a miniaturized low-cost Linux computer that can also interface with external components. First released in 2012, this series of small single-board computers was developed in the United Kingdom by the Raspberry Pi Foundation to promote the teaching of basic computer science in schools and in developing countries. Unlike Arduino, Raspberry Pi hardware is not open source, but much of the software that it runs, including the operating system, is as are the plans for many projects that make use of the Raspberry Pi.

At about the same time as these computers for makers were becoming popular, buzz was also building for 3D printing. 3D printing is a subset of additive manufacturing in which material is selectively deposited based on the instructions in a 3D design file. Imagine thin layers of (typically) plastic printed one at a time until an entire three-dimensional object comes into existence.

3D printing is usually dated to Chuck Hull's 1986 invention of a stereolithography apparatus (SLA). However, from an open source and maker angle, the most relevant date is 2007, when Adrian Bowyer of the University of Bath founded the RepRap project, an open source project intended to build a 3D printer that could print most of its own components.

Over the next few years, commercial 3D printing started to roll out.

3D printing has proven popular as a way to economically create one-off parts. This is handy for a hobbyist wanting to create a one-off case, gear, or just something decorative. However, in addition to its use in certain types of manufacturing, 3D printing is also used to create custom prosthetics and other medical devices.

Arguably, 3D printing hasn't lived up to the hype that's sometimes surrounded it, but it provides another example of how hardware designs can be cooperatively developed and shared.

Opening Culture in Organizations

More radically, we can even ask how and why organizations might change and evolve in a world where open source influences how individuals and organizations work together.

Why Do Organizations Exist Anyway?

"The Nature of the Firm" is a seminal 1937 article[13] by Ronald Coase, a young British economist who would go on to win the Nobel Prize in economics over the course of a long career. Coase asked the questions: Why do people give up some of their freedom to work as they like and become full-time employees? And wouldn't it be more efficient for firms to depend on loose aggregates of private contractors, hired as-needed to perform a specific task? After all, orthodox economics going back to at least Adam Smith suggested that everyone should already be providing goods and services at the best rate available as part of an efficient market. Why hire someone who you might need to pay even at times when you don't have an immediate need for their skills and services?

His answer was that it's to avoid transaction costs associated with using a market-based price mechanism.

You need to find a person who can do something you want done but that you can't or don't have time to do on your own. You need to bargain with them. You need to trust that they will keep your trade secrets. You need to educate them about your specific needs. So firms get created and often grow.

Of course, it's a balancing act. Firms have always used specialist suppliers—think ad agencies, for example—which can be thought of as reducing transaction costs themselves relative to contracting with individuals off the street. As *The Economist* noted on the occasion of Coase's 100th birthday in 2010, however:

> *Mr Coase also pointed out that these little planned societies impose transaction costs of their own, which tend to rise as they grow bigger. The proper balance between hierarchies and markets is constantly recalibrated by the forces of competition: entrepreneurs may choose to lower transaction costs by forming firms but giant firms eventually become sluggish and uncompetitive.*[14]

These ideas were built on by many economists over the years, including Oliver E. Williamson who once observed that it is much easier to say that the organization matters than it is to show why or how; he would also win a Nobel Prize for "his analysis of economic governance, especially the boundaries of the firm," which he shared with Elinor Ostrom.

---

[13]"The Nature of the Firm" by R. H. Coase, *Economica*, November 1937.

[14]https://www.economist.com/business/2010/12/16/why-do-firms-exist

More recently, New York University Professor of Law Yochai Benkler explicitly argued in a 2002 paper that "we are beginning to see the emergence of a new, third mode of production, in the digitally networked environment, a mode I call commons-based peer production." This third mode, the successor to firms in companies and individuals in markets, arose from open source software, he said.[15]

It's at least interesting to ask how online markets, connected communities, and the "gig economy" (think Uber) change historical equations. We've seen the rise of coopetition earlier in this book. There's little doubt that contracting out for certain types of work has indeed become easier for companies—for better or worse. On the other hand, while public clouds have become a generally beneficial option for certain types of computing workloads, there are also plenty of outsourcing horror stories in IT. We should perhaps leave this question at "it depends" and refer back to examples of how open source communities best work as the relevant discussion points for this book.

However, it's also worth considering what open source practices and principles mean *within* a given firm. IBM president and former Red Hat CEO Jim Whitehurst refers to this as the "open organization" in his book of the same name.

Open Organizations

General Motors might seem an odd starting point for this discussion, but, for all its various problems over the years, it provides an interesting study point about the principles of decentralization, which is a component of openness.

Writing in 2018, Steve Blank noted how

> *Borrowing from organizational experiments pioneered at DuPont (run by his board chair), Sloan organized the company by division rather than function and transferred responsibility down from corporate into each of the operating divisions (Chevrolet, Pontiac, Oldsmobile, Buick and Cadillac). Each of these GM divisions focused on its own day-to-day operations with each division general manager responsible for the division's profit and loss. Sloan kept the corporate staff small and focused on policy-making, corporate finance, and planning. Sloan had each of the divisions*

---

[15]"Coase's Penguin, or, Linux and The Nature of the Firm." Yochai Benkler, 112 *Yale Law Journal* (Winter 2002–2003).

start systematic strategic planning. Today, we take for granted divisional-
ization as a form of corporate organization, but in 1920, other than DuPont,
almost every large corporation was organized by function.[16]

GM was still the epitome of a hierarchical organization, of course, in the vein of the companies that William Whyte wrote about in 1956 in his influential *The Organization Man* (Simon & Schuster). A central tenet of that book is average Americans subscribed to a collectivist ethic rather than to the prevailing notion of rugged individualism. The *Fortune* magazine writer argued that people became convinced that organizations and groups could make better decisions than individuals, and thus serving an organization was a better logical choice than focusing on individual creativity.

GM was a hierarchical organization distributed through accounting structures rather than direct command and control.

Today, we see some signs of broader change.

More democratic forms of organizational governance exist. One popular discussion topic is holacracy, which introduces the idea of roles (rather than job descriptions), as part of a system of self-organizing, although not self-directed, circles. The term was coined by Arthur Koestler in his 1967 book *The Ghost in the Machine* (UK, Hutchinson; US, Macmillan). It's now a registered trademark of HolacracyOne although the model itself is under a Creative Commons license. The best-known practitioner is probably Zappos, the online shoe retailer now owned by Amazon. In a 2015 memo, then-CEO Tony Hsieh wrote:

Holacracy just happens to be our current system in place to help facilitate our move to self-organization, and is one of many tools we plan to experiment with and evolve with in the future. Our main objective is not just to do Holacracy well, but to make Zappos a fully self-organized, self-managed organization by combining a variety of different tools and processes.

However, the prevailing wisdom—which reflects practices familiar to open source development practitioners—is not so much about democracy as it is about decentralization and empowerment based on skills and expertise.

In *The Open Organization: Igniting Passion and Performance* (Harvard Business Review Press, 2015), Whitehurst argues that

---

[16]https://steveblank.com/2018/04/23/why-the-future-of-tesla-may-depend-on-knowing-what-happened-to-billy-durant/

Many people assume that if an organization is not top-down that it must be some flavor of democracy—a place where everyone gets a vote. In both hierarchies and democracies, decision-making is clear and precise. It's proscribed and can be easily codified. In most participative organizations, however, leaders and decision-making don't necessarily follow such clear rules, just as it was in ancient Athens, where literally every citizen had the same opportunities to lead or follow others. Some people have more influence than others.

One interesting aspect of such an environment is that it doesn't necessarily mean, as one might assume it would, eliminating managers. Whitehurst writes that "Nothing could be further from the truth. Our managers play a vital role in building, supporting, and moderating the meritocracy. Finding that balance between supporting it and, at the same time, leaving things alone is critical." Think back to our discussion of the role of maintainers like Greg Kroah-Hartman in the Linux kernel, and this dynamic will seem familiar.

The need to delegate and federate decision making isn't a new insight. It was pushed down to the divisional level at GM under Sloan. Management consultant Gary Hamel argues that "building and benefiting from communities at scale requires us to start with 'openness' as a principle, rather than with some particular set of collaborative tools or practices." It's more pervasive than an organizational delegating decision making within a formal structure.

In *Team of Teams: New Rules of Engagement for a Complex World* (Portfolio, 2015), Stanley McChrystal, who commanded the US Joint Special Operations Command in the mid-2000s, describes the basic problem. He recounts how the scientific management system that Frederick Taylor unveiled at the 1900 Paris Exposition Universelle "was so beautiful it inspired people to devote their lives to his vision." It was so impressive for how efficient it was at executing known, repeatable processes at scale. His steel factory model could churn out metal chips at a rate of 50 feet per hour rather than the norm of nine.

However, McChrystal goes on to write that today's world is more interdependent. It moves faster.

This creates a state of complexity, which is fundamentally different from challenges that are "merely" complicated in a technical sense. Complexity in this sense means less predictable. It means emergent behaviors that increasingly need to be reacted to rather than planned for in great detail.

McChrystal argues for pivoting away from seeing efficiency as the managerial holy grail to a focus on adaptability. He distinguishes commands rooted in reductionist perfection from teams that have a connectivity of trust and purpose that gives them an ability to solve problems that could never be foreseen by a single manager—even if they're less efficient in some theoretical sense.

All of this echoes the open source development model in so many ways.

Concluding Thoughts

Open source today is not peace, love, and Linux. OK. Maybe a little bit. Or even more than a little bit. The "free as in speech" aspect of open source is very much worth keeping in mind at a time when there's so much centralized control over social networks, search, personal information, and communication channels generally.

However, as we've seen throughout this book, you don't need to be a hippy to appreciate the value of open source.

It broke down the vertical silos of the computer industry and helped to prevent new horizontal ones from dominating all aspects of the computer industry.

New vertical silos are indeed developing. The global public cloud providers. Apple. The social media giants. All have powerful ecosystems and network effects that exert a strong gravitational pull into their walled gardens. Yet, open source at least provides a counterweight and moderating influence that preserves user alternatives and can ameliorate the most extreme cases of lock-in.

It's also proven to just be a very good software development model. While many successful projects have aspects of the cathedral to them (which is often both inevitable and necessary), the free-wheeling bazaar is also at least lurking. It removes friction associated with individuals and companies working together and has clearly influenced how even proprietary software development takes place in many cases.

Not all aspects of open source have been an unbridled success. Business models built around products that use only open source code have proven elusive for many companies. Some of today's largest tech companies make extensive use of open source for their online services but often don't sufficiently feed back into the virtuous cycle that fuels open source development with the dollars from business value. This includes not only some of the tech giants but also many other giant enterprises that increasingly depend on open source software for the digital services that are an increasingly critical part of the value they deliver to their customers. We see positive signs with the proliferation of open source program offices and open source foundations with widespread vertical industry participation. But the tragedy of the commons remains a lurking concern.

Culture Matters

However, as we've seen in this chapter as well as throughout the book, open source also reflects and informs changes in how individuals come together in order to innovate and otherwise accomplish missions that are important to them. Like most change, it's evolutionary. But organizations are cooperating more. They depend on each other more. We see more standards and therefore better interoperability. Information is more widely shared and collectively created, whether educational resources or knowledge more broadly. Even data to create physical artifacts can be exchanged.

And it's encouraging to believe that the values and thinking that gave birth to open source are being absorbed into how people and organizations act and interact more broadly. That may be hard to believe if you carefully follow the news headlines. But there are significant qualitative differences between how successful organizations operated in decades past and how they do today. Transparency is greater. Decision making is more decentralized. Diversity and inclusivity are becoming more recognized as important attributes. Not everything has to be a zero-sum game.

Among tech companies, consider Microsoft. It once had an executive whose primary mission was to attack Linux at a time when Microsoft was stagnating. Today, under CEO Satya Nadella, Microsoft's fortunes have revitalized in parallel with a legitimate embrace of open source. Is this all because of one person? Probably not. Nor is it absolute. But, as John Seyer put it to me, it's "probably the single biggest change in tone and culture of a tech company in recent history."

Open source collaboration is not immune from these shifts either even as it's helped to drive some of them. As Luis Villa observed earlier in this book, open source software as a formal movement was initially very much focused on user freedoms deriving from a license, sometimes to the exclusion of healthy and inclusive communities working together to create the software in the first place. As open source development has evolved from a fringe activity to a practice at the center of the technology world, it too has had to reconsider many practices and patterns.

This chapter presented some of the opportunities for open that go beyond software. Certainly, not everything is as tailor-made for open approaches as software. There are practical challenges to collaborating on objects that have a physical form. There are political challenges to projects that touch government at any level. Some creative works are almost inherently the work of a single mind or small number of collaborators. Nonetheless, there are many opportunities as we've seen, perhaps most of all with data, its presentation, and its dissemination.

But the most interesting and potentially powerful area for open innovation, which arguably is a prerequisite for everything else, is culture. Open source software has structures and processes that allow for collaborative development and a continually evolving set of practices that optimize the process. However, ultimately it has to take place within a system where people and organizations are, well, open to working in the open—which has often not been the natural state in industrialized societies. Absent cultural buy-in to open, default-to-closed is likely to prevail.

The future is still unevenly distributed. The effects of open are hardly universal. And they're unlikely to ever be so, for good reasons as well as bad. However, open source has taken a large bite out of software and of culture even as software is eating the world.

Index

229

© Gordon Haff 2021
G. Haff, *How Open Source Ate Software*, https://doi.org/10.1007/978-1-4842-6800-1

P, Q

R

Printed in the United States
By Bookmasters